Rethinking Informed Consent in the Big Data Age

In the "big data age", providing informed consent online has never been more challenging. Countless companies collect and share our personal data through devices, apps, and websites, fuelling a growing data economy and the emergence of surveillance capitalism. Few of us have the time to read the associated privacy policies and terms and conditions, and thus are often unaware of how our personal data are being used. This is a problem, as in the last few years, large tech companies have abused our personal data. As privacy self-management, through the mechanism of providing online consent, has become increasingly difficult, some have argued that surveillance capitalism and the data economy more broadly need to be overthrown.

This book presents a different perspective. It departs from the concept of revolutionary change to focus on pragmatic, incremental solutions tailored to everyday contexts. It scrutinises how consent is currently sought and provided online and offers suggestions about how online consent practices can be improved upon. These include the possibility of subjecting consent-gathering practices to ethics committees for review; the creation of visual-based consent agreements and privacy policies to help with transparency and engagement; the development of software to protect privacy; and the idea of automated consent functionalities that allow users to bypass the task of reading vast amounts of online consent agreements. The author suggests that these "small-scale" changes to online consent-obtaining procedures could, if successfully implemented, provide us with a way of self-managing our privacy in a way that avoids a revolutionary dismantling of the data economy. In the process, readers are encouraged to rethink the very purpose of providing informed consent online.

Rethinking Informed Consent in the Big Data Age will appeal to researchers in normative ethics, applied ethics, philosophy of law, and the philosophy of AI. It will also be of interest to business scholars, communication researchers, students, and those in industry.

Adam J. Andreotta is a lecturer in the School of Management and Marketing at Curtin University. His research focuses on the philosophy of self-knowledge and AI ethics. His research has appeared in *Synthese, Review of Philosophy and Psychology, Acta Analytica, AI and Society*, *Big Data and Society*, and elsewhere.

Routledge Research in Applied Ethics

Human Enhancement and Well-Being
A Case for Optimism
Emma C. Gordon

Urban Enlightenment
Multistakeholder Engagement and the City
Shane Epting

Moral Challenges in a Pandemic Age
Edited by Evandro Barbosa

The Ethics of Drone Design
How Value-Sensitive Design Can Create Better Technologies
Dylan Cawthorne

New Omnivorism and Strict Veganism
Critical Perspectives
Edited by Cheryl Abbate and Christopher Bobier

Human Freedom in the Age of AI
Filippo Santoni de Sio

Procreative Responsibility and Assisted Reproductive Technologies
Davide Battisti

Ethics and Situational Crime Prevention
Thomas Søbirk Petersen

Rethinking Informed Consent in the Big Data Age
Adam J. Andreotta

For more information about this series, please visit: https://www.routledge.com/Routledge-Research-in-Applied-Ethics/book-series/RRAES

Rethinking Informed Consent in the Big Data Age

Adam J. Andreotta

Routledge
Taylor & Francis Group
NEW YORK AND LONDON

First published 2025
by Routledge
605 Third Avenue, New York, NY 10158

and by Routledge
4 Park Square, Milton Park, Abingdon, Oxon OX14 4RN

Routledge is an imprint of the Taylor & Francis Group, an informa business

Library of Congress Cataloging-in-Publication Data
Names: Andreotta, Adam, author.
Title: Rethinking informed consent in the big data age / Adam J. Andreotta.
Description: Abingdon, Oxon [UK] ; New York, NY : Routledge, 2025. | Series: Routledge research in applied ethics | Includes bibliographical references and index. | Contents: Informed Consent in the Medical Context : Lessons and Practical Applications—Informed Consent Gone Awry—Impediments to Online Informed Consent—The Limits of the Law and Soft Governance Approaches—On Comics and Consent—On Automated Consent—Looking Into the Future of Informed Consent—On The Privacy Paradox.
Identifiers: LCCN 2024035880 (print) | LCCN 2024035881 (ebook) | ISBN 9781032625966 (hardback) | ISBN 9781032626086 (paperback) | ISBN 9781032626048 (ebook)
Subjects: LCSH: Informed consent (Medical law) | Big data.
Classification: LCC K3611.I5 A87 2025 (print) | LCC K3611.I5 (ebook) | DDC 344.04/12—dc23/eng/20240806
LC record available at https://lccn.loc.gov/2024035880
LC ebook record available at https://lccn.loc.gov/2024035881

ISBN: 978-1-032-62596-6 (hbk)
ISBN: 978-1-032-62608-6 (pbk)
ISBN: 978-1-032-62604-8 (ebk)

DOI: 10.4324/9781032626048

Typeset in Sabon LT Pro
by Apex CoVantage, LLC

Contents

Acknowledgements

I am deeply indebted to many people who helped me while I was completing this book. The book represents my thinking on the topic of informed consent, in the online personal data collection and use context, over the past five-year period. During this time, I have presented the ideas from the book in various seminars and lectures, as well as in conversations with countless colleagues and students. I learned a great deal from many conversations, audience questions, and peer-reviewed feedback along the way.

Some of the ideas in this book were first introduced in journal articles. I would like to thank Nin Kirkham and Marco Rizzi, my coauthors with whom I authored my first article on the topic "AI, Big Data, and the Future of Consent", which was first published *online* in 2021 in *AI and Society* (see Andreotta et al., 2022). I learned a lot from the discussions I had with Nin, who is a philosopher, and Marco, who is a legal scholar, about the importance of looking at this topic from an interdisciplinary perspective. While the paper was short, it inspired me to develop the ideas featured in the paper and look to other ways of improving online consent.

I would like to thank Anne Schwenkenbecher and Tim Flanagan, from Murdoch University, for inviting me on several occasions to take part in their philosophy seminar series over the past few years. In 2023, I gave a talk on some of the ideas from Chapters 5 and 6 and received excellent feedback and recommendations from Anne and Tim. I would also like to extend my appreciation to Henk van den Belt and Monica Seeber, who were in the audience and suggested some books and articles that greatly assisted me.

In 2023 and 2024, Richard Hamilton invited me to take part in a panel discussion on medical consent at Notre Dame, Fremantle. There I spoke about how automated consent and comic contracts could help with some of the problems associated with long consent forms and privacy policies. I would like to thank Richard and the medical students in attendance for their excellent questions.

In 2023, I presented an early version of Chapter 7 at the Australasian Association of Philosophy (AAP) conference—in the Australian Association for Professional and Applied Ethics (AAPAE) stream—in Melbourne, Australia. I would like to thank Hugh Breaky, the president of the AAPAE, and other members of the audience there, for their helpful comments. I would also like to thank Benjamin Winokur for reading Chapter 7 and providing insightful comments.

For her assistance and guidance on the topic of comic contracts, I would like to thank Camilla Baasch Andersen, from the University of Western Australia, who is also the original creator of them. I would like to thank her for the permission to use two images from contracts she developed (see Chapter 5) involving Aurecon and Bankwest. Chapter 5 of this book benefited greatly from Camilla's suggestions and recommendations on the extant literature. I would also like to thank Camilla and Nin for discussions about two-way consent, which briefly features in Chapter 5. I would like to thank my brother, Jordan Andreotta, for helping me design and create the two comic-styled image samples involving Spotify and Meta that feature in that chapter.

I would like to thank Björn Lundgren for numerous discussions on the topic of automated consent, which eventually led to a coauthored article on the topic. Some of the ideas in Chapter 6 were first introduced in our article "Automated Informed Consent", which was published in *Big Data and Society*. I would like to thank three anonymous peer reviewers for their comments on the paper.

Two of my oldest friends, Ben Salleo and Holly Fraser, who work in healthcare, deserve a special mention for taking the time to explain to me how informed consent is understood and operationalised in the medical context. Ben and Holly helped me to see the connections between informed consent in the medical context and informed consent in the online context. Their suggestions helped to improve Chapter 1. I would like to thank David Rutledge of the ABC, and Sam Baron of the AAP, who helped to facilitate an episode of "The Philosopher's Zone" on ABC Radio National in Australia, which aired in early 2023. There, I was interviewed by Jacqueline Boaks from Curtin University, whom I would also like to thank. There we discussed several ideas that feature in this book. I would also like to thank Alan Tapper, who gave me excellent feedback on the interview and made some comments and objections that I discuss in Chapter 1 of the book.

I first pitched the idea of doing this book to Andrew Weckenmann at the American Philosophical Association's 2023 Central Division Meeting in Denver, Colorado. I would like to thank Andrew for taking the time to meet with me to discuss the possibility of doing the book. His guidance and suggestions at the early stage of the proposal were invaluable. I would also like to acknowledge the editorial guidance provided by Rosaleah Stammler during the production process. Two anonymous peer reviewers commented on my initial proposal and made excellent suggestions, such as including a chapter on the privacy paradox and clarifying the differences between medical consent and consent in the online context. I would like to thank my academic institution, Curtin University, for their continued support, in particular Amy Tian and Julia Richardson.

Finally, I would like to thank my wife, Tanya, who read the entire manuscript and made several insightful comments and suggestions. Her encouragement and support were invaluable throughout the entire process of writing this book.

Preface

Imagine that you have just stepped into a doctor's office to discuss the possibility of undergoing a major medical procedure. The doctor greets you as you take a seat. As you discuss the details of the procedure, the doctor pauses occasionally to check to see if you understand the key steps. You are then asked to explain the procedure in your own words. Without using any technical language, you provide your understanding. The doctor, once satisfied that you understand what will occur, then explains the potential benefits of undergoing the procedure and the risks associated with it. Ethically bound, the doctor also refrains from invidiously influencing your decision. For example, the doctor is aware of certain cognitive biases such as "loss aversion"—a bias which makes us less likely to choose an option when it is described in terms of the harm it will cause rather than the benefits it will bring (see Kiener, 2021, p. 4292; cf. Kahneman & Tversky, 1972). They know that informing you that a medical procedure has a 10% chance of failure might lead you to think of it more negatively compared to saying that it has a 90% success rate, even though the two are logically equivalent. Thus, your doctor is mindful of *how* you are informed. Finally, your doctor suggests alternatives to the procedure. With much to consider, you engage in a meaningful discussion with the doctor and eventually give your *consent*. Aware of the risks, you proceed confidently, confidentially, and *informed*.[1]

Now, let us compare this consent process with the ones that occur online, such as the ones associated with the websites that we use daily or the apps on your smart phone. Imagine that you have just downloaded and installed TikTok. Upon clicking on the installed app for the first time, you are asked if you would like the app to connect to devices on your network. You decide not to allow it to and proceed. Next, you see a screen which explains that by tapping "agree and continue" you will be agreeing to the company's terms of service, that you acknowledge that you have read the company's privacy policy, and that you have learned how they collect and share your data. You are curious about what the terms of service are, and think that you should read the privacy policy, but do not recall being presented with them. You could go out of your way to look for them since, after all, they should be somewhere on the website or within the app. But you decide not to. Eager to use the app, you decide instead to click "agree and continue" and are presented with the next screen which asks you to choose your interests. You select "comedy", "sports", and 'animals", and click to proceed to the next screen, which has a "start watching" button. If you are using an Apple iPhone, you are prompted with a screen that asks you whether you would like the app to track your activities across other companies' apps and websites. Privacy conscious, you select "Ask app not to track" thinking to yourself that you have done all you need to do to protect yourself. The videos then start to play. You chuckle as you watch a video of a dog chasing people in the first one you watch. For a moment, you think back to the terms of service and the privacy policy, but your mind returns to the videos you are being presented with. As you continue scrolling, and watching the videos, thoughts of the privacy policy and terms of service drift from your mind. You consider seeking them out but convince yourself that there would not be much point. TikTok is surely bound by the laws of your country not to violate your privacy. Plus, even if they did collect your personal data, surely no one would be interested in it. What could be done with the knowledge that you like watching videos of dogs? You decide it is not worth reading the privacy policy—there are better things to do with your time.

If you are like most people, you choose not to read them and move on to other things. A recent study suggested that only 6% of Australians read all the privacy policies that they received online in a year (Nguyen & Solomon, 2018). Another study found that only 22% of Europeans always read them (FRA, 2020). When we think about how much time it would take to read them all, these figures are not surprising. A 2008 study estimated that it would take the average person 244 hours to read all the privacy policies they encountered in a year (McDonald & Cranor, 2008). An estimate given today would no doubt be much higher, given the greater number of devices we use that connect to the internet (e.g., smartwatches, smart fridges, and so on), and the growing list of stakeholders who buy and sell our personal data.

The fact that informed consent on the internet is not taken as seriously as it is in the medical context may not strike you as that surprising. After all, you might reason, it needs to be taken very seriously in the medical context because of the risks to human health, since people's bodies are being operated on, or treated, and there is a chance for death or injury to occur. Opening an app like TikTok or Googling where the next Olympic Games will be held, does not seem to carry the same risks. However, while the probability that your next Facebook login will put your life at risk is low, this does not mean that the large-scale collection and use of personal data is harmless.

As I will discuss in the book, there is much to be concerned about when it comes to personal data collection. As such, I argue that it is important that informed consent is taken much more seriously than is currently the case. While it remains a matter of controversy about how best to define "informed consent", or what constitutes it, I think few would argue that many of us actually give informed consent when using the internet. Ask yourself the following questions. Do you know what your favourite app, or website, does with the personal data it collects about you? Are you aware of the potential risks that face you when your personal data are collected? Have you taken the time to read all the privacy policies associated with each of the apps you use or websites you visit? If you have, do you feel like you've truly understood them? If you've answered no to any, or all, of these questions, then it may be that you often fail to give informed consent to the companies that are collecting your personal data. This, I will argue in this book, is a problem.

Now of course, it is true that we all understand risks differently. Two people both might be aware of the risks of skydiving and yet make very different choices about whether jumping out of a plane is a good idea. Similarly, some people might be quite happy with their personal data being collected and sold, whereas others may not want any of their personal data sold. The problem, as I explain in the book, is that people are not always sufficiently aware of how their personal data are being used, so it is hard to see how we can give *informed consent*. Take TikTok, for example. Consider the actions of the UK Cabinet Office, who banned ministers and civil servants from using the app on their work phones. The reasoning that justified this decision stemmed from the fact that TikTok requires users to give them permission to access stored data on the device (Sabbagh, 2023). As with many apps, TikTok can access personal data from a user's device such as their contact lists or geolocation data. From a government agency's perspective, it is understandable why they might not want ministers' and civil servants' mobile phones providing such data. The risks of confidential information being collected pose a security threat that, in this case, was deemed too high.

What are the risks to the average internet user, however, and how can you ensure that you are aware of the kinds of personal information apps like TikTok collect from you? While you might not be a government official, shouldn't you still be aware of how your personal data are used? This is where things get complicated for the average internet user. Since only a small percentage of people read and understand privacy policies, or terms and agreements, a large number of people fail to give informed consent online. Furthermore, companies are often not transparent about how they use your data, so it can be hard to actually know, even if you try to find out. And what is true for TikTok is also the case for Facebook, WhatsApp, and even smaller-scale apps, like ones you might use for parking. For example, a parking app collects personal information about you such as your license plate details and movements (see Powles, 2024). If you do use parking apps, and thus share such data, are you aware of how these data are used, or whether they are being safely secured?

In this book, I will argue that we need to rethink the way that consent is typically given online. By examining how informed consent is viewed in the medical context, I will suggest that we can extract valuable, and most importantly, practical solutions that can be applied to the online context. However, it is important to acknowledge at this early stage that applying the medical model of consent to the online context is neither practical nor feasible. Requiring a professional consultation for every TikTok session, Facebook login, or Google interaction would be inconvenient and would discourage people from using these services. This is certainly not the approach I propose in the book.

Nonetheless, change is imperative. Consider the Facebook-Cambridge Analytica Scandal, which became public in 2018 after whistleblower Christopher Wylie leaked information about Cambridge Analytica's unauthorised collection and use of over 80 million Facebook users' personal data. These data were then used to send targeted advertisements to US voters in an attempt to influence the 2016 US election. This scandal resonated deeply with the public because it showed just what can happen when our personal data are misused, namely, democratic processes have the potential to be undermined. As the capacity to collect our personal data increases over the next few years—through the proliferation of personal devices such as "smart" watches, fridges, and cars—so too will the risks of data being used in ways that could potentially harm us.

In recent years, significant literary contributions have highlighted the ethical concerns associated with personal data collection, as evidenced by Shoshana Zuboff's (2019) *The Age of Surveillance Capitalism*, Julie Cohen's (2019) *Between Truth and Power,* Carissa Véliz's (2021) *Privacy is Power*, and Sarah Lamdan's (2022a) *Data Cartels*, to name only a few examples. These seminal works shed light on the "hidden commercial practices of extraction" and "data harvesting" that are prevalent in the commercial utilisation of personal data.

Zuboff, for example, notes the different kinds of harms that large-scale personal data collection causes—such as the invasions of privacy, the capacity for behavioural manipulations, and the potential undermining of democracy. As a result, Zuboff boldly advocates the monumental task of overthrowing surveillance capitalism. Cohen, similarly, has also characterised some of the misuses of personal data and in her book, she calls for "countermovements" (2019, pp. 269–271), to address these pervasive issues. And Véliz takes a strong stance and says that the "surveillance economy has gone too far, it has abused our personal data too many times in too many ways" (2021, p. 141). In her view the "grand experiment" of personal data collection and use is one that is "too dangerous to be continued" (2021, p. 141).

I agree with these authors that our personal data are [i] being collected in ways that we would not always consent to if we were fully informed about how they were being used and [ii] being used in ways that harm us. Yet, I remain unconvinced about the efficacy of their solutions. Zuboff's goal of overthrowing surveillance capitalism strikes me as overly ambitious. Cohen's suggestion that we should form counter-movements raises questions about how exactly these should take place. And Véliz's suggestion that the collection and use of personal data should be *discontinued* goes too far in my view, as there are benefits of personal data use.

In what follows, I sketch a slightly different perspective, which departs from the concept of revolutionary change to focus on pragmatic incremental solutions tailored to everyday contexts. My goal is to scrutinise the way that consent is given, and the way that it is sought, online and provide suggestions on how such practices can be improved. Central to this approach is the enhancement of consent procedures through the incorporation of visuals, in order to help transparency and comprehension; the utilisation of automated consent functionalities, in some cases aided by artificial intelligence (hereafter, "AI") and machine learning, that can provide consent on behalf of users, thus saving them from going through thousands of privacy policies; and also the possibility of ethics review committees who would be responsible for reviewing the consent procedures that companies employ. By exploring the potential implementation of these solutions, I argue that informed consent can be better secured online.

As a result of this approach, I take a somewhat more neutral stance towards personal data collection and use, as practices in themselves—that is, I am not going to argue that the data economy is intrinsically immoral. While I agree with the above authors that many companies have failed to act ethically with respect to their personal data collection and use practices, I also think there are benefits from the collection and use of personal data which are important not to forget.[2]

A parallel might be drawn here with contemporary debates about AI, and whether we should be optimistic or pessimistic about its development. For example, in their recent book, *Moral AI*, Borg et al. (2024) note that there is room for both optimism and pessimism when it comes to the future of AI. They argue that there are reasons for *optimism* when it comes to transportation, since AI can power driverless cars, which can help people who cannot see travel; but there is also room for *pessimism* as driverless cars have been responsible for the death of passengers. Similarly, they argue with the military use of AI: there is room for optimism as AI-augmented bomb disposal robots can detonate bombs so that humans don't have to risk their lives; yet there is room for pessimism as AI weapons can go out of control and hurt and kill the innocent.

When it comes to the collection and use of our personal data, I think the same is true. While acknowledging the inherent risks and concerns, I believe a balance can be found. Personal data collection offers numerous advantages, especially when managed carefully. Consider the potential for improved healthcare, the promise of autonomous vehicles, and ease of decision-making when it comes to entertainment such as recommendations of music and movies. While there are positive signs, such as the introduction of the General Data Protection Regulation (GDPR), there is room for a greater focus on how informed consent is understood online. What we ideally want is control over what is being done with our personal information. If individuals were more informed about how their data are used and they had more control of what was happening with their data, then some of the problems identified here would be minimised.

My thinking on the topic of informed consent goes back several years, but it was not until I co-authored a piece published in *AI and Society* with my colleagues Nin Kirkham and Marco Rizzi from the University of Western Australia (Andreotta et al., 2022) that I fully appreciated the need to rethink the way that informed consent is understood in the online context. Our starting point for the paper was, like for many, the observation that privacy policies and terms and conditions are rarely read and understood by users, and that while they may be of interest to lawyers, they are typically unhelpful for regular internet users. Despite its brevity, our article hinted at some possible ways that consent could be better secured online. In the years since the publication of this article, I have had the chance to develop my thoughts on the topic through seminar presentations, class discussions, radio interviews, and further collaboration with colleagues. The book represents the thoughts I have developed on the topic over the past few years. I hope the work can encourage others to develop new ways of securing online informed consent.

I have structured the book and my subsequent argument in the following way: in Chapter 1, I provide a brief history of informed consent, and explain how the concept is currently understood and operationalised by medical practitioners. I then suggest that there are several important lessons to learn from the medical context that can be applied to the online context. In Chapter 2, I examine some of the harms that can arise from the misuse of personal data. I go through several recent examples of personal data collection that have occurred without informed consent. In Chapter 3, I outline three of the central barriers that prevent informed consent from being given and received online. These include: the Transparency Problem, the Re-purposed Data Problem, and the Meaningful Alternatives Problem. Chapter 4 starts to address these problems. I give examples of some of the large legal fines that have been recently issued to companies for misusing personal data, and then discuss some limits of the law. This discussion then gives rise to a subsequent one about "soft governance" approaches. There I discuss the possibility that companies could subject their personal data-gathering procedures to ethics review, in the same way that researchers in universities submit their research projects to ethics review before proceeding with them.

Chapter 5 draws inspiration from so-called "comic contracts", in order to illustrate how online consent procedures could be shortened and made more engaging by adding visuals to them. I explore some of the recent literature on the topic, and then present two of my own examples that apply to Spotify's targeted advertising system, and another to a VPN service that was run by Onavo Protect, a company owned by Meta. In Chapter 6, I consider the concept of automated consent, which is the idea that software could be set up to offer consent on our behalf, thus preventing us from reading all the privacy policies that apply to us. In addition to suggesting some of the technology's potential benefits, I also emphasise the need for oversight as it develops. Chapter 7 looks to the future of consent. There I examine emerging technologies that complicate the providing and receiving of informed consent. These include issues that arise from: emotional AI, deepfakes, GenAI, Bluetooth trackers, and blockchain technologies. Finally, in Chapter 8, I address the "privacy paradox", which is the phenomenon that arises when people claim to care about privacy while also giving away large amounts of personal data, nonetheless. I argue that the phenomenon is not so paradoxical at all and suggest that people exhibit such behaviour due to the difficulty of privacy self-management. I provide a response to Solove (2021), who claims that privacy self-management has become an impossible to undertake task. I suggest that the small-scale changes to consent gaining procedures, of the kind outlined in the book, could, if successfully implemented, provide us with a way of successfully self-managing our privacy.

The rapid pace of AI expansion need not "end" privacy as some have suggested (cf. Walsh, 2023a). There are risks in allowing our personal data to be collected and shared, of course; but there are also many benefits.

What we should ultimately want, I will argue here, is better control over such processes.

A note on terminology: in this book, I will focus on the collection and use of personal data that occurs on the internet during our daily interactions, such as those on our smartphones or while browsing online. When I use the term "personal data" in this context, I am referring to the information about us that is collected during these interactions. This is in line with the European Commission's definition of "personal data" which is: "any information relating to an individual" (European Commission, D-GJC, 2016); and the GDPR's, which says, "[p]ersonal data are any information which are related to an identified or identifiable natural person" (European Union, 2016, Article 4). Examples include: your name, age, photo, post code, income, IP address of your devices, your locational data, social media posts, web searches, and so on.

The collection and use of personal data is not new. However, in the so-called "big data" age, its collection and use give rise to substantial privacy concerns. As more devices collect information about us, and AI and machine learning become more sophisticated, there are issues about who has access to these data, what they might reveal about us, and what they might be used for. The term "big data" is widely used today, and has been featured in book titles, journal names, and industry reports over the last few years. Writing in *The New York Times*, Steve Lohr notes that while the term "big data" is a "meme and a marketing term" it is also "shorthand for advancing trends in technology that open the door to a new approach to understanding the world and making decisions" (2012). Big data is often discussed in association with the rise of the "Internet of Things", the term which describes the billions of devices all over the world that connect to the internet such as cars, smart kitchen appliances, and Fitbits (to name just a few).[3]

But what *specifically* is big data? One answer is that it is just a *lot of data*. Luciano Floridi (2012), for example, notes that it is estimated that humanity accumulated 180 exabytes of data between the invention of writing and 2006.[4] Between 2006 and 2011, the total grew 10 times to 1,6000 exabytes. And he notes that it is expected to grow fourfold every three years. That is a *lot of data*. Yet, Floridi suggests that "it is unclear what exactly the term 'big data' means and hence refers to" (2012, p. 435). After all, Floridi notes, the term "big" is a relational predicate. A cat is *big* compared to an ant, but *small* compared to a giraffe.

In a recent study, Favaretto et al. (2020) asked over 30 researchers to define the term and found that "[n]o univocal definition of Big Data was found among the respondents and many participants admitted uncertainty towards giving a definition of Big Data" (p. 1). A definition of "big data" may indeed be elusive. An ostensive definition, however, may be more easily discerned and provide us with a more workable definition. Such a definition is offered by the European Commission, who define "big data" as

> *[L]arge amounts* of different types of data produced from various types of sources, such as people, machines or sensors. This data includes climate information, satellite imagery, digital pictures and videos, transition records or GPS signals.
>
> (European Commission, D-GJC, 2016, my emphasis)

While there is still ambiguity with this description—that is, "large" is a synonym for "big"—the definition does point to a real phenomenon, namely the large amounts of personal data, which are increasingly giving rise to the kinds of privacy concerns that have been much discussed as of late.

The collection of personal data, and risks associated with its use, did not emerge with the rise of big data, or the invention of Google in the 1990s, as Barnes (2013) points out. It is the scale of contemporary data collection and use today, however, and the computational power now available to process these data that gives rise to new kinds of privacy risks. The main question I take up in the book is how we can better self-manage the collection and use of these data by focusing on how we give consent online.[5]

In the book, I will use the terms "consent practices", and at times the more specific "consent procedures", to refer to the ways that companies gain permission, or authorisation, from us to collect and use our personal data (or sometimes fail to gain consent from us). For example, you might give consent to a company to track you across websites by clicking "I accept" or "agree" after being presented with a privacy policy or terms and conditions agreement. That would be a specific *procedure* you would go through to provide consent. I will use the term "consent practices" to refer to the more general actions that companies undertake, such as being transparent, or failing to provide users with choices. Essentially, I am concerned with the "consent agreements" of the kind that "regular internet users", as Chomanski and Lauwaert (2023) put it, encounter on a daily basis.

The reason it is important to clarify this is because we do not often encounter *consent forms* online, of the kind one might encounter before one gets an operation or partakes in a research experiment. For example, you might click "I agree" or click "accept all cookies" when a pop-up window appears on a website. And in some cases, you may even give your consent to a company to collect your data by "remaining on the site without leaving or changing", as Jones et al. (2018, p. 66) put it. In such a case, online consent may even be given unconsciously.

Those familiar with Manson and O'Neill's (2007) book, *Rethinking Informed Consent in Bioethics*, will immediately notice the similarity between their book title and mine: *Rethinking Informed Consent in the Big Data Age*. I have given my book this title because, like Manson and O'Neill, I want to suggest that we need to rethink the very notion of informed consent. My focus is on the *online context*, however, not the *medical context*, so our approaches, topics examined, and conclusions are of course very different. Yet like Manson and O'Neill, I want to suggest that in order to improve informed consent we need to question its purpose and critique existing consent-gathering practices.

The provision of online consent is often seen as an obstacle to overcome, rather than something to help us self-manage our personal data. As a result of the failure to read and understand online privacy policies, we sometimes have little idea about what we are agreeing to when we provide online consent. For example, in 2017, 22,000 people unknowingly agreed to 1000 hours of community service, some of which included cleaning toilets and scraping chewing gum off seats, when they signed up for free Wi-Fi while at a music festival (see Hern, 2017). This was due to there being a "gag clause" in the terms and conditions, which Purple, the Wi-Fi company involved, inserted in it. A prize was offered to anyone who read the terms and conditions. According to Hern (2017), only one person came forward.

This may be a humorous example, but it raises a serious point, namely, that privacy policies and terms and conditions, and the consent we provide after receiving them are typically ineffective methods for providing informed consent. As Jones et al. (2018) say, "digital consent has been repeatedly criticised as being an unworkable, empty procedural act" (p. 65). If the purpose of consent is to help us control our personal data, or protect us from being exploited, and at present we struggle to provide informed consent online, then this is something that needs to change. To do that, we first need to rethink the purpose of online consent.

Notes

1 This may be thought of as a normative aspiration—that is, how things ought to be. I am not claiming that this is true of all medical consultations.

2 A good example of this can be found in Eric Topol's (2019) book *Deep Medicine*, which explains how AI can assist with medical decision-making and reduce errors in medical diagnoses. Large amounts of personal data will be required for the facilitation of this, of course. See also Suleyman and Bhaskar (2023, pp. 61–66), who discuss some new and emerging uses of AI, such as improving the efficiency of electrical grids, detecting fraud, and creating a safer transportation infrastructure. Large amounts of personal data will be required to facilitate such uses.

3 The term "big data" is often attributed to John Mashey, who coined it in the 1990s.
4 An Exabyte (EB) is: one billion gigabytes. For more information, see: https://www.techtarget.com/searchstorage/definition/exabyte.
5 See Hummel et al. (2021) for a discussion on the idea that data subjects should be the owners of their personal data. The authors show that there are problems associated with claiming that we "own" our personal data. Regardless of whether we own our data or not, I will argue that a more important issue is how we control the use of personal data. This is where informed consent becomes important.

1 Informed Consent in the Medical Context

Lessons and Practical Applications

In this book, I argue that the consent practices that apply to the commercial use of personal data can be enhanced. I begin, in this chapter, by looking at the way that consent is viewed in the medical context, in order to extract some key insights and valuable lessons that I believe can be applied to the online personal data collection and use context. By "medical context" I have in mind consent procedures that encompass the traditional health industry—which includes surgeries and treatment with certain high-risk medicines—as well as the elective health procedures, such as cosmetic procedures, which have become widespread in society.

I look to the history of informed consent, in Section 1.1, in order to draw out some of these lessons. However, as I mentioned in the Preface, we need to be selective, as there are important differences between these two contexts. It would be impractical, for example, to require a sit-down consultation session for every TikTok or Facebook login. In Section 1.2, I articulate some key differences between express consent and informed consent, suggesting that at present, much of the consent that we give online fails to constitute informed consent. In Section 1.3, I examine some current controversies surrounding the question of what constitutes informed consent in the medical context. I suggest that the same controversies exist in the personal data collection and use context and argue in Section 1.4 that a pluralistic approach should be taken. In Section 1.5, I consider the *asymmetry objection*, which states that it is mistaken to look to the medical world for inspiration. In Section 1.6, I briefly consider a further objection to a key premise in the book's central argument, which says that current consent procedures on the internet are not that ethically problematic.

1.1 A (Very) Brief History of Informed Consent

In order to show why online consent procedures should be taken more seriously than they currently are, it is essential that we examine informed consent's historical and practical significance within medical ethics. First,

DOI: 10.4324/9781032626048-1

it is important to recognise that informed consent has not always been centrally figured in medical ethics. In their seminal work, *A History and Theory of Informed Consent*, Faden and Beauchamp (1986) provide an expansive overview of the history of informed consent and point out some of the key *paradigm shifts* that have occurred over, approximately, the past two thousand years.[1] For instance, they note that while the Hippocratic Oath (or oaths) developed by the Ancient Greek Physicians provided practitioners with an important set of professional responsibilities to uphold, acquiring informed consent was not one of them. The Hippocratic Corpus (*The Corpus Hippocraticum*), as a result, fails to address the role of communication, disclosure, or permission-giving in the patient–physician relationship (Faden & Beauchamp, 1986, p. 61). Indeed, as they also point out, withholding information from patients was sometimes recommended.

A similar observation is made in their discussion of Enlightenment era medicine where Faden and Beauchamp note how the *deception* of patients was recommended if it led to favourable results, such as in instances where deceiving a patient could calm them down. In Faden and Beauchamp's discussion of Benjamin Rush, a prominent figure in 18th-century medicine, we see an example of someone even recommending deception when dealing with the so-called "unenlightened patients" (1986, p. 65).

It was not until the mid-20th century, however, with the creation of the Nuremberg Code, that the importance of informed consent was fully appreciated in medical ethics. The Code followed the atrocities of World War II, and the subsequent Doctors' Trial in 1947 and is generally seen, as Manson and O'Neill suggest, as the "first authoritative statement of consent requirements in biomedical ethics" (2007, p. 2). The Code's ten points address the atrocities that occurred during World War II (e.g., the Nazi medical experiments) and highlight the importance of gaining consent. For example, the first point of the Code states that "The voluntary consent of the human subject is absolutely essential" (British Medical Journal, 1996); the fourth states that "The experiment should be conducted in a way that avoids all unnecessary physical and mental suffering and injury" (British Medical Journal, 1996); and the sixth states that "The degree of risk to be taken should never exceed that determined by the humanitarian importance of the problem to be solved by the experiment" (British Medical Journal, 1996). Faden and Beauchamp (1986, p. 86) explain, further, that informed consent was not truly integrated into American medicine until the late 1950s.

Several other key events are worth noting. One is the creation of the Declaration of Helsinki Report in 1964, which was developed by the World Medical Association (WMA). This initiative outlined a set of ethical principles for research, placing consent at its core. While not a legally binding document, it put forward a set of guidelines and principles for practitioners to follow—wherever they might be in the world, and whatever the legal requirements of their country were. There are several mentions of *informed consent* in the declaration, but here are two that I believe are the most relevant to our discussion. The first comes from Article 25, which says that

> Participation by individuals capable of giving *informed consent* as subjects in medical research must be voluntary. Although it may be appropriate to consult family members or community leaders, no individual capable of giving informed consent may be enrolled in a research study unless he or she freely agrees.
>
> (WMA, 1964/2013, my emphasis)

That a person needs to "freely agree" before being included in a research study may seem like a simple and obvious requirement today, but it is worth pausing for a moment to think about (i) how recent this requirement is, and also (ii) how personal data collection and use on the internet fails to meet this standard. Ask yourself whether you have *freely agreed* to let all of the different companies collect and use your personal data.

The second article I wish to draw attention to is Article 26. It importantly requires that human subjects not only *agree* to take part but are *informed* about what they are agreeing to.

> In medical research involving human subjects capable of giving informed consent, each potential subject must be adequately informed of the aims, methods, sources of funding, any possible conflicts of interest, institutional affiliations of the researcher, the anticipated benefits and potential risks of the study and the discomfort it may entail.
>
> (WMA, 1964/2013, my emphasis)

This article is significant because it encourages medical researchers to be transparent about what they hope to achieve by doing the research, and it also encourages them to clarify the risks associated with taking part in the research project. Without knowledge of such risks, it is hard to see how one can give informed consent. For anyone currently involved in medical research, this may seem like a standard practice that may seem obvious to secure. But again, it is worth thinking about how recent in human history these changes are and how infrequently this occurs with respect to personal data collection and use on the internet. If you feel like you do often give consent "freely" online, ask yourself how frequently you feel you have been informed about the anticipated benefits or potential risks of sharing your personal data. If you are like most internet users, I suspect there would have been numerous occasions that you have shared your personal data without such knowledge.

In the years that followed the Declaration of Helsinki, further changes occurred in medical ethics. One was the shift from the "Doctor Knows Best" paradigm—the idea that the doctor is best placed to make decisions, when it comes to what is the right course of action for a patient to take—to a more "Autonomous" paradigm, which emphasised a more significant role for the patient to play, when it comes to deciding what treatment is best for them. As Robert Baker (2019) has described, two important documents can be thought of as the catalysts for this change in perspective. One was the publication of the *Belmont Report* in the late 1970s (NCPHSBBR, 1979), which identified and made the case for a greater focus on respect for persons, beneficence, and justice; and the second was the *Principles of Biomedical Ethics* in 1979 by Beauchamp and Childress (1979/2008), which focused on establishing the importance of four ethical principles: autonomy, non-maleficence, beneficence, and justice (cf. Page, 2012). If we look at contemporary guidance documents about how medical practitioners ought to act, we see the legacy of such works. For example, in the "Clinical Governance Advice No. 6" consent guidance document from the Royal College of Obstetricians and Gynaecologists (RCOG)—an organisation with over 17,000 members worldwide which helps to improve women's healthcare—it is advised that healthcare practitioners need to ensure that patients are "able to understand information provided", "not be coerced or influenced by carers, family or friends", and can understand the "benefits and risks of the intended procedure" (RCOG, 2015, p. 9).[2] Here we can see a focus on patient autonomy, beneficence, and justice.

Why is it important to consider this history? For one reason, it suggests that meaningful change seldom occurs overnight. Transformations often follow impactful events, like the aftermath of World War II; instances where individuals advocated for change; and periods of stagnation where things remained static. A second reason has to do with our current project, which is about trying to improve consent procedures on the internet. My hope is that by looking at the way that informed consent has become increasingly valued in the medical context; there will be some lessons that can be applied to the personal data collection context, where it is not currently valued as highly.

I see an important role for scholars to specify these lessons and how they can be generalised. Recall, I am not suggesting that every Google login requires a sit-down appointment with a data scientist, but I do believe that looking at the history of informed consent can help us to find ways to improve informed consent practices on the internet. We do not need to fully re-invent the wheel to do this; there exists an established body of guiding principles, norms, and legal requirements regarding informed consent in the medical context informed by rich ethical and philosophical traditions. How exactly we draw from the medical context is a task that I take up in this book.

In looking to the history of informed consent, we might also pay attention to the structure of how change occurs. One key lesson from Robert Baker's (2019) work on ethical *revolutions* is that old ethical paradigms are superseded by new ones in specific ways. In his discussion about the change that occurred from the "Doctor Knows Best" paradigm to a more "Autonomous" consent model (which I mentioned above), he notes that criticism alone did not bring about change. The two important publications of the late 1970s, the *Belmont Report* and the *Principle of Biomedical Ethics*, that brought about this change were not simply criticisms. Both texts gave a positive account by sketching an alternative paradigm to the Doctor Knows Best paradigm. As Baker suggests in the following:

> [N]o insurrection—or, to be circumspect, none that I have analyzed—has successfully destabilised a dominant moral or scientific paradigm without offering an incompatible alternative paradigm. Our intellectual natures abhor conceptual vacuums.
>
> (2019, p. 173)

Baker's point here is that one must do more than offer criticism; one must also provide alternatives. Even if a current paradigm or way of doing things is unpleasant or unworkable, we might become resigned to it, if we believe there are no alternatives. Of course, it is still vital to point out the problems with current paradigms. For example, it is still necessary, as many have done, to highlight the ways that Facebook or TikTok collect and use our personal data are often ethically flawed. But this cannot be all we do. We need to start outlining alternative paradigms in which a data economy may operate. The more detailed and coherent these proposals are, the more likely it will be that meaningful change can actually occur.

As we saw in the Preface, there are many criticisms of "surveillance capitalism", whereas solutions or alternative paradigms are much harder to come by. For many, it may seem hard to even imagine how things could be different. However, I think such historical examples of the kind examined above, should encourage us to try. In the 1970s, the paternalistic Doctor Knows Best paradigm understood the act of obtaining *informed consent* as a mechanism to protect researchers. When this paradigm was superseded by the Autonomous paradigm, informed consent was seen in a very different way. It was understood as a process that could facilitate patient's autonomy, dignity, and choice (see Baker, 2019, p. 175).

Analogously in the online commercial data context: consent is often seen as a way to protect a company, such that it is collected for the purposes of providing evidence that a person actually consented to a privacy policy or terms and conditions agreement. That there is often no attempt to make sure that the person has *understood* the data collection process, and thus given *informed consent*, is an ethical shortcoming that exists in contemporary online consent-gathering practices.

1.2 Express Consent Versus Informed Consent

Consent has the ability to alter the morality of an action. As Heidi M. Hurd aptly puts it, consent is a kind of *magic* that can turn trespassing into a dinner party, theft into a gift, or an invasion of privacy into an intimate moment (1996, p. 123). The notion of consent thus holds paramount importance in contemporary medical ethics, as it can allow medical practitioners to operate on our bodies in a way that might be considered assault if it were not for the consent we have given. The administering of a powerful drug for treatment, for example, could be considered poison without consent (Manson & O'Neill, 2007, p. 75). You might think that consent itself may be fairly easy to obtain. One may say "yes", sign a document, or click an "accept" button online. These kinds of actions are instances of "express consent" and are relatively unproblematic in terms of their ability to authorise something. Either one gives consent or one does not. Yet things get complicated the moment that we also require that the consent needs to be *informed*. It is trivially easy to know if one has given consent to a doctor operating on one's body by saying "yes", or by looking at a signed document, but that same person will need to do a lot more than any of these acts to also show that they have given *informed consent*.

A challenge in the medical context is to specify the conditions upon which informed consent is given. As mentioned earlier, if a patient is tricked into saying "yes", or a patient was not told about the risks of a procedure, but still agrees to it, they will not have given informed consent. Similarly, many of us may give *express* consent online, often without knowing much about what we are consenting to, which is to say that we often fail to give informed consent. This might seem like a trivial point, but within the data economy, this distinction becomes important. This is because we spend so little time reading privacy policies and terms and conditions. In circumstances where we do give consent, it is often nothing more than express consent. Think about how many times you have scrolled to the bottom of a terms and conditions document and clicked "agree" without any knowledge of what you were agreeing to. If you have not read or understood anything, we can hardly say that you have given informed consent.

Personal data collection processes, just like dinner parties, are not inherently bad. Of course, there is a lot of misuse of personal data out there, but personal data collection has the potential to benefit people's lives too. The problem here is whether people actually *know* what they are consenting to. We not only want to be in charge of what personal data are collected, but also know who is collecting it, and how it is going to be used. To return to our dinner party example, your decision to allow a guest over is hardly informed if all you know about the person is that they were born in Australia. Ideally, you want to know who the person is, before you invite them into your home. Analogously, if you have little idea about how your data are being used, the fact that you gave express consent is certainly relevant, but by itself fails to fulfil the *purpose* of consent.

Suppose Facebook asks you to agree to a recent change to their privacy policy. If you click "yes" or "I agree", this means you have given express consent. From a legal perspective, this might give Facebook all the permissions it needs to use your personal data in the ways outlined in the privacy policy. But from a moral perspective, if this is all you have done, this is problematic. If you have not read their privacy policy, or if the privacy policy does not explain everything that could be done with your data, as well as the risks involved with sharing your data, then you will not have given *informed* consent. But what risks should be disclosed? One possibility is *all of them*. This is unworkable, however, as there could be hundreds, if not, thousands of risks. What about only the serious ones then? This seems more workable but immediately raises the question of what counts as "serious", however. Consider the following from Edward L. Raab, who talks about risk disclosure in the medical context.

> Must all risks be disclosed? The law requires disclosure only of material, not trivial, risks that are reasonably foreseeable. "One in a million" occurrences, risks obvious even to a layperson, and those that clearly would not result in refusal of treatment had they been disclosed constitute other exceptions. As in malpractice, these situations turn on their particular fact contexts.
>
> (2004, p. 227, emphasis in original)

Of course, in order to determine what the material risks of a certain procedure are, one will be required to know the specific context in which it arises, and one may need to know something about the patient too. For example, a procedure that carries with it a risk of blood clot might seem like a trivial risk to one patient, but it may seem like a huge risk to a patient of a certain age and medical history. While a medical professional can take the time to explain risks to patients and determine how best to assess them, this is hard to achieve in the online context. First, not only do we lack any kind of data professional to communicate with us online, but personal data can often be used in ways that go beyond the purpose that they were originally given consent for, and thus introduce new risks that were never known to the user as discussed in Chapter 3.

1.3 What Constitutes Informed Consent?

As we have seen, informed consent is central to health and medical ethics.[3] But what exactly is it? While the question might initially appear straightforward—the disclosure of information to patients before they give their consent—it becomes more puzzling when we start to ask how much information should be provided. Furthermore, a glance into the literature on medical informed consent reveals an ongoing debate about its nature. For some, informed consent is more than simply information transfer (see, e.g., Manson & O'Neill, 2007). Thus, if we are to extract lessons from the way that informed consent is viewed in the medical context, we must grapple with some of the complexities of the concept, before attempting to apply it to the online context.

Suppose you speak to a medical professional, in order to get an important procedure done, and the only thing that the medical professional tells you is that the procedure involves surgery but fails to tell you anything else. You agree, and the procedure takes place. Does that count as informed consent? I think most people would say no, since you do not really know anything about the procedure, such as the risks associated with it. But this raises the question of what amount of information suffices for informed consent. You might think that the solution is to give people more and more information until some threshold is met. It might be hard to imagine what that is, but in principle, we might come to the optimum amount of information. However, as Tom Walker (2012) suggests, this leads to practical problems. One problem concerns how demanding a task this is. He states, "[i]t takes more time and effort to ensure patients or research participants understand information than it does simply to disclose it, and the more information on the list the more demanding this becomes" (2012, p. 50). The second problem he identifies has to do with our ability to comprehend what we are told or read. He states, "there is now considerable empirical evidence to suggest that patients and research participants do not understand all of the information they are given" (2012, p. 50). This is a problem because if you do not understand the risks, you might underappreciate them.

This is an especially big problem with personal data collection and use on the internet, as we have already seen, since it might take you weeks or months to read through all the privacy policies or terms and conditions you encounter in a year. Think about your own case: how many times have you skim read, or completely dismissed, a terms and conditions agreement online? Now, even if you do manage to read some of the agreements or privacy policies that you encounter online, the nature of personal data usage makes it hard for users to keep up to date about how their personal data are *now* being used. The terms and conditions you spent hours reading and understanding (assuming they were sufficiently transparent) last year might now be out of date. As Helen Nissenbaum has pointed out, "the realm is in constant flux, with new firms entering the picture, new analytics, and new back-end contracts forged" (2011, p. 36). New data broker companies may have an interest in collecting your data that did not exist at the time you consented to the collection of your personal data.[4]

So far, I have discussed some of the issues with informed consent that relate to the "disclosure of information". Many regard this as central to informed consent because disclosure of relevant information seems necessary for us to make informed decisions. Manson and O'Neill characterise this as the *standard view* about informed consent and say, "[o]n the standard view that informed consent is required in order to respect autonomy, these 'informational' obligations are seen as justified because they protect and enhance individual decision making" (2007, p. 27). On the standard view, Manson and O'Neill claim what matters from an ethical perspective is that "the patient or research subject *choose* or *decide which* course of action she favors, or *whether* to proceed with a certain course of action" (2007, p. 27, emphasis in original). Again, information seems necessary for this. However, Manson and O'Neill argue that this is not all there is to informed consent. A better reason to focus on consent in their view is that it provides a way of protecting the patient. They say, "[c]onsent is a way of ensuring that those subjected to invasive interventions are not abused, manipulated, or undermined or wronged . . . in serious ways" (2007, p. 82). If our focus, or aim, is just to provide information to subjects, this might not necessarily take place. Think about how much information is given to us via privacy policies online. Does this information transfer really protect us from harm? In Manson and O'Neill's view, the prevention from abuse, manipulations, or wrongdoing cannot be achieved by the transfer of information *alone*. They claim that if our aim is to protect patients, then this "aim cannot be secured by making consent disclosures more and more 'complete'" (2007, p. 82).[5]

This is a key point and one that is directly relevant to our concerns about personal data collection. If we look at the contemporary problems with informed consent through the lens of information transfer, then it might seem like our problems can be solved in the commercial use of personal data context by providing more detailed privacy policies or terms and conditions. But if the aim of informed consent is to protect against certain abuses, and longer and longer privacy policies do not achieve this, then our strategies and methods of obtaining informed consent need to change. Moving away from a sole focus on "information transfer" also forces us to think about other relevant questions such as who informs, and how they inform us. This is an important consideration because power discrepancies, say between patients and physicians, can affect a patient's decision-making capacity (see Nimmon & Stenfors-Hayes, 2016). If our focus is only on information transfer, then we may not pay attention to this.

In suggesting that "information transfer" might not be the only thing we focus on in attempting to secure informed consent, I do not mean to suggest that it is irrelevant. We can be concerned with multiple aspects of consent at the same time, as is shown in the following definition of informed consent by Tom Beauchamp. In the context of medicine, clinical practices, and biomedical research, Beauchamp says, "[a] person gives an informed consent . . . if and only if the person, with *substantial understanding* and in *substantial absence of control by others*, intentionally authorizes a health professional to do something" (2011, pp. 517–518, my emphasis). There are two elements worth noting here: the first is Beauchamp's requirement that one needs to understand what they are consenting to; and the second is the absence of control by others. This means that a health professional ought not to coerce you into doing something you would normally not want to do, or something that is against your best interests.

Beauchamp's first point is important in that it emphasises "substantial understanding", instead of simply information transfer. This pertains to the *purpose* of informed consent, which as we have seen ought to assist patients in decision making. As Tendler et al. (2023) point out, in clinical trials in the United States, informed consent documents are there to help subjects decide whether they should take part in the trial. Thus, they ought to present information in a clear way, "not merely provide a list of isolated facts", in order to "facilitate comprehension" (2023, p. 8).

It is of course one thing to say that this is how informed consent ought to be understood in the medical context, but is it also the case that this tracks the normative requirements of informed consent online? After all, in the medical context, a doctor will be able to check to see if a patient understood a certain procedure; there does not seem to be any equivalent in the online context to ensure that "data subjects" understand what they consenting to. Here I borrow the term "data subject" from the GDPR, which also uses the term "personal data" to mean "any information relating to an identified or identifiable natural person ('data subject')" (European Union, 2016, Article 4). If we also look to the GDPR, the "toughest privacy and security law in the world" (Wolford, n.d.-a), which was put into effect in 2018 in the European Union, we see two other important groups of stakeholders that are defined, which I now consider. These are the so-called "data controllers" and "data processors". Might these groups of stakeholders have a responsibility to ensure that data subjects understand what they are consenting to?

To answer this question, let us look to see how both are defined. First, "data controllers" are defined as follows:

> A data controller determines the purposes and means of processing personal data. In other words, the data controller decides the how and why of a data processing operation. A data controller can be a legal person, for example a business, an SME, a public authority, an agency or other body.
>
> (EDPB, n.d.)

A "data processer", on the other hand, "acts under the instructions of the controller only, by processing personal data on behalf of the controller" (EDPB, n.d.). To see the difference between the two consider a brief example. Suppose you run a company that sells Blueberry Jam and suppose as part of your business you collect personal data, such as your customers' email addresses, their age, buying habits, and so on. You would be a *data controller*. As someone in this role, you might then sell their personal data to a "data processor", who would process these data in a certain way. As the GDPR states in Article 4, Definition 8, a processor means "a natural or legal person, public authority, agency or other body which processes personal data on behalf of the controller" (European Union, 2016). The GDPR states, furthermore, that both sets of stakeholders have certain legal responsibilities to use your data in an ethical way (European Union, 2016, Articles 24 and 28).

So, could we modify Beauchamp's definition so that it describes the relationship between data subjects and controllers/processors in a similar way to the relationship between patients and medical practitioners? Here is what that might look like:

> *Beauchamp's modified definition.* A *data subject* gives an informed consent online if and only if the *data subject*, with substantial understanding and in substantial absence of control by others, intentionally authorizes a *data controller* or *data processor* to do something.

This revised definition may provide us with a good starting point, but there are some problems with accepting it outright. First, to state the obvious, data controllers and processors are not medical professionals. Even when they claim to have altruistic aims (e.g., to "change the world"), their primary function is to operate within a legal framework of a data economy.[6] This is not to say that ethical norms do not apply to them, but their general aims are quite far removed from medical practitioners, who are not only bound by some general ethical and legal standards to preserve human health but also by the specific ethical standards and practices of their profession.

Consider the practice of targeted advertising—for example, a form of online advertising that uses personal data to allow companies to reach those who might actually be interested in a certain company's product or service. Here the primary aim is to convince a person to buy something they might not otherwise have bought. In some cases, the more one *understands* how this process works, the "creepier" they might find it, and thus less effective the advertisements might be due to mistrust (cf. Herder & Zhang, 2019). In some cases, then, "understanding" might be in tension with certain commercial interests.[7]

Another issue relates to the way in which one is supposed to verify that "substantial understanding" has occurred. In the medical context, a doctor or physician could simply ask their patients, in order to see if they understand. However, in many online cases, consent is given at the end of a long privacy policy or terms and conditions document, which gives little to indicate to a data controller or processer that the data subject has understood anything. Of course, there would still be evidence of express consent (e.g., evidence that one clicked "I agree"), but as our earlier discussion has shown, this is insufficient to show that understanding has occurred. Considering that many people fail to read privacy policies, as I will discuss in more detail in the subsequent chapters, such people cannot possibly give informed consent if they are unaware of what is occurring with their data. How exactly a data controller or processor could ensure that people do understand, even if they wanted to, remains a challenge.

We have seen that there are some challenges with applying the concept of informed consent from the medical context to the personal data economy context. A further complication pertains to the concept of informed consent itself, as there are debates in the literature about what constitutes it. For example, there are those such as Tom Walker (2022) who suggest that informed consent can provide a kind of symbolic value for patients. He argues that "[i]n some circumstances, it is having the opportunity to choose, not the act of choosing, that is valuable" (2022, p. 61, my emphasis). Walker draws on work from the philosopher Thomas Scanlon (1998, pp. 251–256) to highlight the fact that being deprived of a choice in certain circumstances, when others have been given a choice, can be demeaning. By giving a patient a choice, you can recognise them as competent and equal members of society. In Walker's view, there are implications of accepting such a view, namely, it should move one away from the current focus on autonomy in medical ethics. Walker's emphasis on the value of choice is relevant to our current concerns due to the widespread collection of our data without our awareness. The fact that we are not properly consulted or given a proper choice might be seen as just as morally problematic as the fact that we do not give informed consent when completing online agreements. The fact that we do not even get a chance to make meaningful choices might have a negative impact on us.

A brief review of some of the different explanations of informed consent reveals that there are ways of thinking about informed consent that go beyond "information transfer". Furthermore, these ways appear to be relevant and applicable to some of the problems that face those whose personal data are collected and used online. Although there are controversies here, I think there is a clear lesson that emerges from this discussion—that is, by only focusing on information transfer, we lose sight of the purpose of informed consent.[8]

1.4 What Grounds Informed Consent: A Pluralistic Approach

There are, as we have seen, several competing explanations for what constitutes informed consent in the medical context. While the accounts we have looked at above stress different aspects over others, all were in agreement that reducing informed consent to information transfer is problematic. If these approaches are to guide us in our task of improving informed consent practices online, then what should be said about these different perspectives? Given the relative infancy of the attempts to improve informed consent online, I think we should be less concerned with debating which of these is the most important at this stage and be more concerned with ensuring that they all play some role in our focus on informed consent.

While I agree that informed consent in the personal data collection context should not be reduced to mere "information transfer", I will refrain from prioritising any of these elements here, and instead adopt a more pluralistic approach, considering all of these various elements. In my view, starting with a more pluralistic approach makes the most sense. In more mature contexts, such as the medical, variations and distinctions become more evident as the field matures and reaches a consensus on specific issues. However, since informed consent in the online context is often lacking and considering the diversity of factors involved, I believe that it is best to take all aspects seriously at this early stage.

In searching for an account of informed consent that is fit for purpose in the online context, then, there are four conditions I will keep in mind as we progress. First, for a "data subject" to give informed consent online, they should be given a say in what happens to their personal data and thus be recognised as a rational agent whose decision can either permit or block the sharing of some type of personal data—call this the "autonomy/respect for persons condition". Second, informed consent should also serve to prevent abuse to data subjects; it should ensure that individuals are aware of the risks associated with consenting and facilitate a way of protecting themselves from harm—call this the "harm condition". To achieve this, the information that data subjects receive should be communicated to them in a manner that truly provides an understanding of the associated risks—call this the "communication condition". Finally, data subjects should ideally have a sufficient degree of knowledge about what they are agreeing to when they provide consent. To restate, these four conditions are as follows:

1. The Autonomy/Respect for Persons Condition
2. The Harm Condition
3. The Communication Condition
4. The Knowledge Condition

While our list could be expanded, and further refined, it provides us with a way to start assessing current consent practices in the personal data collection context. And we do not have to look far to find cases where these conditions have failed to be secured. For example, in her recent book, *Privacy Is Power*, Carissa Véliz presents many examples of companies who have misused our personal data. She notes that "[f]or years, Facebook allowed Microsoft's Bing search engine to see Facebook users' friends *without their consent*, and it gave Netflix and Spotify the ability to read and even delete Facebook users' 'private' messages" (2021, p. 17, my emphasis). Facebook's other controversies about privacy have been well documented in the media too. For example, according to Dance et al.'s article in *The New York Times*, Facebook "permitted Amazon to obtain users' names and contact information through their friends, and it let Yahoo view streams of friends' posts [as early as summer 2018] despite public statements that it had stopped that type of sharing years earlier" (2018).

In these examples, we see all four of the conditions outlined earlier fail to be satisfied. The respect for persons/autonomy condition is not satisfied because data subjects were not actively involved in the choice to share their personal data; furthermore, since they did not understand what was happening to their data, they could not assess the risks associated with sharing their data—such types of data sharing could possibly cause harm to them, after all (the harm condition). The communication condition fails to be satisfied because the companies did not make meaningful attempts to explain to the data subjects what was happening with their personal data. This leads to the failure of the fourth condition—the knowledge condition. The data subjects involved clearly lacked knowledge about what was happening with their personal data, as their consent was not even sought in the first place.

It may seem that with the introduction of legislation such as the GDPR, we will start to see some changes in the behaviour of companies, and thus the law will be able to provide the solution. Consider, for example, Article 4 of the GDPR, which features a discussion about consent:

> '[C]onsent' of the data subject means any *freely given*, specific, *informed* and unambiguous indication of the data subject's wishes by which he or she, by a statement or by a clear affirmative action, signifies agreement to the processing of personal data relating to him or her.
>
> (European Union, 2016, my emphasis)

Now, while this is certainly well and good, questions arise about how well this description of consent can meet all of the four conditions that were raised above. It is clearly a good thing that the consent described here is required to be "informed", but what might "freely given" mean? Does one freely give consent when their decision is influenced by others, for example? Furthermore, how can data controllers or processors ensure that people actually do understand what they are consenting to, and are not just blindly giving express consent? Alternatively, might companies simply be obligated to provide the information to data subjects, and whether they read it or understand it is a choice they are responsible for and not the company? Before launching into a discussion of these questions, I will end the chapter with two objections to my overall proposal.

1.5 The Asymmetry Objection

My contention in this book is that we can draw lessons from the way that informed consent is utilised in medical contexts for the commercial use of personal data on the internet. There is a vast medical consent literature that can be drawn from to help us with some of the problems we face with online personal data collection. An objection that is important to address at this early stage of the book is whether my project is based on a mistaken assumption about the commercial sector. It may be objected that informed consent is so important in the medical context because human lives and our general well-being are at stake. Furthermore, it may be argued that medical professionals have certain responsibilities to patients that go beyond mere financial transactions between medical professionals and patients. This is not the case in the commercial sector.[9] With these kinds of concerns in mind, one may make the following objection:

The Asymmetry Objection

> The medical world has standards and practices, as it literally deals with life and death, but the commercial world of personal data collection operates within the free market, which, while regulated, requires data subjects to take responsibility for what they consent to. Businesses do not exist to protect the well-being of citizens, and it is a mistake to try to attribute to them the aims and goals of medical practitioners.[10] Doing so places unrealistic expectations on the market and, in the process, halts progress. Businesses like Facebook or Google are not medical practitioners or researchers, and it is a mistake to think that they need to start acting like they are. Furthermore, not much harm can come about from personal data collection.

It might be objected that businesses, like the so-called "big tech" companies, do not have the kinds of moral obligations of the kind that apply in the medical context. Their moral, or normative obligations, consist of whatever is required by law, and whatever is good for business. One could, further, adopt as a motto the title of Milton Friedman's (1970) infamous essay in *The New York Times* "The Social Responsibility of Business Is to Increase Its Profits". One might think it naive, or even fundamentally at odds with the aim of business, to look to the medical world for any kind of inspiration that could potentially curb profits.

Of course, it should be stated that with the introduction of the GDPR in Europe, and countries like Australia updating their privacy laws, it is becoming harder for companies to do whatever they like with people's personal data.[11] Nevertheless, you might think that going over and above what the law dictates, or what is good for business, places unnecessary limits on these companies. During a conference I once attended, I was giving a talk on data privacy and ethics. After the talk, someone from the private sector came up to me and objected to my framing of the problems, of the kind discussed here, as ethical ones. In his view, as long as businesses were following the law, and customers were still sticking with the company, then that is all they needed to do. "We call it reputation management", he told me.[12]

One problem with such a view is that it is not very forward-looking and risks not taking into account the well-being of all the stakeholders involved. However, even if one is inclined to accept this view, there may still be important reasons to care about ethics—that is, even those who are convinced that "the business of business is business" might still think that "good business is good ethics", as Stephen Cohen (1999) puts it.

Companies and brands can ruin their reputations if they are associated with scandals or are shown to have partaken in deceptive practices or have broken the law. Consider what happened to Cambridge Analytica after the 2018 scandal broke, for example (though it is also worth noting how Facebook was able to continue on relatively unscathed.) Good business may require "good ethics".

Recent studies indicate that people, especially the current generation, care deeply about ethical considerations. For example, as a university lecturer who teaches young adults, I often hear from students who say that they have stopped using products because of a certain company's behaviour. We see this kind of response reflected in reports too. A 2018 McKinsey & Company report found that 70% of Gen Z responders—who they call the "first generation of digital natives"—"purchase products from companies they consider ethical" (Francis & Hoefel, 2018, p. 9) and "[a]bout 80 percent [of Gen Z responders] refuse to buy goods from companies involved in scandals" (Francis & Hoefel, 2018, p. 9). A 2023 Edelman Trust Institute (ETI) report, furthermore, which surveyed over 13,000 people from 14 countries made a similar finding. One interesting result was that 62% of responders in the ages 18–26 category agreed with the following statement "[i]f a brand doesn't communicate its actions to address societal issues, I assume it is doing nothing or hiding something" (ETI, 2023, p. 12). A second question looked at whether "[i]t is more important to trust the brands I buy or use today than in the past" (ETI, 2023, p. 11). Gen Z (the 18–26 age group) scored the highest of all other participants, with 79% of this group answering "yes" to the question. Thus, even if one takes a cynical view, with respect to companies going over and above what is required of them by the law, there are still prudential reasons for companies to care about ethics.[13]

A second reason to reject the asymmetry objection has to do with an outdated view of stakeholder management that I think is implicit in it.[14] If we go back to the 1960s, Albert Carr (1968) famously argued that business bluffing is ethical, suggesting that it may be acceptable in the context of business. However, if this holds true, if it ever did, it advances a very negligent and dangerous way of conducting business. As John R. Rowan (1998) suggests, there is a real need for members of the public to know what they are buying because if there is a safety flaw, or harm could come to people if they do not have all the facts, then that could be quite dangerous. They need to know what they are buying or signing up for and have knowledge of "available alternatives" (1998, p. 102). He adds:

> Without such knowledge, [the public] are not in a position to exercise their rational capacity and make a decision consistent with their goals. In other words, the *consent*, in addition to being given voluntarily and by a

> competent public, must be *informed*. Because business professionals recognize (or should recognize) that the public does not possess equivalent knowledge and expertise with respect to the product or service in question, they are obligated to disclose to the public all information relevant to that good or service, and then allow a choice to be made.
>
> (1998, p. 102, my emphasis)

Rowan here talks about an "ethical obligation" that companies have, which is not solely grounded in economic benefits. For Rowan, it stems from an imbalance between what the company knows and what the public knows. This is something that I will develop over the course of the next seven chapters. Technology companies will be aware of the fine-grained details of data collection (e.g., what personal data are collected, and where it goes), but the public often has a poor understanding, putting them in a vulnerable position, that can potentially lead them to become exploited, due to their lack of knowledge. The knowledge imbalance between companies and the public thus becomes very dangerous and is something that informed consent should be able to help protect. If companies do not do a good job of obtaining informed consent, this knowledge gap remains and is ripe for exploitation.

1.6 On the Right Not to Know

In this book, I accept the "prevailing view" in the recent literature—that online consent practices on the internet are ethically flawed. This chapter proposed some initial steps to rectify these flaws. However, it is important to identify one of the key premises in my argument that is not accepted by everyone, namely, the truth of the *prevailing view*. For example, Chomanski and Lauwaert (2023) have criticised an earlier attempt of mine to defend the view (see Andreotta et al., 2022), as well as the work of several others.[15] Chomanski and Lauwaert claim that "[u]ninformed consent to online terms and conditions (what we will call, for short, 'online consent') is less ethically problematic than many scholars suppose" (2023). According to them, there is nothing ethically problematic with a data subject clicking "accept" at the bottom of a privacy policy without understanding what they have consented to. In their view, users have a "right not to know" what is happening to their data if that is their preference. Chomanski and Lauwaert state that

> It is likely that typical internet users exercise their RNTK [Right Not to Know] prior to agreeing to the terms and conditions of various websites (they certainly act as if they do). Their consent, then, ought to be presumed meaningful in all of the senses under consideration.
>
> (2023)

Furthermore, the authors assert that when data subjects provide such consent, they "exercise their RNTK, and thus their subsequent *uninformed* consent is, at least presumptively, valid" (2023, my emphasis). While there are certainly some situations where people do exercise their RNTK online (e.g., one might try to avoid seeing negative comments about oneself online), I find this interpretation implausible, when applied to the psychology of regular internet users providing consent online. For this to be true, I think we would first have to establish that users do not care about how their personal data are used and are also unconcerned about the kinds of privacy violations that have been widely reported on lately.

The question is do people really exercise their RNTK when clicking "I agree", or might they be placed in a seemingly impossible situation where there are simply too many privacy policies and terms and conditions to navigate, and not enough time? Even if we do accept Chomanski and Lauwaert's view as an account of how rational adults act online, cases of consent without knowledge have implications for other people who can be impacted by the consent another gives. It might be, for example, that an adult clicks "I agree" and this allows targeted ads to be sent to their children, or non-consenting family members, colleagues, or friends. Or, in cases where you exercise your RNTK and then, without realising it, you give away your contacts' information such that they too can be advertised to—something they would never give consent to.

At present, people may click through the privacy policies that apply to them, but I do not think that this automatically shows they have exercised their right not to know. There is real harm that can come to data subjects who provide "uninformed" consent. Once these harms are fully appreciated (the task of Chapter 2), then I believe that the implausibility of this position can be shown. Online consent procedures are certainly, at the moment, problematic, and attempting to go through thousands of long policies and terms and conditions is a near-impossible task. This much we all should agree on. However, I believe that if we can work on improving consent practices, then people might stand a better chance of self-managing their own privacy.

1.7 Conclusion

In this chapter, I have argued that in order to improve informed consent practices and procedures online—which involves the collection and use of large amounts of our personal data—we can look to the medical world for inspiration. We need to be selective, however, in the lessons we apply. We do not need to turn TikTok or Facebook sessions into doctor's office visits. Nevertheless, we can attempt to improve consent by moving away from a model which focuses merely on the "transfer of information". Such a model is, as I will show, ineffective in securing data subjects' informed consent online. We should attempt to make sure that consent practices involve respect for persons, actually communicate information to consenters, provide the consenter with an awareness of potential risks, and thus provide consenters with knowledge of what is occurring with their data. In order to see why this is a pressing ethical issue, I now turn, in the next chapter, to the harms that can come about from failing to secure informed consent online, to build the case for a greater focus on informed consent on a strong ethical foundation.

Notes

1 The concept of a paradigm shift was popularised by Thomas Kuhn in his seminal work, *The Structure of Scientific Revolutions*. Kuhn was concerned with paradigm shifts in the context of scientific revolutions (1962/2012). See Baker (2019) for an application of this idea to medical ethics.

2 For more information about RCOG, see their website: https://www.rcog.org.uk/about-us/what-we-do/.

3 See Manson and O'Neill (2007, p. 5) for an important discussion about situations in the medical context where it would *not* be appropriate to withhold treatment before informed consent has been given. They state that "[p]atients who cannot give informed consent can hardly be denied treatment . . . Very many patients are unconscious or too ill, cognitively impaired or mentally confused, too young or too frail to grasp the relevant information, so cannot give informed consent to their medical treatment" (Manson and O'Neill (2007, p. 5). In research ethics, on the other hand, they note that informed consent may be a "universal" requirement (Manson and O'Neill (2007, p. 5).

4 Sarah Lamdan (2022a, p. 28) notes that there are two types of data brokers that exist today. The first are "commercial" data brokers, which are the ones associated with companies like Facebook and Google, who are interested in our personal data for the purposes of targeted advertising. The second type is "institutionalized" data brokering, in which companies sell personal data to governments and other institutions, who are then able to make decisions about whom to criminalise and whom to surveil. This book will focus on the former.

5 In an earlier paper, Onora O'Neill argued that a "better reason for taking informed consent seriously is that it provides assurance that patients and others are neither deceived nor coerced" (2003, p. 4).

6 As Kara Swisher notes, many large tech companies, like Facebook, "began with a gauzy credo to change the world" (2018).

7 For a discussion of the history of surveillance and capitalism in the United States, see Lauer and Lipartito's (2021) recent edited volume.

8 For an excellent summary of the recent philosophical literature on informed consent, see Eyal (2019).

9 A separate objection arises from the fact that personal data collection in the commercial context differs fundamentally from the medical context, since personal data can be used for long periods of time. As Mittelstadt and Floridi (2016) note, consent in the medical context is typically obtained for a single study or procedure, whereas personal data can be used and sold multiple times for different purposes and to new stakeholders. This means that repeated consent may

be required. I address this concern in my discussion of the Re-purposed Data Problem in Chapter 3.

10 See Broadbent (2019), Chapter 2, for a discussion on the "goal" of medicine.

11 See Paltiel (2023) for a discussion of the recent amendments to the Australian Privacy Act—specifically, the recently passed *Privacy Legislation Amendment (Enforcement and Other Measures) Act 2022 (Cth).*

12 See Pollach (2011) for a study of whether and how IT companies are motivated to care about online privacy as part of their corporate social responsibility (CSR). Pollach's research shows the existence of three different ways in which companies state they are motivated to care about online privacy. One stems from moral concerns—that is, some companies acknowledge that people have a right to privacy; a second from relational concerns—that is, some companies acknowledge that people have a desire for privacy; and a third is instrumental—that is, some companies recognise that promoting privacy is a way to improve the reputation of the company.

13 There are, of course, tensions between what people say about privacy and their behaviour, a phenomenon known as the "privacy paradox". I examine this paradox in Chapter 8.

14 See Freeman (1984) for an influential account of stakeholder theory.

15 The "prevailing view" is held by authors such as Zuboff (2019), Solove (2013a), Pascalev (2017), and others.

2 Informed Consent Gone Awry

A significant amount of personal data is collected and used online without *informed* consent. Why is that an issue? This chapter provides an answer to this question by examining some problematic ways companies have collected and used our personal data in recent years. As we shall see, there are multiple ethical concerns that arise from the improper use of personal data, so it will be important to review several examples in order to clarify what these are. Given the ubiquity of ways we operate on the internet, I can only scratch the surface of them here.

One aim of the chapter is to adequately respond to the objections that arose in Chapter 1. Recall the *asymmetry objection*, which claims it is misplaced to look to the medical world for inspiration in our attempt to improve informed consent practices online. This is because the commercial and the medical contexts are fundamentally different. In health and medicine, the main aim is to improve human well-being, whereas in the commercial world, the aim is to make money.[1] The second was the *right not to know objection*—the claim that when people click through privacy policies, or terms and conditions agreements, without reading them, they are exercising their *right not to know* what is happening to their personal data. This makes it ethically unproblematic that data subjects fail to give informed consent. I show that both objections lose their force when we consider the types of harm that can arise from the improper collection and use of personal data.

In Section 2.1, I provide a brief overview of the moral methodology that I will employ. In Section 2.2, I go through several examples of data collection and use that have occurred without informed consent, and identify how such practices have harmed data subjects. In Section 2.3, I draw a connection between informed consent and the self-management of one's privacy. Finally, in Section 2.4, I discuss the extent to which nudging might undermine informed consent.

DOI: 10.4324/9781032626048-2

2.1 On Moral Justification

The central thesis of this book is that contemporary consent practices on the internet are morally problematic. One question you may have regarding this thesis concerns the moral commitments or assumptions that guide my argument—that is, which moral principles or theories underpin my belief? My argument in what follows does not rely on one particular moral theory, though I will appeal to various moral concepts or ideas that have featured in different major moral traditions. These include appeals to *harm* (as prioritised in consequentialism and utilitarian theories), appeals to *respect for persons* and *autonomy* (as prioritised in Kantian ethics), and appeals to the *character* or *virtue* of individuals (as prioritised in virtue ethics). Where possible, however, I will attempt to appeal to moral principles that are widely accepted and be transparent about any controversial aspects from an ethical perspective.

As I will be taking this broader approach, I will not be as concerned with addressing specific issues and puzzles that arise for each moral theory or make any assumptions about which view needs to be accepted.[2] For consequentialists, or utilitarians, online data collection without informed consent might be deemed immoral because of the negative consequences that arise from it (e.g., the harm caused to millions of data subjects versus the small amounts of happiness felt by the relative few who make large amounts of money from it). However, as Kieron O'Hara has pointed out, specifying these harms can be a challenge. He says, "calculating the consequences of the operation of big data techniques is not easy" (2020, p. 19) especially when so much data collection is done covertly.[3] Was a consequence of Cambridge Analytica's data collection practices that it undermined democracy for example? One does not need to be a consequentialist to be concerned about the large-scale harms that occur from personal data collection and use.

Deontologists—those who claim that acts are morally permissible, necessary, or forbidden based upon the nature of the acts themselves, rather than the consequences of the act—might seem to have an easier time identifying what is morally objectionable about data collection and use without informed consent.[4] This is because collecting personal data for the purposes of making money, without proper informed consent, seems to undermine an agent's autonomy, or use them as a "mere" means to an end. As Kant—the most well-known deontologist—puts it, an act is unethical if it fails to adhere to the Categorical Imperative, which states, "[a]ct only according to that maxim whereby you can at the same time will that it should become a universal law" (1785/1993, p. 421). There are several formulations of the Categorical Imperative, but perhaps most relevant to our discussion is the Formula of Humanity, which states, "[a]ct in such a way that you treat humanity, whether in your own person or in the person of another, always at the same time as an end and never simply as a means" (1785/1993, p. 429).

It might seem that contemporary personal data collection practices fail to meet this condition since companies are using our personal data to make money. However, this need not necessarily be the case. For example, Bowie (1999) asks what Kantian ethics might say about the mass layoffs of the 1990s, which occurred after big companies started downsizing. Bowie asks whether these layoffs are immoral from a Kantian perspective. One might think they are, since such layoffs might not seem to respect the autonomy of the people involved. But Bowie disagrees—he says, "[s]o long as the relationship was neither coercive nor deceptive, there would be nothing immoral about layoffs" (Bowie, 1999, p. 8). Such considerations are relevant to our discussion. It encourages us to focus on whether data subjects are coerced or deceived into giving their data away, or whether they understand what they are doing when they share personal data. But again, one need not be a deontologist or Kantian to be concerned with coercive or deceptive consent-gathering practices that occur online.

A third view is virtue ethics, which focuses, as Robert Solomon says, "on the person's *character*, or alternatively, on those traits of character expressed in this and other actions, his or her *virtues*" (1999, p. 30 emphasis in original), and not the consequences of actions or acts themselves. In the context of personal data collection and use, virtue ethics would require us to examine the individuals involved and consider their character traits, motivations and intentions. We might ask whether data controllers or processors intentionally set out to deceive data subjects or coerce them, in order to make money—that is, are their actions motivated by vices such as greed? Furthermore, one could also focus on how data collection without informed consent impacts the character traits of the data subjects themselves, and whether it prevents them from flourishing. These are important scholarly questions, but one need not be a virtue ethicist to ask them. Regardless of the moral theory we accept, we can still be concerned with how data collection practices impact the characters of the stakeholders involved.[5]

Each of these three moral perspectives provides a different framework to assess the moral challenges of personal data collection. However, we need not make any assumptions here about which theory is the "correct" approach to ethics—insofar as doing so is possible—in order for the central argument that I am making here to proceed.[6] For example, even if you are not convinced that the consequences are *all* that matter morally speaking—that is, it is the consequences of an action that determine its moral properties—you should still think that large-scale harms that stem from the misuse of personal data are ethically problematic.[7]

2.2 Ethical Shortcomings in Contemporary Consent-Gathering Practices

In order to support the claim that current consent-gathering practices on the internet are ethically flawed, I will consider several recent data scandals. I use the term "data scandals" here quite loosely because while many of them were *scandalous* in the sense that they were newsworthy, many were not "data breaches" in the sense that the companies involved were hacked. Take, for example, the Facebook-Cambridge Analytica Scandal (which we will discuss in more detail later). In responding to a claim that a "data breach" occurred at Facebook, Paul Grewal, the VP & Deputy General Counsel for Facebook, stated at the time:

> The claim that this is a data breach is completely false. Aleksandr Kogan requested and gained access to information from users who chose to sign up to his app, and everyone involved gave their consent. People knowingly provided their information, no systems were infiltrated, and no passwords or sensitive pieces of information were stolen or hacked.
>
> (Grewal, 2018)

Even if Grewal is correct here, it does not exculpate Facebook or Cambridge Analytica. The issues, for the most part, with contemporary data collection practices arise from the business practices adopted by companies—though it will be important to review data breach cases too (see Section 2.2.6). In each case that follows, I will discuss how informed consent failed to be achieved and explain why this is ethically problematic.

2.2.1 Bounty and the Sharing of Sensitive Data

In 2019, the UK-based parenting club Bounty—a company which offers services and products to new parents—was fined £400,000 by the Information Commissioner's Office (ICO) for sharing customer data with marketing agencies without customers' permission or consent. While not the largest fine we have seen in the last few years, it is important to discuss for several reasons.[8] One has to do with the scale of what occurred, with more than 14 million people who were affected (Kunert, 2019). Bounty collected these personal data from its app, its website, and from new mothers in hospitals (BBC News, 2019). These data (over 30 million customer records) were then shared with data brokers such as Acxiom, Equifax, and Sky (Hern, 2019). Given the sensitive nature of these data, there was an important need to secure informed consent from users. The director of the ICO's investigation, Steve Eckersley, who issued the fine, had the following to say:

> Bounty were not open or *transparent* to the millions of people that their personal data may be passed on to such large number of organisations. Any *consent* given by these people was clearly not informed. Bounty's actions appear to have been motivated by financial gain, given that data sharing was an integral part of their *business model at the time.*
>
> (as cited in Wolford, n.d.-b; cf. Hern, 2019, my emphasis)

The director's point about Bounty's motivations here is important, as it is common today to see business models built around data sharing. How companies who operate in the data economy, who make money from data sharing, can be transparent about how they operate is a question I address in subsequent chapters.

What specifically was problematic with Bounty's data collection practices then? According to Laura White (2019), there were several issues. One relates to the opt-in policy Bounty used. White notes that those who made offline registrations—which accounted for almost 70% of registrations—had no choice but to *agree* to share their data with third parties. Second, those who registered "offline" did not have access to Bounty's privacy policy when they registered. And third, those who registered "online" were not informed that large data broker companies (e.g., Acxiom, Equifax, and Sky) might have access to their data. Any kind of consent that users provided to Bounty cannot really be thought of as informed, given that users would have large gaps in their knowledge when it comes to how their data were being used (recall our discussion of the importance of the knowledge condition in Chapter 1).

Even before looking at the consequences of Bounty's actions, it seems there are at least two fundamental ethical issues here, namely, that the company did not do enough to *inform* users about how their data were being used, and second, users were not given much *choice* about how their data were being used. A deontologist may suggest that this in itself is ethically wrong, regardless of the consequences that followed because it fails to treat users as autonomous agents, capable of making a choice. In other words, the business model appears morally objectionable since it relies on opacity to generate revenue. As demonstrated in the previous chapter, it is important to uphold transparency so that users can assess the associated risks.

It is hard, of course, to ignore the harmful consequences that arise from collecting and using these data without informed consent. What specifically is wrong with having your data sold to data brokers such as Acxiom, Equifax, and Sky? Again, we may look to what the ICO director said:

> Such careless data sharing is likely to have caused *distress* to many people, since they did not know that their personal information was being shared multiple times with so many organisations, including information about their pregnancy status and their children.
>
> (as cited in Wolford, n.d-b., my emphasis)

While it is difficult to know how each individual felt, given the amount of people involved, we can assume that a great number of people felt significant amounts of distress. Furthermore, some members of the public, when they learned that this occurred, may have continued to feel distress when contemplating whether they are still at risk. Some Bounty users could have also felt dehumanised, as they were not properly consulted about the data use, and thus not informed about the risks of having such data collected and used. Some may have felt that their own preferences were not seen as important. As Walker has pointed out, with reference to medical consent, sometimes it is having the "opportunity to choose, not the act of choosing, that is valuable" (2022, p. 61). This is because, he continues, "that opportunity conveys how one is seen" (2022, p. 61). Some Bounty users, then, may have not only felt distressed that sensitive data were shared but also because they were not even consulted, which they could have seen as "potentially demeaning" as Walker also puts it (2022, p. 61).

2.2.2 *The Opacity of TikTok's Data Collection*

I opened this book with an account of someone installing and using TikTok for the first time. I described a scenario involving someone who failed to read the terms and conditions before using the app. Of course, I could have picked any popular smartphone app and told a similar story, but I chose TikTok because at the time of this writing, it is one of the most used apps in the world. Like many apps, TikTok has the capacity to access personal data from a user's device such as their contacts, location data, age, device settings, and its cookies can track internet behaviour (BBC News, 2023). One of the problems that surrounds this type of data collection is that very few of us have knowledge about how companies like TikTok use it. To what extent do TikTok share data with data brokers like Bounty did for example?

As we also saw in the introduction, such uncertainty has led to concerns. You may have heard that TikTok shares personal information with the Chinese Government or that it takes your personal data so that it can spy on you. While TikTok has denied allegations that they give users' data to the Chinese Government (BBC News, 2023), there are still concerns about how it uses personal data. In 2023, the UK government, for example, banned ministers from using TikTok on their work phones (BBC News, 2023). In explaining why they did this, Oliver Dowden, Chancellor of the Duchy of Lancaster, said "The security of sensitive government information must come first" (Cabinet Office & Dowden, 2023). The risk of sensitive data (e.g., sensitive government information) being shared was thus deemed greater than any enjoyment the app might have given.

The question of whether *you* should delete the app is a bit more complicated of course. It is one thing for ministers to be prohibited from using the app, due to the sensitive nature of their work, but are there similar risks for the general public? Consider one risk of using the app, that was reported in the *Guardian* in 2023, namely, that TikTok had updated its privacy policy in order to inform "European users that their data can be accessed in China—in specific circumstances" (Milmo & Hern, 2023). Should this alarm us? Alan Woodward, who is a professor of cybersecurity at Surrey University, said "The bottom line is that if there is a cybersecurity issue for the government users, the same applies to all of us" (as cited in Milmo & Hern, 2023).

Whether or not such risks matter to you might come down to your individual preferences, of course. One of the problems that faces the average internet user with making an informed decision about whether to use the app, despite such risks, is that it is difficult for them to know the extent of data collection and use, and what the potential risks are of allowing such sharing. According to a 2022 report in URL Genius (Klais, 2022), TikTok shares your data more than any other social media app. The study was based upon data derived from Apple's recent privacy feature, "Record App Activity", which allows users to see information about what each of the apps on their iPhone are collecting (if you have an iPhone, it can be found in the device's settings). Yet despite the transparency offered by Apple, issues remain. Commenting on the results of the URL Genius report, the researcher Brian Klais, said that "[c]onsumers are currently unable to see what data is shared with 3rd party networks, or how their data will be used" (Klais, 2022). Thus, it is "essentially impossible to know who's tracking your data or what information they're collecting" as Tom Huddleston (2022) notes in CNBC.

In terms of informed consent, this lack of transparency is a problem. Even if you knew *that* personal data were being used, you might still be concerned about *how* they were being used. We might also bring into question the attempts made by TikTok to help you understand what occurs with your personal data. At present, people can learn about what happens by reading TikTok's privacy policy. There users can find out the kinds of personal information collected, which is good in terms of transparency. For example, the following kinds of "technical Information" are collected, as is stated in their privacy policy:

> IP address, user agent, mobile carrier, time zone settings, identifiers for advertising purposes, model of your device, the device system, network type, device IDs, your screen resolution and operating system, app and file names and types, keystroke patterns or rhythms, battery state, audio settings and connected audio devices.
>
> (TikTok, 2024)

While TikTok put this on their website, they failed to inform users, as stated earlier, where exactly these data go, how they will be used, and the kinds of risks that are associated with each type of data collection. To pick just one example, what are the risks associated with sharing keystroke patterns, if any? Are these risks distinct from the ones associated with the collection of location information? It might be objected that the privacy policies are long enough and that adding all of these details would make privacy policies simply too long to be of any practical benefit. While that might be true, the fact remains that without such knowledge, or the ability to negotiate the terms and conditions, it is hard to see how people can give informed consent.

As there have been accusations that TikTok performs "aggressive" data harvesting (see Touma, 2022), some data subjects may feel frustrated with their lack of ability to self-manage their data, which itself may cause them harm. At present, directing users to privacy policies, which are often long and vague about who is using the data, does not provide them with a good way of understanding what will be done with their data, and what risks they may face from allowing their data to be shared. Furthermore, it is difficult for users to keep up to date with changes to privacy policies. Of course, the fact that users typically have no means of negotiating these policies hardly encourages them to read them—assuming they have the time to do so.

2.2.3 YouTube and Vulnerable Stakeholders

Suppose for the sake of argument that it does not bother you that TikTok collects and uses your personal data in ways you are *unaware* of. Suppose, furthermore, that Chomanski and Lauwaert (2023) are right that in giving *uninformed* consent you exercise your right not to know what TikTok is doing with your personal data. You might reason, furthermore, that privacy is not so important anyway, and make what is sometimes called the "nothing to hide" argument, which states that only those with something to hide (e.g., one's criminal activity or one's infidelity) should be concerned about privacy.

A central problem with "nothing to hide" type arguments is that they are extremely shortsighted. As Edward Snowden once put it, "when you say I don't care about the right to privacy because I have nothing to hide that's no different than saying I don't care about freedom of speech because I have nothing to say" (as cited in Rusbridger et al., 2015). Not only might you have something to say in the future, but there may be many others who might have something to say right now. Analogously, in the context of informed consent: to say that uninformed consent is morally unproblematic because users exercise their right not to know, or the harms are small, ignores the problem that there might be others who are affected by the "uninformed" consent you provide. Suppose as a result of your uninformed consent, you give consent for a certain type of personal data, such as your location data, to be made available to a third party, which is then used to identify the whereabouts of someone close to you, which causes harm to them.[9] There are also cases where consent pertains to those in *vulnerable* groups such as children, which I now turn to.

In 2019, YouTube (owned by Google) were fined $US170 million (AUD 250 million) by the US Federal Trade Commission (FTC) for collecting children's personal data, for the purposes of advertising, without first getting consent from their parents (Associated Press, 2019). The fine followed an investigation into the way that YouTube used the personal data of children under 13 (Associated Press, 2019). An issue was raised because under Federal Law in the United States, the collection and use of data from children under 13 requires "consent" from parents. The problem was, however, that, many children under 13 were not only actively using the site, but also being targeted. FTC Chairman Joe Simons said that YouTube "refused to acknowledge that portions of its platform were clearly directed to kids" (as cited in FTC, 2019). Since YouTube is one of the most popular sites on the planet, there would have been a lot of children affected.

One type of harm that could have arisen from this kind of non-consensual personal data collection is that children could have been shown ads that would not have met the approval from parents. Children are vulnerable stakeholders as they can be easily manipulated or influenced by what they see. Targeted advertising can be harmful due to their "immature critical thinking skills and impulse inhibition" as Radesky et al. (2020) put it. Parents thus might have felt frustrated and disappointed to learn that their children were targeted without their consent. And given the number of users of the site, many parents are likely to have been affected. As FTC chairman, Joe Simons, notes, "YouTube touted its popularity with children to prospective corporate clients" (as cited in FTC, 2019). Parents might not have wanted their children to receive targeted ads (e.g., for certain foods which have been linked to childhood obesity), since such ads might have made children more receptive to certain products compared to non-targeted ads. YouTube's actions, then, may have caused a lot of harm. Failing to obtain informed consent here also seems to violate certain deontological and virtue ethics requirements, as it may seem to treat children merely as means (in other words "just using them to make money"), and such advertisement practices may even reveal the deceptive intentions on the part of the platform's management team.

As Feller and Burroughs (2022) note, YouTube responded to the large fine by making changes to their site, such as discontinuing personalised ads for children's videos and disabling comments for them.[10] Yet, we may still wonder how well the site currently informs parents about how their children will experience the site. If parents are not aware of the risks their children face while using the site and give "uninformed" consent, it might still be an issue. The FTC "crackdown" has placed limitations on YouTube's capacity to advertise, thereby restricting what the site can ask consent for.

However, as noted by Feller and Burroughs (2022), while YouTube has stopped targeted advertising with respect to children, this does not mean it has eliminated advertising directed towards them altogether. In their recent article, they discuss the rise of companies such as Pocket Watch which specialises in helping transform YouTube "child stars" into global brands (Feller & Burroughs, 2022). These so-called "kidfluencers" can get millions of views from their videos and can endorse products from prominent child brands. However, Feller and Burroughs note that "Pocket Watch's exploitation of children as advertising spokespeople for global products via embedded advertising fails to adequately disclose such commercial material relationships and thereby falls under the category of deceptive advertising" (Feller & Burroughs, 2022, p. 588). This should prompt us to ask how YouTube helps to communicate any new risks and works with parents to establish consent, and how informed parents would be. If a parent believes that the FTC has prohibited all advertisements for their children on this site and that it is free of targeted advertising, then there are complications with the consent they give and whether it can be considered informed.

2.2.4 *Cambridge Analytica and Democracy*

One of the most widely discussed "data scandals" in recent years is the Facebook-Cambridge Analytica scandal. This incident has been explored in books written by those involved in it such as Christopher Wylie's (2019) *Mindfuck: Inside Cambridge Analytica's Plot to Break the World* and in Brittany Kaiser's (2019) book *Targeted: The Cambridge Analytica Whistleblower's Inside Story of How Big Data, Trump, and Facebook Broke*

Democracy and How It Can Happen Again. Additionally, a Netflix documentary, the *Great Hack,* which was directed and produced by Noujaim and Amer (2019) exposed the case details to a large audience. The scandal has been widely discussed in the past few years and has stirred debate about the extent to which Cambridge Analytica's actions influenced the 2016 US Presidential Election. Here, my focus will be on the way that informed consent failed to be secured.

First, a quick recap. In 2018, the "whistleblower" Christopher Wylie, a former employee of Cambridge Analytica, publicly disclosed documents revealing how millions of Facebook profiles were "harvested" by the company so that it could send targeted ads to their profiles as part of a political campaign. In early 2018, it was reported that the number of profiles harvested was 87 million (Solon, 2018). How did the company get access to all of these data? In 2013, Aleksandr Kogan led a team from Global Science Research, in collaboration with Cambridge Analytica, to develop a personality test app called "thisisyourdigitallife". As Olivia Solon reported in the *Guardian*, "[h]undreds of thousands of users were paid a small fee to take a personality test and they *consented* to having certain personal data collected" (2018, my emphasis). Cambridge Analytica was then allowed by Facebook to access the raw personal data from the personality test app users' Facebook friends. Once in possession of these data, Cambridge Analytica could, with the aid of machine learning, send targeted ads to potential American voters. Not everyone responds the same way to ads of course; so certain ads were tailored to suit different people who the company predicted would be most receptive to them.

There is much to say about this case from the perspective of the privacy violations that occurred. And there is also much to say about the ethics of targeted advertising and whether it crosses into a grey area of behaviour manipulation. But there is also much to say about the consent procedures used here. First, as noted in the *Guardian*, consent was granted by the users of the personality test app. We may wonder whether this consent was actually informed, of course, and if users read the privacy policy associated with it, and actually understood what would occur. But what is particularly noteworthy is how the consent that was received functioned—specifically, the consent of the 320,000 users of the "thisisyourdigitallife" app effectively enabled Cambridge Analytica to "use their data and *that of their friends*" as described by Schneble et al. (2018, p. 1, my emphasis). The fact that app users could consent to the use of their friends' data is "unusual" (Schneble et al., 2018), and not something that we typically see in medical or research ethics of course. But as this example shows, it is something that is possible when dealing with big data. If it is not feasible to get the consent of over 80 million users, due to the sheer number of people involved, then the best course of action may have been not to collect the data at all.

Another issue with the case is that Facebook does not seem to have given informed consent either. As the *Washington Post* reported, not even Facebook read the terms and conditions (Romm, 2018). When Jo Stephens, a member of parliament, asked Facebook about whether they read them, Facebook's Mike Schroepfer said "[w]e did not read all the terms and conditions" (as cited in Romm, 2018). Here we observe a breakdown in informed consent from all parties involved. We have users giving consent that impacts also their "friends", additionally, we have platforms not adequately reviewing these terms. While much attention has rightly focused on affected users, it's crucial to acknowledge the breakdown between Facebook and Cambridge Analytica as it might represent a general problem with data collection and use online. If companies are unaware of how personal data are utilised, whether for potential sale or third-party use, it becomes challenging for them to inform their users accurately about the processes involved.

What were the consequences of this non-consensual data collection? It is hard to know whether the ads were effective, but there has been speculation that the targeted ads influenced people's voting behaviour. In his book *Zucked: Waking Up to the Facebook Catastrophe*, Roger McNamee (2019) suggests that there is a real chance that Cambridge Analytica's data set influenced the election outcome. He says, "it is virtually impossible that it didn't" (2019, p. 185).[11] Others, however, are sceptical of the efficacy of the targeted ads. Political scientist Eitan Hersh, for example, told the U.S. Senate Judiciary Committee in 2018 that there was little data to suggest that Cambridge Analytica swayed the election one way or the other. In his own words, he stated "[n]o evidence has been produced publicly about the firm's profiling or targeting to suggest that its efforts were effective" (as cited in McNeil, 2018). Whether or not Cambridge Analytica was effective, we might think about what these companies *tried* to do (a question a deontologist or virtue ethicist might ask). Not only was there a disregard for informed consent, but we can also scrutinise their intentions in attempting to sway an election, regardless of whether they succeeded. And indeed, the Federal Trade Commission did suggest that this was the case. The official ruling, which came 18 months after the scandal broke, was that "Cambridge Analytica deceived consumers through its data-gathering practices" (Lecher, 2019). Deceptive practices, as such, are clearly in tension with the notion of informed consent. As we saw in the previous chapter, informed consent is a mechanism that is supposed to offer protection against deception. Such practices provide another reason why uninformed consent poses such a problem.[12]

2.2.5 *Some Further Problems With Securing Informed Consent Online*

Could the above problems be solved by making privacy policies or terms and conditions more detailed? One problem, among many, with this potential solution is the cognitive load this would place on data subjects. First, there is the issue that privacy policies can become outdated relatively quickly. It is one thing to read a privacy policy and give informed consent when one first joins a website, for example, but what makes things difficult is when that website makes subsequent changes. When consent is given in the medical context for a procedure, it pertains to that specific procedure, and not to future ones (though this could differ in medical research, of course) (cf. Mittelstadt & Floridi, 2016). In the online personal data context, however, one's data collection and use may be ongoing, and the conditions under which data are used could change when the privacy policy or terms and conditions change.

Consider the case of X (formerly "Twitter"), who recently updated its privacy policy in 2023 to include information about collecting "biometric data" (Roth, 2023). As is stated in X's privacy policy, this addition reads as follows: "Biometric Information. Based on your *consent*, we may collect and use your biometric information for safety, security, and identification purposes" (my emphasis).[13] Now while there are certainly important use cases of biometric data, such as fingerprint authentication processes (Roth, 2023), the larger problem here is that there are also risks which relate to identity theft, as well as the potential for these data to be sold. Since X can be sure that only a small percentage of people will read its privacy policy, it is questionable that an update on its website is the best way to communicate this change (recall the communication condition from Chapter 1).

If informed consent requires a communicative element (see Chapter 1) between two parties, then updates, which even if go to email addresses, remain problematic, since companies cannot guarantee that they will be read or understood. When biometric data are collected, new risks arise which pertain to the misuse or theft of the data that users should be aware of (cf. Kindt, 2013). The point here is not that there is something wrong with biometric data collection, the issue lies in the difficulty of "privacy self-management"—in Solove's (2021) terminology. It becomes difficult for users to keep informed about such changes. How exactly companies should efficiently update users of course is a tricky question—one that will be explored in subsequent chapters. Nevertheless, it is an issue that one of the main tools used to provide informed consent—privacy policies and terms and conditions—has this flaw.

This issue is exacerbated by the fact that some privacy policies can be quite confusing or misleading. For example, in 2023, Katherine Kemp examined the privacy policies of 12 of the most popular fertility apps—to pick one kind of app that deals with the collection of sensitive personal data. In her analysis, she found several major flaws with the apps—specifically, they contained confusing and misleading privacy policies, did not offer users much choice about the collection and use of their data, employed inadequate de-identification measures, and retained data for years (Kemp, 2023). These are all important issues in their own right but let us focus on the idea of misleading "messaging" that the apps conveyed. In her analysis, Kemp found that five of the twelve apps she looked at stated "that they do not sell data or that they "never" sell data", in either the privacy policy or in the app messaging (2023, p. 13). She notes that one *app* called "My Calendar" by SimpleInnovation stated that "[w]e do not and will never sell your data as it is against our beliefs and mission", while the *privacy policy* stated that

> If we are involved in a merger, acquisition, reorganization, restructuring, or other sale or transfer of all or any portion of our assets or business, that could involve your Personal Information and User Data being transferred to the buyer or surviving entity.
>
> (as cited in Kemp, 2023, p. 13)

As Kemp rightly points out, this policy is not what one would expect from an app claiming it will "never sell your data". Furthermore, as seen in the Bounty case, there is an additional concern due to the nature of the personal information involved—specifically, data about users' menstrual cycles, mood fluctuations, or health conditions. Misusing these data could cause great harm; some individuals might experience embarrassment if the data are shared with third parties, while others could face strained relationships if certain types of data are made public. In severe cases, financial or mental health could be greatly affected. The potential for harm is substantial.

We also might question the intentions of the companies responsible for these consent practices. Kemp (2023) concludes her study by calling the privacy practices "unfair" and "unsafe", but she also raises an important point about consent practices more generally. She says, "privacy practices of fertility apps illustrate the extent to which modern data practices disregard the value and importance of privacy" (2023, p. 27). Furthermore, it can be pointed out that the disregard for informed consent and the failure to help users understand how their data are being used—especially in cases where the nature of that data is extremely sensitive—reveal a widespread problem with consent practices online, rather than isolated exceptions to an otherwise well-functioning consent-gathering system.

2.2.6 *Data Breaches*

Lastly, I will consider the harm caused by "data breaches", which occur when information is accessed without permission, and often associated with cyber-attacks. You may be aware of how harmful they can be, but you may wonder what they have to do with informed consent. This is because the companies involved are better thought of as victims, rather than the ones actively involved. Nevertheless, data breaches still require us to consider how informed consent is applied. Consider, for example, a recent case involving Optus, one of the largest Telecommunications companies in Australia. In 2022, around 10 million customer records from its database were exposed—thus constituting one of the worst data breaches in the country, in terms of the number of people affected. The stolen data went back to 2017 and included customer names, email addresses, and, in some cases, passport, and driver's license details (see Williams et al., 2022). Notably, even *former* customers of Optus were affected, as Australian law requires that companies keep data for two years (Williams et al., 2022). The harm to customers (and former customers) could have been quite significant. As Williams et al. (2022) stated in the *Conversation*, it was likely that

> [T]he data will be distributed across the dark net (sold at first, but eventually available for free). Cyber criminals use these data to commit identity theft and fraudulent credit applications, or use the personal information to gain your trust in phishing attacks.
>
> (Williams et al., 2022)

Naturally, customers were "angry" and "felt powerless" (Kurmelovs, 2022).

You might agree that data breaches have the potential to cause great amounts of harm but fail to see what the connection to informed consent is. Optus, after all, did not trick customers, nor was the breach due to a misleading privacy policy. While all of this is true, there are some other issues which relate to informed consent that are important to raise. The first pertains to the length of time that customer data is held after a customer leaves the company. One important thing to question here is whether customers were made aware of this, and what options they were given with respect to the length of time the data would be held for. There are clearly risks associated with data storage, as the breach showed, and users could have been given more of a say in what was occurring with their data, especially if they were former customers.

A second issue here concerns how well companies protect personal data. After all, customers place enormous trust in companies, and presumably sign up because they *believe* they are secure.[14] Ask yourself how long you would stay with a company that suffered data breaches every month. In this case, Optus stated that it had "multiple layers of protection in place" (see Murphy, 2022) and did not deliberately put customer data at risk. Clare O'Neil, who is the Home Affairs Minister gave a slightly more critical perspective, however, and said Optus has "left the window open" (as cited in Murphy, 2022) for cyber criminals. Regardless of whether this later claim is accurate, there is certainly a responsibility that companies have to protect its users, especially since they sign up and give consent for their data to be collected on the basis that companies will secure them, or at least take *reasonable* measures to do so.

I have discussed a case from Australia, but we face the same problem globally, as Solove and Hartzog (2022) explain in their book *Breached!: Why Data Security Law Fails and How to Improve It.* The authors note that in the 15 years prior to 2022, there was over 9,000 reported data breaches involving over 11 billion records, with potentially many more going unreported (p. 28). While cybercriminals are primarily responsible for these illegal activities, the authors also point out that some of the blame lies with the companies themselves. Solove and Hartzog explain the role that human error plays in managing data security, as well as the problems associated with the retention of personal data—such as when former customers' data are kept longer than necessary (see 2022, p. 32). This is relevant to informed consent, again, because of what customers believe when they sign up. If there are indeed risks to data subjects, or personal data will be held even after customers leave the company, then it seems that data subjects should be informed about the risks, or consulted about such data use, just as patients should be informed about the risks of a procedure before they agree to undertake it.

How exactly these companies should get informed consent is, of course, a difficult problem. With every new consent request, the cognitive load gets heavier for data subjects. As Solove and Hartzog discuss, many say that they want "perfect security" (2022, p. 69), but this simply isn't possible or desirable. Every new level of security may add time to users' experiences and make the use of a service inconvenient. They suggest that the "biggest costs of many security measures are that they can reduce functionality, make things inefficient and inconvenient, and be difficult and time-consuming" (2022, p. 11). Similarly, with informed consent: if we were required to keep track of all the companies holding our data and were required to provide consent for every decision a company makes using our data, it would not take long for us to suffer from "consent fatigue" (cf. Schermer et al., 2014; Choi et al., 2018).

In some cases, however, companies not only fail to get informed consent, but ignore users' choices altogether. Take, for example, the Ashley

Madison breach of 2015, where personal data were made available, that should not have been stored in the company's data repository in the first place. For instance, some users paid to have their profiles deleted, yet their personal data were still compromised in the breach (Horton, 2024). The storage of these data was unauthorised, since users did not give consent to the company to retain them. Furthermore, the site used "fake security icons" on its website to deceive people into believing the site was safe to use. These are clearly deceptive practices, making it difficult for data subjects to provide informed consent for their personal data to be collected and used under the false belief that the site is secure. As with many data breaches, the harm caused to the people involved can be significant, especially when it involves banking details, marital, or financial information. In the Ashley Madison case, lives were also literally lost (cf. Horton, 2024).[15]

2.3 On Our Desire for Privacy

I have examined some of the specific harms that can arise from the failure to secure informed consent online. In addition to these harms, there is a more general desire for privacy that I think is important to recognise too. One problem with addressing the issue solely through these individual harms is that some of us might differ in our preferences about what we want to share and what we want to keep private. As psychologists and philosophers have pointed out (see, e.g., Prinz, 2011; Bloom, 2016), it can be difficult to put yourself in the shoes of another if they are quite different from you. You might find it hard to imagine why anyone would care about receiving targeted advertisements since you are fine with them, for example. However, you might not want someone going through your emails or personal letters in your own home. If we acknowledge a more general universal desire for privacy, that of course will look different for each of us, we will be better placed to appreciate the importance of informed consent.

You might have heard the provocative claim that "privacy is dead" or heard of Mark Zuckerberg's 2010 claim that "[p]eople have really gotten comfortable not only sharing more information and different kinds, but more openly and with more people" and his subsequent comment that the "social norm [of privacy] is just something that's evolved over time" (as cited in Popkin, 2010), which suggests that privacy is something that may no longer be highly valued.[16] In the last few years, privacy scholars have shown this position to be untenable. Neil Richards, in his book *Why Privacy Matters*, for example, has shown how privacy gives us control over our lives, as he says in the following:

> Put simply, privacy is about power. Privacy is about the rules governing the extent to which human information is detected, collected, used,

> shared, and stored and how those activities can be used to affect our lives. It's not just about who knows what about us, but about what rules apply to what they know. Thus, a "secret" is still a secret once it is shared with a confidant, and we still continue to care about what we share.
>
> (2021, p. 3)

Privacy is a distinct concept from consent, of course, but Richards's point about control underscores their important connection. The issue of targeted advertisements, for example, is both a privacy issue and a matter of informed consent because it revolves around choices you make about your personal data usage. If privacy is about control, then consent becomes the mechanism that facilitates that control. Therefore, it is crucial that consent is informed.

Recent survey data reflects this. In 2020, a study by the Office of the Australian Information Commissioner (OAIC), titled "Australian Community Attitudes to Privacy Survey" looked at different ways in which Australians view privacy (OAIC, 2020). The survey revealed that 70% of the participants said that privacy was a major concern for them (OAIC, 2020, p. 17). Furthermore, 87% stated that they wanted "more control and choice over the collection and use of their personal information" (OAIC, 2020, p. 7). This latter finding is significant, as it shows that a large percentage of people lack control over something which is important to them. A 2023 follow up report showed similar trends in Australia. It found that 84% wanted more control over their data, down from 87% in 2020 (OAIC, 2023). With respect to the problem of how to protect personal data, the 2023 report found that 51% of participants felt like they knew how to protect their data, up from 49% in 2020 (OAIC, 2023, p. 16).

Polling results from around the world show something similar. In the United States for example, a 2022 Ipsos poll found that "70% of Americans agree that controlling who can access their online personal information has become more challenging" (see Llyod & Jackson, 2022, p. 1). If one of the fundamental ways in which we manage or control our privacy is through informed consent, and this is becoming harder to do, then this is a problem that needs to be addressed since privacy is so fundamental to our lives.[17]

2.4 On Voluntary Consent

The final issue I will address pertains to the nature of the consent that we provide online. We have mostly viewed consent as an attitude that permits some course of action. However, it is important to recognise that simply being informed about what is likely to occur if one consents is not all that is required. Someone who is coerced into making a choice does not clearly give informed consent. This is something that is mentioned in the GDPR, in a section titled "Consent". It says, "Consent must be *freely given*, specific, informed and unambiguous. In order to obtain freely given consent, it must be given on a *voluntary* basis" (European Union, 2016, my emphasis). The notion of a "free choice" is a philosophically interesting concept, however. Does it mean without influence? The answer "without influence" is surely not right, as every decision you make is influenced to some degree by various factors. For example, your decisions are *influenced* by the culture you grew up in, or your biology. The issue here concerns factors that may invidiously influence you, thereby undermining your voluntary consent, rather than the everyday influences on decisions. One example of such influence is nudging.

To understand the concept of "nudging", consider, Thaler and Sunstein's (2008) book *Nudge,* which gives an overview of the topic. Here is an example discussed in the book. Consider Carolyn, a director of food services, who oversees hundreds of schools, and Adam, a management consultant, who are discussing strategies to influence students' food choices. Thaler and Sunstein explore various ways that their decisions could affect the students' choices. For instance, by strategically placing healthy foods, such as at eye level, Carolyn and Adam could "nudge" students towards selecting certain items. Thaler and Sunstein define Carolyn and Adam as "choice architects" (Thaler & Sunstein, 2008, p. 3) who must decide where to place foods, and what kinds of choices they should try to encourage. Should they place foods in ways that promote students' health, at random, to match the students' own preferences, in ways that satisfy the interests of the suppliers, or to maximise profit (Thaler & Sunstein, 2008, pp. 1–2)? The students are of course free to choose whatever they like, but the choices Carolyn and Adam make will influence them.

Determining when it would be unethical to nudge someone to do something is, of course, a vexed question. Would it be right to nudge everyday supermarket shoppers to buy healthier foods if it were possible? Would it be ethical to take advantage of shoppers' emotions to increase profits? After all, individuals may be more likely to purchase items when in a certain emotional state. A business that could detect such factors could employ nudging successfully. These are difficult questions to answer, as such cases may involve individuals who feel they have made a free and informed choice. It would not necessarily mean they have been morally wronged, though. Thaler and Sunstein suggest that nudges "must be easy and cheap to avoid" (Thaler & Sunstein, 2008, p. 6). Putting healthy foods at eye level would count as a nudge but prohibiting junk food from supermarkets would not count.

This distinction is helpful for demarcating nudges from non-nudges, but it may be less useful for determining when a nudge has drifted into the grey area of behaviour modification. Nudging is not new—it occurs currently and has been employed for a long time. However, the more data you have about someone, the easier it becomes to nudge them. For example, consider the advertisements you might receive on Facebook about lawnmowers after you conduct a Google search for them; this can nudge you into buying something you might not have otherwise bought. You can of course avoid buying the lawnmower—nothing compels you to buy it. But what happens when that nudging gets more and more specific so that you receive lawnmower advertisements when you are at your most vulnerable? This question is at the heart of Shoshana Zuboff's (2019) book, *The Age of Surveillance Capitalism*. There, she suggests that the types of nudging that now occur online can undermine human freedom. In her view, vast amounts of personal data collection can lead to "behaviour modification" which she sees as the necessary evolution of the surveillance capitalism means of production (see Chapter 10, pp. 292–293).[18]

An important question that confronts us, in our task of rethinking informed consent online, is the question of when nudging actually undermines voluntary consent? To help answer this question, we can look to the work of Maximilian Kiener (2021, 2023), who has sought to address this question in the medical context. Recall that he notes that a doctor can influence a patient by presenting a treatment as having a 90% chance of success rather than a 10% chance of failure (as discussed in the Preface, these are equivalent, but due to the cognitive bias loss aversion, they may be perceived differently). Suppose a doctor tells a patient that a procedure has a 90% chance of success, and the patient freely chooses to undergo it, thus presumably exercising their informed consent. In this case, we might ask: did the patient truly give informed consent, since they were nudged?

In his recent work, Kiener has provided an answer to the question by arguing that "nudging undermines voluntary consent if and only if it cannot be 'interpersonally justified' to the patient" (2021, p. 4201). What Kiener means here by "interpersonal justification" pertains to the *influence* that, say, a physician has over a patient. Kiener suggests that a physician's influence should be "made transparent but also *justified to the person affected*" (2021, p. 4216, emphasis in original); and he also states that "an influence needs to respect the consenter's entitlement to pursue their own conception of the good" (2021, p. 4216). This may work well in the medical context, but it is difficult to see how it could work in the online context.

Kiener notes that interpersonal justification in the medical setting requires (i) a trusted partner—that medical professionals need to honour their patients' trust—and that they need to have (ii) equal moral standing with them and (iii) assist in their decision-making (2021, pp. 4218–4219). One of the challenges in extending the concept of interpersonal justification to the online context is that online consent procedures are often opaque, as this chapter has demonstrated. Privacy policies and terms and conditions frequently fail to communicate to users how their data are being collected and processed. It is difficult to envision how "company influence" could be explained to data subjects online, especially if doing so could undermine the efficacy of certain technologies (e.g., targeted advertising).

While a doctor can take the time to justify decisions to patients and explain the influence they have over their patients, it is difficult to see how something equivalent could occur online. Not only do we often have to provide consent multiple times a day, but the business practices adopted by some companies conflict with Kiener's idea of interpersonal justification. As this chapter has shown, some companies' practices can be quite opaque, and at times be deceptive. Thus, within the current paradigm, it is challenging to see how interpersonal justification can occur with respect to decisions data subjects make online. The risk here is that even when we give consent, even if informed, we could be nudged into consenting in ways that undermine our capacity to make "free" choices. In subsequent chapters, I look at whether technological solutions could help to address this problem.

2.5 Conclusion

This chapter has only scratched the surface of the kinds of harms that are associated with the online collection and use of our personal data. Once these harms are fully appreciated, it becomes clear in my view that there is indeed a significant problem with "uninformed online consent". The widespread failures of informed consent practices point to larger issues, however, with respect to the way that informed consent is currently understood in the online context that we will need to address. In the next chapter, I propose a framework designed to tackle these issues. Once we have identified the problems, we can start to evaluate potential solutions.

Notes

1 This is not to say that economic concerns are irrelevant to medical professionals, of course. See Feiler et al. (2018) for an edited volume featuring essays on how the market can affect healthcare.

2 For an overview of how each of these three theories—as well as a fourth view, Social Contract Theory—can be employed in the analysis of the ethical issues that come about from big data use, see Herschel and Miori (2017).

3 For example, it might be especially difficult to argue from a *utilitarian perspective* that someone was harmed due to their personal data being collected if they

were not aware of the data collection, and thus did not experience any pain from it.

4 O'Neill (2002), for example, argues that Kant's view of autonomy can provide a strong foundation for upholding trust in bioethics.

5 See Driver (2012, pp. 92–94), for example, who describes a view called "virtue consequentialism", which construes "right actions" through the lens of the virtues and the consequences they bring about.

6 See Mackie (1977), for example, for an argument that there are no mind-independent moral facts in the world to get "right". According to his famous Error Theory, moral judgements (e.g., "stealing is wrong") are never true.

7 I am not suggesting that ethics is simply a "combination" of all three views, as such a position would lead to contradictions. The question of what *grounds* an ethical judgement is distinct from the question of what is morally objectionable about a certain action or set of behaviours. For example, a utilitarian could argue that it is important to have respect for persons, and even to encourage human flourishing, *because* doing so maximises utility.

8 Since the data sharing occurred before 2018, the fine was only £400,000. If it had occurred after 2018, after the implementation of the GDPR, fines would likely have been much higher.

9 To give a concrete example: in 2018, Public Transport Victoria (PTV) released the data from 15 million de-identified records pertaining to the use of a Melbourne passenger smart card ticket system called "Myki", as part of a data science competition (Culnane et al., 2019). Within only a few months, three academics from the University of Melbourne and the University of Surrey were able to reidentify some of the records. The authors pointed out that such records can reveal home and work locations, and "it can also tell us who card holders travel with, like family members or ex partners, or if they travel alone—like unaccompanied children returning from school often do" (Culnane et al., 2019). If one gave uninformed consent to reveal their data, it could have an impact on others.

10 Furthermore, while YouTube stated that it would not use targeted advertising with respect to children, there have been some indications that this type of advertising may still exist. For example, *The New York Times* reported that in 2023 a Canadian bank employed a YouTube campaign, which used an "ad-targeting system from Google that employs artificial intelligence to pinpoint ideal customers" (Grant et al., 2023). The advertisement found its way to a Barbie-themed children's video that a user viewed in the United States. When the user clicked the video, they were taken to the bank's website, which tagged the user's browser with tracking software. *The New York Times* reported that hundreds of thousands, or even millions, of people could have been affected by this.

11 Christopher Wylie notes that when testifying in Congress, he was asked whether he believed the data were used to sway the American electorate. He stated that he did believe so (2019, p. 5). This suggests an intention to deceive.

12 Relatedly, see Coeckelbergh's (2024) recent book, *Why AI Undermines Democracy and What to Do About It*, which describes how AI poses a threat to democratic processes.

13 See https://x.com/en/privacy#twitter-privacy-1

14 See Richards and Hartzog (2021) for a discussion on the prospects of imposing a "duty of loyalty" on companies who collect and process personal data.

15 For a useful taxonomy of the types of "privacy harms" that can occur, see Citron and Solove (2021). They describe seven different types of privacy harms: (1) physical harms; (2) economic harms; (3) reputational harms; (4) psychological harms; (5) autonomy harms; (6) discrimination harms; and (7) relationship harms. Informed consent, as I described it here, ideally allows people to protect themselves against such risks. When one fails to give informed consent, they fail to properly self-manage the risks associated with these harms. Relatedly, see a recent discussion by Carissa Véliz on the so-called "surveillance delusion", which is "the assumption that surveillance has no significant moral costs" (2023, p. 555).

16 Richards also references Pulitzer Prize-winning journalist Thomas Friedman, who declared in 2014 that "privacy is over" (2021, pp. 1–2).

17 See Müller (2009) for a discussion of the privacy concerns associated with data mining, even when performed by machines.

18 Jones (2021) places the origins of Surveillance Capitalism in the year 2000, when ads were set up and managed by a company later to be called AdWords. As Jones also points out, while Google was a pioneer in this space, they borrowed from existing practices (Jones, 2021, p. 184).

3 Impediments to Online Informed Consent

In the previous chapter, we examined some of the challenges associated with providing and gaining informed consent online. In this chapter, I offer a framework designed to address these pervasive issues. I characterise three fundamental problems with contemporary online consent practices that will guide our discussion throughout the book. With a focus on practicality, I will then look to solutions, in subsequent chapters, that are capable of addressing these problems. My hope is that this framework provides us with a way to evaluate new and emerging ways of gaining informed consent.[1] In Section 3.1, I examine the Transparency Problem. In Section 3.2, I address the Re-purposed Data Problem, and in Section 3.3, the Meaningful Alternatives Problem. In Section 3.4, I introduce a test case, involving the use of tracking cookies, to illustrate how the framework can be applied in practice.

3.1 The Transparency Problem

As we saw in Chapter 1, transparency plays a key role in contemporary medical informed consent practices. Transparent consent practices not only allow patients to become *informed* about the potential *risks* of the procedures that they undergo, but they can also help to build *trust* between medical practitioners and patients.[2] For example, Queensland Health, the health service from the state of Queensland, Australia, has outlined some key requirements of informed consent in their "Guide to Informed Decision-Making". The document notes that for consent to be valid, certain principles need to be fulfilled, one of which states that "the discussion between the patient and the health practitioner is *transparent*, well balanced, and involves two-way communication which is sensitive to the situation" (Queensland Health, 2023, p. 8 my emphasis).

Since the central argument I am making in this book is that there are lessons about informed consent that we can extract from the medical context, a promising place to start in our goal of improving consent practices online

DOI: 10.4324/9781032626048-3

is to focus on making them more *transparent*. This sounds simple in theory but actually turns out to be quite difficult in practice, for the reasons I go into below.

Even if we could motivate companies to be transparent in their consent-gathering practices, how would they do it? In the medical context, a patient can, and is often encouraged to, engage in discussions with their physician. Doing so allows patients to understand what will occur in the procedure, and also allows them to comprehend the risks of proceeding. This can lead to a discussion about available alternatives if those risks are deemed too great. This does not straightforwardly translate to the online context. Companies like Google and Facebook are not likely to start hiring people to help you understand how their site collects and uses your personal data. It is worth remembering, however, that transparency was not always central to medical ethics, as we saw in Chapter 1. Therefore, just because it is difficult to imagine how transparency could be achieved in the online context, it does not follow that it cannot be achieved.

3.1.1 Business Models

The business models adopted by some companies are one type of obstacle that stands in the way of achieving greater transparency. In certain contexts, being too transparent could cost you money. For some, deception in the business world may be simply "part of the game". Consider Albert Carr's infamous claim from the 1960s: "[w]hatever the form of the bluff, it is an integral part of the game, and the executive who does not master its techniques is not likely to accumulate much money or power" (1968, p. 153). According to this perspective, the honest used car salesman might be seen as naive for being too transparent, potentially losing a sale. Conversely, if they "forget to mention" flaws in a car before they sell it, they might increase their sales. Whatever we might say about the economic benefits of this approach, it is clearly morally objectionable. Selling a car with faulty brakes, without disclosing this information, can put lives at risk. The response that "that is just how business is done" appears weak and ignores the kinds of concerns we looked at in Chapter 1 about corporate social responsibility. You might think that "business bluffing" represents an outdated way of operating, or that consumer protection laws prohibit such egregious forms of deception.[3] However, we continue to witness instances of non-transparent practices in the online context.

A notable example of this can be found in journalist Steven Levy's (2011) book *In the Plex: How Google Thinks, Works, and Shapes Our Lives*. Levy describes how in the early days of Google, there was a deliberate attempt to hide their business model. Levy notes that former CEO Eric

Schmidt even had a name for Google's attempts to remain opaque, namely, "the hiding strategy" (Levy, 2011, p. 69). What was Google trying to hide? According to Levy, Google had "cracked the code" on how to make money on the internet and was keen to prevent competitors from discovering how they had done it. Levy notes that David Krane, one of Google's early press agents, was tasked with redirecting questions away from journalists who attempted to find out how they had done it (Levy, 2011, p. 69). The hiding strategy persisted until 2004, when the company went public. Levy notes how surprised investors were when they found out just how much money was being made. Virtually everyone at Google knew the secret and were instructed to "keep their mouths shut about it" (Levy, 2011, p. 69) as Levy puts it. As we now know, the company made such large amounts of money by selling personal data for the purposes of advertising.

On the one hand, this is understandable. If Google's competitors knew how they had "cracked the puzzle" of making money on the internet, then this could have impacted Google's ability to grow their business. Trade secrets give businesses competitive advantages after all. On the other hand, we should not forget that Google's competitive advantage was facilitated by personal data from real people. If these data were being used without proper informed consent, regardless of the consequences, we might worry that people were being used as *mere* means to an end, as a Kantian might put it. Given that websites like Google were novel to people in the 1990s/early 2000s, and given that Google was not completely transparent, it is interesting to speculate about the psychology of someone during that time. What, for example, did people believe was being done with their personal data, and could this have been enough to facilitate informed consent?

In their article in *The New York Times*, Warzel and Ngu (2019) compare Google's privacy policy in 1999, which was a mere 600 words, to its 2019 version which was 4000 words. The 1999 policy is interesting for a couple of reasons. Not only is the brevity worth noting, but so is the nature of what was collected and how it was used. Warzel and Ngu note just four types of data that were collected by Google, namely, "search activity", "personal information provided", "click-through information", and "cookies". Initially, Google's privacy policy stated that they care about user privacy, and that: "we only talk about our users in aggregate, not as individuals" (Warzel & Ngu, 2019). However, as Warzel and Ngu note, the phrase was removed only three months later in the next revision of the policy. Between 1999 and 2019, there would be 30 versions of the policy. In the over 20 years since this first privacy policy was created, the internet has become significantly more complicated, and Google's lengthier privacy policy reflects this. Still, we might ask how well Google's hiding policy impacted users in its early days—that is, whether it prevented them from providing informed consent, since the service was novel to many users, and many users may not have appreciated the implications, or the risks, of these early data collection practices.

While awareness of the risks associated with personal data collection is growing today, issues with transparency persist. Even with privacy policies in place, businesses might not be motivated to reveal how data are used and shared. Some reasons may stem from concerns about protecting trade secrets; whereas others may arise from a concern that people may be less likely to use the service if they really knew how their data were being collected.

In her recent book, *Data Cartels* (2022a), Sarah Lamdan, for example, explains how data analytics companies like Reed Elsevier LexisNexis (RELX) and Thomson Reuters are selling our personal data in ways that we may not be so comfortable with. She notes that when one fills out a dating profile or posts something on social media, one would generally prefer that such information does not go to employers, landlords, or police (2022a, p. 2). Yet that is what sometimes does occur, she says, *without your consent*. In an article adapted from her book (see 2022b), Lamdan provides a discussion of RELX, which she notes is lesser-known than the so-called "big five" (Amazon, Google, Facebook, Microsoft, and Apple), but just as significant. She says, "[y]ou might not be familiar with RELX, but it knows all about you" (2022b). Intriguingly, Lamdan notes that RELX's income rivals that of the big tech companies: it is a billion-dollar business. She adds that

> Even if you don't feel like you have close, personal ties to RELX, one of the company's dossiers probably has your name on it—and that information may be used to make decisions about your everyday life.
>
> (Lamdan, 2022b)

Several questions might come to mind when you read this quote. Is information about you in their dossiers? What decisions are being made that relate to you? Furthermore, do you have any control over these data, or is avoiding giving data even possible? From a business perspective, it is certainly advantageous that such data practices are not well understood, given growing concerns about privacy.

How can transparency be improved here? One way to make companies more transparent would be to establish stricter privacy laws.[4] Lamdan, for example, notes that "only government intervention can stop it" (2022a, p. 23). One might feel pessimistic, or powerless, after reading these words, given that Lamdan's answer implies that self-managing one's privacy will be a challenge. That there are companies that many of us have never heard of before, using our data in ways we are unsure about, raises concerns about how motivated these companies are to be transparent in the first place.

Consider another common use of personal data online: targeted advertising, which is becoming more sophisticated and widespread. For example, you might notice advertisements on a social media site for dining tables, after making several web searches for them. Understanding the basics of how this process works might be easy enough, but what level of understanding is sufficient for giving informed consent to companies to collect and use your data in this way? In a recent discussion of this topic, April Falcon Doss (2020) explains how the IAB (Interactive Advertising Bureau) created and maintained Open Real-Time Bidding (Open RTB), which is one of the main ways that targeting advertising works online. How does it work? As Doss explains (pp. 86–88), first you go to a website, which generates a "bid request". Once the bid request is created, it is then sent to an AdTech channel, such as OpenRTB. These bid requests contain personal information such as your IP address, your device details, any personal details from previously collected data (like browser cookies showing what other sites you've visited), and "behavioural profile information" that may have been purchased from a data broker (Doss, 2020, p. 87). Next, as Doss explains, all of that information (which is included in the bid request) is sent to an online auction, where prospective advertisers can then bid for the chance to advertise to you. The "winning bid" then gets the chance to put an advertisement on the page in front of you. All this happens, Doss says, "before the page is loaded into your browser window" (Doss, 2020, p. 87).

Consider two individuals: one familiar with OpenRTB and one who only possesses a vague understanding that their personal data are being used by online advertisers. Suppose, further, that both provide consent for a website to collect their data. Do both comprehend what is occurring with their data to an extent that would constitute informed consent or would only the one who understands the process in some detail exercise informed consent? At first pass, we might say that both do, even though only one has a basic idea of how it works. To draw a parallel to medicine, you do not need to understand how the lungs work in detail to give informed consent for a surgeon to operate on them. Similarly, in the context of online advertising, one could argue that failing to understand how OpenRTB works doesn't necessarily mean you cannot give informed consent. On the other hand, we might say that both fail to give informed consent since it might be very hard to have a full understanding of the data collection and use process.

In 2022, for example, complaints were made against the Interactive Advertising Bureau Europe (IAB Europe), for violating certain provisions of the GDPR. The complainant's said:

> The OpenRTB ecosystem is so extensive that it is *impossible* for data subjects to give an informed consent to the processing of their personal data, or to object in an informed manner to the processing of their personal data on the basis of a legitimate interest.
>
> (Autorité de protection des données, 2022, p. 99 no 425, my emphasis)

Belgium's Data Protection Authority ruled against IAB Europe, stating that their reliance on OpenRTB conflicted with certain parts of the GDPR. This ruling is a positive step forward for privacy concerns, but it presents companies with a difficult dilemma. If it is "impossible" for data subjects to give informed consent in such situations, it seems companies will either need to (i) abandon the requirement for receiving informed consent online or (ii) prohibit the use of OpenRTB. Requiring companies to obtain informed consent would significantly impact their profitability. Thus, as Doss (2020) points out, the IAB lobbies governments worldwide to continue using these systems. According to her, they achieve this through policy papers and recommendations. However, if successful, these companies would effectively be choosing to disregard informed consent in favour of financial gains.

The law will clearly continue to play an important role in restricting the use of certain data collection practices. In the previous chapter, we saw how Bounty was heavily fined because it did not fully inform its customers about how their data were being used. The director of the ICO, Steve Eckersley, as we saw in the previous chapter said, "Bounty were not open or *transparent* to the millions of people that their personal data may be passed on to such large number of organisations" (as cited in Hern, 2019, my emphasis). As Eckersley also noted, any consent that was given was clearly not informed. Importantly, recall that Eckersley commentated on how Bounty's actions appear to have been motivated by financial gain, given that data sharing was an integral part of their business model at the time. From an economic standpoint, it is not hard to understand why companies do this.

However, returning to an earlier point, we might wonder how *transparency* is supposed to be achieved. While it may be true that people have some idea that their personal data are being collected, it remains difficult for them to become informed about some of the important details. Consider a 2018 report from the Consumer Policy Research Centre (Nguyen & Solomon, 2018). The report looked at how Australians were impacted by some of the emerging trends and issues in the personal data collection context. Several findings are worth stating. First, the report stated that "91% of the Australians surveyed "understood that companies have the ability to follow their activities across many websites" (2018, p. 28). This may seem to suggest that most people who *consent* to have their data collected have the capacity to *understand* what is happening. However, in focus group feedback from the participants, we see a lack of deeper understanding of how this occurs. One participant said, "I don't know how I can decipher where my data goes and how it's used. It concerns me, but it's not transparent to me" (2018, p. 28); a second said, "[o]nce you share your information, you cannot trace it" (2018, p. 28); and a third participant said, "I don't see how or why they are using the data, and I'm more frustrated with this" (2018, p. 28). So, even if most people knew their data were being *used*, a lack of transparency about what specifically is done with the data, means it is hard to see how they can provide informed consent.[5]

As our discussion has shown, companies have economic reasons to prioritise profit over enabling informed consent. At times, this can drift into deceptive behaviour, however. For instance, in 2023, an Australian court fined Meta 20 million AUD (14 million USD) for failing to disclose how one of its apps, Onavo Protect, collected and used users' personal data (Kaye, 2023). Onavo Protect was a VPN service that Meta operated on Apple and Android phones and was downloaded over 270,000 times (Kaye, 2023). The fine came about because of the way the app was advertised, namely, as a way to protect privacy. Like many apps, it had the capacity to collect users' location data, websites visited, and other personal data. These data were then sent to Meta so that they could be used for commercial purposes. However, for an app that marketed itself as privacy friendly, this is not something that its users would have expected. It is worth considering the beliefs of the people who used the app. Some might have downloaded it because they were concerned about privacy, and only gave consent for the app to collect their personal data on the basis of that belief. Judge Wendy Abraham said of the case that the

> The failure to make sufficient disclosures . . . may have deprived tens of thousands of Australian consumers of the opportunity to make an informed choice about the collection and use of their data before downloading and/or using Onavo Protect.
>
> (as cited in Kaye, 2023)

From a purely economic perspective, it might seem like a good idea for a company not to disclose such information. After all, many users are becoming increasingly concerned about privacy. The more one knows about how one's personal data are being collected and used the less likely one may be to sign up for such an app. From an informed consent perspective, however, this is deeply problematic. Recall from Chapter 1, that informed consent is supposed to provide the consenter with protection from abuse (see Manson & O'Neill, 2007). If someone signs up to use a VPN service, they may do so because they value their privacy and do not wish to share personal data with third parties.

3.1.2 Complexity of the Problem

Suppose that companies could be convinced to become more transparent and avoid deceiving data subjects. Even in such cases, the transparency problem is still substantial. One problem is that online personal data-gathering practices can be complex, and so companies need to determine how best to present information in a way that data subjects can understand. A privacy policy that is completely transparent (in the sense that it does not deceive) might still contain words or phrases that are unknown to the data subject, and thus be difficult to fully comprehend. Consider for example, findings from a recent report from the Consumer Policy Research Centre and UNSW (Kemp et al., 2024). It states that "[m]ost consumers appear to have no understanding of terms commonly used by industry in privacy notices including "pseudonymised information" (81%), a "hashed email address" (74%) or an "advertising ID" (67%)" (Kemp et al., 2024, p. 5). If it is the responsibility of companies to ensure that users understand what they are consenting to, then they may need to allocate significant resources to ensure that the consent procedures they provide are comprehensible.

While one does not need to understand every detail of a process to give informed consent, a basic level of understanding seems necessary, though not sufficient. Consider an analogous case in the medical context: a doctor does not have to explain the intricate workings of the heart or lungs to a patient in order to obtain their informed consent for a medical procedure. What matters is that the patient has enough information to make an informed decision. Thus, a *complete* understanding of something is neither desirable nor morally necessary to provide informed consent. For example, in order that one have a *complete* understanding of how a website uses one's data, such as Google or Netflix, an understanding of the programming language used to make the website, such as Python, might be required. That is certainly not what I am suggesting should be understood as a prerequisite for informed consent. Yet if we are to take seriously the knowledge condition from Chapter 1, then one should possess knowledge of *certain facts*. The knowledge of Python might not be one of them, but there will be some that are not well known at present.

Of course, those facts will be context dependent. A basic understanding of "pseudonymised information", might be required in certain contexts in order to give informed consent whereas not in others.

It may seem that I am constructing a notion of informed consent that is impossible to achieve and thus of low practical value. This conclusion need not be drawn, however. If we consider ways that tend to make it harder to gain informed consent online, as looked at above, then companies could simply avoid them and try to design more effective consent-gathering practices (assuming they could be motivated to). To focus on something small, companies could put more thought into how they present information to data subjects in privacy policies. For example, Tendler et al. argue that at present, consent forms for *clinical trials* are often designed on "intuition and opinion rather than evidence" (2023, p. 9). As a result, they are increasingly long and legalistic, and thus ineffective in communicating to the subjects what they need to know about the trial. In the authors' view, their design should be based on a "data-driven approach to improving consent documents" (2023, p. 9), in order to make them shorter and more readable. This means that the consent forms should be subjected to empirical analysis, to see how well they facilitate understanding and engagement. One suggestion that the authors offer, for clinical trials, involves an approach which removes "the exhaustive list of potential side effects from each individual drug or procedure and instead combines the risks into a summary table" (2023, p. 8). In their view, doing so could help reduce the length of certain consent forms; for example, they describe one that was reduced from 4,500 words to 1,113 words. This may not strike you as a groundbreaking change, but if there are many small changes that can be made to current consent practices, whether they be in clinical trials, or online consent practices, then larger changes may be possible. Along these lines, I consider how adding visuals to consent procedures could help with transparency in Chapter 5.

Even if online consent-gathering practices could be simplified to some extent, a substantial problem would remain, namely, that online data collection and use practices are complex by their nature. Suppose a company is convinced of the need to be transparent. And suppose they try to simplify their consent-gathering procedures as much as possible. The task of understanding what is happening with one's data would still be substantial, as Helen Nissenbaum says:

> [C]onsider what might need to be conveyed to users to provide notice of what information is captured, where it is sent, and how it is used. The technical and institutional story is so complicated that probably only a handful of deep experts would be able to piece together a full account; I would hazard that most of the website owners who contract with ad

networks providing targeted advertising services are not among such experts.

(2011, p. 35)

Furthermore, even if one could get a complete idea of how their data are currently being used—unlikely as this may be—one's knowledge of what is occurring may quickly become outdated. As Nissenbaum also says, "the realm is in constant flux, with new firms entering the picture, new analytics, and new back-end contracts forged" (2011, p. 36). The consent practices associated with the commercial use of personal data on the internet are somewhat distinct from consent practices in the medical context then (though similar issues may arise in medical research), as they do not necessarily correspond to a single procedure (e.g., an operation).

Another type of complexity problem goes by the name of the "Black Box Problem", which has been widely discussed by privacy scholars in recent years (see, e.g., Pasquale, 2016; Burrell, 2016; Mittelstadt et al., 2016). One of the benefits of AI is its ability to analyse "big" data sets and discover novel patterns that human beings would find difficult to identify, due to the size of the data sets involved. The problem that this gives rise to is that not even the creators, or those most familiar with the AI algorithm in question, may know why or how it works in the way it does. As Brożek et al. put it, "we often do not know *how* or *why* the algorithm got to the proposed solution" (2024, p. 427, emphasis in original). Similarly, as Judea Pearl says, many users will say about an algorithm that "it 'works well and we don't know why'" (2019, p. 15).

How is this relevant to informed consent? Suppose you are considering whether to provide consent to a website to collect and use your personal data—a site that uses advanced AI algorithms to send targeted ads to you. In some cases, the black box problem may prevent you from gaining a full understanding of how this occurs, since no one may be able to explain how the AI algorithm responsible works.[6] This issue may also raise legal concerns, such as for those in the EU who enjoy a statutory "right to an explanation", as stated in the General Data Protection Regulation (European Union, 2016). One issue that complicates the application of this legislation, however, as noted by Brożek et al. is that the "[l]aw itself does not define explainability" (2024, p. 428) (cf. Selbst & Powles, 2017). This introduces challenges to the enforcement of the right to an explanation from a legal perspective, as we should expect it to mean different things in different contexts.

On the other hand, as mentioned above, it is not clear that a data subject needs to know everything about how an algorithm works, in order for them to provide informed consent. Questions remain about how much transparency, or how detailed an explanation, is desirable or necessary.

And clearly, this will differ from context to context. There are, however, some technical solutions to the black box problem that hold promise, such as those offered by "Explainable AI", the term given to the techniques being developed that allow humans to understand the outputs of AI and machine learning (see Holzinger et al. (2022) for an overview of some of these).[7]

3.2 The Re-Purposed Data Problem

Over the past few decades, advances in AI and machine learning have enabled data analysts to detect patterns in large data sets that otherwise would have been extremely difficult to see. As a result of these "big data" analyses, novel insights have been gained that would have been hard to predict or anticipate from the outset. From a perspective of gaining knowledge about us and the world, this is a feature. However, from a perspective of informed consent, there are challenges that arise when personal data are used in ways that go beyond the purposes for which the consent was originally given. For example, you might give consent to Facebook collect your "likes" so that you can be recommended groups, but you might take issue with Facebook then analysing those likes, in an attempt to try and determine what advertisements you might be persuaded by. As Kosinski et al. point out, "Facebook Likes, can be used to automatically and accurately predict a range of highly sensitive personal attributes including: sexual orientation, ethnicity, religious and political views, personality traits, intelligence, happiness, use of addictive substances, parental separation, age, and gender" (2013, p. 5802).

A similar problem arises in the medical context. In a recent article, Green et al. (2023), for example, discuss how the function of health records has changed over the last few years—that is, they were once used for clinical record keeping and communication purposes. Now, however, electronic health records are increasingly being used for "quality analysis and management, financial administration, as well as research and innovation" (Green et al., 2023, p. 120.) There may be nothing unethical with such uses, but unless those people were informed about these new uses, when they became implemented, then it is hard to see how they can have given informed consent for their records to be used in such ways.

Of course, this problem is not new. Floridi (2019) provides an example involving UK postcodes. The original purpose of collecting them, as Floridi notes, was to aid in the sorting of mail. However, Floridi points out that today they can be used to "calculate insurance premiums, designate destinations in route planning software, and allocate different levels of public services" (2019, p. 110). Someone who is using a post code to calculate insurance premiums is re-purposing the data. This may not be a problem of course. But it can be if consent was not given to use the information in such a way.

This can become a significant issue in the personal data collection context since AI and machine learning can analyse large sets of data to find patterns that may have been hard to predict. For example, it may be hard to imagine how data from a smart water meter could help to reveal information about gender or pregnancy. Yet, as Mejias and Couldry (2024, pp. 26–27) point out, pregnant women tend to use the toilet more frequently, which could indicate that a person is pregnant; conversely, sudden decreases could indicate that an abortion has occurred. The purpose of collecting such data may have originally been to determine how much water was used. However, these data could be re-purposed in ways that will be concerning to those involved.

In terms of informed consent, this is an issue if you are not aware of such additional uses at the time you give your consent. There is thus a need for consent to be specific, and not apply too generally, say for "various uses", as different uses carry with them different risks. Since data can be used and sold for many different purposes after its initial acquisition, this raises a challenge about how we can ensure that consent is collected not only at the time the data are collected but also for its future uses. A good example of the risks of re-purposed data is shown in a case involving Netflix. In 2006, Netflix launched a competition open to the public, challenging competitors to design the best algorithm for recommending content to its users. A one-million-dollar (US) prize was offered to the winner. In order to win the competition, individuals or teams needed to build an algorithm that was 10% more accurate than the system Netflix was using at the time: Cinematch (see Hallinan & Striphas, 2016).

To run the competition, Netflix released approximately 100 million movie ratings from approximately 500,000 users. Competitors could then use these data to test the efficacy of their algorithm. To their credit, Netflix was careful not to include any personal data, such as users' zip codes, personal IDs, or usernames. The company excluded anything that they thought could identify a user. However, not long after the release of the competition, PhD student, Arvind Narayanan, and his advisor Vitaly Shmatikov, found out a way to deanonymise the users (Hallinan & Striphas, 2016). They discovered that Netflix users could be cross-referenced with users from IMDb, a popular website which contains information about films, and allows users to post film ratings along with their real names. Despite Netflix's effort to uphold users' privacy, the data were able to be deanonymised.

If the users' movie ratings were publicly available from IMDb, along with users' names, then why was this an issue? As Kearns and Roth (2019) point out in their book *The Ethical Algorithm*, users may have only rated a small percentage of these movies on IMDb yet rated *all* the movies on

Netflix. So, by connecting the two data sets, one could know all of the movies they rated, even the ones users may not have wanted to be publicly known. Kearns and Roth suggest that this shows how hard it is to anonymise data. Furthermore, such deanonymisation attempts could cause harm to people. For example, a lesbian mother was reportedly "outed", as a result of the data release, as she had rated gay and lesbian films on Netflix (see Hallinan & Striphas, 2016). This incident led to a lawsuit—Doe v. Netflix, Inc.—where the defendant claimed that she suffered "economic and psychological harm" as a result of Netflix's actions, according to Ryan Singel (2009) of *Wired*.

What *should* Netflix have done here? Should they have obtained informed consent from almost half a million users, perhaps by contacting each one and asking whether they would be comfortable with allowing their movie ratings to be used to facilitate a competition? Should they have also explained the potential risks of providing consent? Quite possibly, but doing so of course would have been challenging given the amount of users. Some users, furthermore, might ignore requests to provide consent: they might not check their emails, for example, and thus delay the process and potentially reduce the size of the data set. On the other hand, these concerns do not seem like good moral reasons for not getting informed consent.

The case is complicated because Netflix does not seem to have been aware of the risks associated with sharing the data set, despite taking measures to protect privacy (i.e., removing user details). Could such an oversight have prevented users from giving informed consent, even if they were informed about the data sharing? Possibly, but we should remember that not even a physician is required to provide every possible risk to a patient in order to obtain informed consent. Nevertheless, one approach they could have taken is to mention the general risk of de-anonymisation, even if they were uncertain about how it could occur. Again, however, determining how they should have handled it remains a difficult question, as predicting how data may be used in the future can be challenging.

One recently discussed technical innovation that holds much promise for addressing such concerns is called "differential privacy". The basic idea behind the technology is that known amounts of randomness can be inserted into a data set so that the integrity of the data set can be preserved while also maintaining privacy. As Kearns and Roth say, "[d]ifferential privacy requires that adding or removing the data record of a single individual not change the probability of any outcome by 'much'" (2019, p. 37). The technology promises, then, that whether you are included in the data set or not should make no "difference" to the risk of being de-anonymised. Thus, in the example above, the risk of your movie ratings being found out would be the same whether you were in the data set or not, if differential privacy was used. Inserting randomness may seem to compromise the usefulness of data sets, but as Fang Liu says, "[o]ne can still learn aggregate information and population parameters from a data set with any individual in the data set being replaced by any other individual from the same population" (2022, p. 52). For these reasons, it has been used in real-world applications, such as by the U.S. Census Bureau, and Apple uses it too (2022). However, even if differential privacy can mitigate the kinds of risks we have been discussing, we might still wonder if there is value in seeking consent, from a symbolic perspective, before releasing data sets containing personal information (cf. Walker, 2022).

Consider another example of the re-purposed data problem, involving the collection of "location pings"—the signals your smart phone sends to cell towers, which are necessary for the location data that enables maps or weather apps, for example. In 2019, Thompson and Warzel (2019) described how the Times Privacy Project obtained a data set containing over 50 million location pings from the phones of over 12 million people (this was a random sample between 2016 and 2017). Within minutes, the authors claim, and with the help of publicly available data, they were able to deanonymise these location data and actually track the whereabouts of then President of the United States, Donald Trump (see their article for the maps of the routes).

As the authors note, we share a lot of these data in our everyday interactions. For instance, if you want to know if your walk to work will be affected by rain, you need to know the weather in your *current location*, and your phone needs to "know" where you are located. Similarly, when using maps for real-time guidance, location data are essential. However, there are risks associated with these data being re-purposed for other uses. As Thompson and Warzel say, "the vast location files are vulnerable to hacks, leaks or sale at any point along that process" (Thompson & Warzel, 2019). In the case involving location pings, the authors were able to track the whereabouts of a political figure, which raises questions about national security. However, it also raises concerns about how ordinary citizens could be harmed from the re-purposing of such data, especially since such data can help to determine your daily movements, which many people would not be comfortable with sharing.

When it comes to informed consent, the re-purposing of location data presents a problem. You might consent to share the location of your phone for your maps to function, but not for those same data to be sold to data brokers. To provide informed consent for third-party data collection, subjects would not only need to be aware that this is what was occurring, but ideally should be aware of the possibility that data leaks could occur, or their whereabouts could potentially be revealed later. How can companies ensure that informed consent is received?

One suggestion would be to find ways to increase data literacy, so that people are better informed about the risks of data being re-purposed. In recent work, Ortega et al. (2023) recruited participants to take part in a "data donation journey", a research project of theirs which required participants to donate some personal data and then be assisted to understand how the data were used. The experimenters required participants to download data from Google, the first step of the data donation journey. They then encouraged participants to understand the types of data collected by Google by prompting them to answer questions about their awareness of how Google collects and stores "speech records", the information collected and stored by voice assistants (e.g., Google Assistant).

The researchers concluded that the exercise empowered participants, and actually encouraged them to reassess or reflect upon their ongoing participation. One problem with the idea of extending this idea to everyday internet users is that it is difficult to see what would motivate people to embark on a "data donation journey" in order to understand how their data are used online, especially given some of the problems discussed in this chapter. Even if one makes a legitimate attempt to understand how their data are being used, they will be immediately faced with several problems, such as the sheer number of sites that use their personal data, each with their own privacy policies and terms and conditions. And second, there is the problem that data can be re-purposed, meaning that data subjects may need to give consent on multiple occasions for the same type of personal information use. So, while we should welcome ways to improve data literacy, there seems to be practical limits to how well we can self-manage our own privacy.

For instance, it is often quite difficult to self-mange data re-purposing. As Bart Custers points out: "[c]onsent is usually asked for when registering, but rarely is consent renewed. As a result, consenting once often implies consent forever" (2016, p. 1). This is a problem, as we have seen, because consent can become "outdated" fairly quickly. For example, when a company reuses a type of personal data in ways that were not disclosed when someone initially gave consent to share the data, as shown in the Netflix case, or when your values evolve over time (cf. Custers, 2016). When you first signed up to Facebook a decade ago, your privacy values may have been quite different to what they are now. However, the site might use your data in different ways than it did in the past, for example. Yet your privacy settings might remain the same as when you first signed up.

Should there be more attempts for users to review privacy policies in order to deal with the problem of re-purposed data? This is simply not practical in many cases, as most people do not thoroughly review existing policies the "first time" when they encounter them. Staying informed and providing consent for further uses seems impractical, then. Thus, keeping individuals informed about changes to the way their data are used becomes challenging, especially when new stakeholders become involved. This is especially a concern in cases where company ownership changes, such as in the case of Google acquiring Fitbit in 2021.

3.3 The Meaningful Alternatives Problem

Supposing that a company is transparent about how it proposes to use your personal data. Suppose also that the company in question has provided you with its terms and conditions and privacy policy, which you have not only managed to read in their entirety, but for the sake of argument, also understood them. You then provide consent. Furthermore, let us suppose that the company does not re-purpose your data in ways that go beyond what you originally consented to. Does this count as informed consent? Possibly not yet.

As we saw in Chapter 1, informed consent in the medical context emphasises that patients should not be *coerced* into making a decision. One way that this is achieved in the medical context is by offering *meaningful alternatives*, where possible, so that a meaningful choice can occur. Consider the following passage from the second edition of NSW Health's "Consent to Medical and Healthcare Treatment Manual" (Consent Manual) which includes guidance on how to promote informed consent. The following is from Section 4 of the manual, "Requirements for consent" and says

> Health Practitioners have a duty to provide the patient with enough information to enable them to gain a genuine understanding of the nature and effects of the operation, procedure or treatment, the risks associated with it and any *alternatives* to the proposed treatment.
>
> (NSW Health, 2024, p. 14, my emphasis)

In the medical context, providing patients with alternative treatments allows them to assess the costs and benefits of different treatments or procedures and ensure that a meaningful choice is actually made. This can help to ensure that they are not forced into doing something. If I am right that we can look to the medical context for inspiration, in our attempt to improve consent practices online, then we will also need to address this issue.

Earlier I looked at data from a report conducted by Roy Morgan Research in 2018, commissioned on behalf of the Consumer Policy Research Centre in Australia (CPRC) (Nguyen & Solomon, 2018). The report suggested that only 6% of Australians read all the privacy policies for all the products and services they had signed up for in the last 12 months. In the section of the report that explored why people give consent without reading privacy policies, several mentioned the lack of meaningful choices. One participant said, "[h]ow can we achieve 'privacy' unless you cut yourself off from useful things?" (Nguyen & Solomon, 2018, p. 31). And another said, "I'm not comfortable with them having any of my information, but if you want to be involved in whatever the site is about, you don't get options" (Nguyen & Solomon, 2018, p. 38). Here we can see that users may not be comfortable giving away their personal data, but choose to give it away because of a lack of alternative options available to them. Nguyen and Solomon note that findings contained in their report are consistent with a European survey which found that people do not read privacy policies "because they felt a sense of helplessness" (Nguyen & Solomon, 2018, p. 31).[8]

These kinds of responses are unsurprising, but they provide us with an explanation of why people may not be motivated to engage with privacy policies. If you cannot negotiate with Instagram or Facebook when you sign up for their platforms, then why bother familiarising yourself with their privacy policies? You might argue that your only choices are to accept the terms and conditions or not use the platform at all. Being informed might only succeed in making you feel uncomfortable; it might not necessarily empower you to choose differently. Of course, in the medical context, the idea of meaningful alternatives is something taken much more seriously. When you seek medical care, you typically have options, and you can carefully evaluate them. The more informed you are about your medical options, the better equipped you are to make choices that align with your preferences and values.

Another problem with there being a lack of meaningful alternatives in the online context is that it creates situations where people can be taken advantage of. For example, in Australia, third-party apps and websites are used within the real estate industry to process rental applications and manage properties (Terzon & Xiao, 2023). Despite not feeling comfortable with doing so, some Australians have uploaded their personal data to these apps (e.g., passport details and payslips) in hopes of securing a rental property in a time of shortage. Some people claimed to have done so, even though they had "concerns about data retention, applicant profiling, rental bidding, and unnecessary fees", as Terzon and Xiao (2023) note. After being rejected for a property by a real estate agency, one person (as reported by Terzon & Xiao, 2023) noted that they felt pressured to upload such data to a third-party website and added, "[i]t feels very wrong. I am the kind of person that doesn't like sharing those kinds of data. But in this case, you have to do it" (Terzon & Xiao, 2023).

At first pass, we might say that people who have uploaded such data exercise a free choice and even provide informed consent to companies to collect and use their personal data. After all, they are not *forced* to upload the data. On the other hand, it is hard to see how they can give informed consent to the companies to collect their data if we are employing a broader conception of informed consent—one that goes beyond mere information transfer. In such cases, we might say that people are being coerced into providing these data, since if they do not, they might not have a place to live. Such people are not given meaningful alternatives. If, as Manson and O'Neill (2007) suggest (as examined in Chapter 1), one of the purposes of informed consent is to protect people from harm, then a lack of meaningful alternatives may indeed prevent informed consent from occurring.

We need to be aware of the "illusion of choice" as Tepper and Hearn (2018) describe in their book, *The Myth of Capitalism*. This occurs when large companies, such as Amazon or Meta, dominate certain sectors of the market, which can have the effect of limiting users' choices, even though it seems like consumers have meaningful alternatives to choose from. Suppose one is reviewing Amazon's data collection policy before deciding whether to provide consent to Amazon to share their personal data. Suppose they are uncomfortable with providing consent to Amazon for them to use the data in the ways specified. What options does such a person have? It may be that for some services, or products, their options are either to accept Amazon's terms and conditions or refrain from using the online store. So, while you might object to the way that Amazon treats its workers, or the way it collects your data for targeted advertisements, you might still opt to use the service, and thus give your consent, since refraining from using the service may not be a live option for you.

Despite these problems, there are some promising signs on the horizon that I believe are encouraging. As I mentioned in the introduction to this book, Apple has actually started asking people if they want to be tracked across apps. In their iOS 14.5 update in 2021, Apple introduced a feature where users were given the option to "Ask App Not to Track" or "Allow". As Brian Chen (2021) points out, two things happen when you ask the app not to track. The first is that an Apple device identifier is disabled. As he states, this is a "random string of letters and numbers that is assigned to our iPhones and is used to track our activities across apps and websites" (Chen, 2021). The second is that a communication is sent to app developers indicating that one does not want to be tracked. While this choice is meaningful for participants, there are still concerns, as Chen points out, namely, that apps may have other methods to track data subjects besides device identifiers. However, this move is still significant, and I believe the more the public knows about these practices, the better. By introducing meaningful alternatives, users could become more motivated to learn about their privacy options, and they might become more invested in their decisions as a result.

Another promising idea is that of paid services. Meta, for example, recently announced that they were launching a paid subscription model, that would mean that users do not see ads on Facebook and Instagram in the European Union (Kastrenakes, 2023). For those worried about targeted advertising, this gives users a meaningful alternative, since they can pay to protect their privacy. However, such solutions may not be possible for everyone. Some may worry that this creates an illusion of choice for those already invested in the platform but lacking the financial means to afford it. There is also the concern that while ads may not be seen on Facebook, personal data could still be collected and used in ways that the subject does not consent to.

One final perspective inverts this model: it is not you that should pay Facebook, but Facebook that should pay you. In the computer scientist Jaron Lanier's (2013) book, *Who Owns the Future,* he suggests that ordinary people could be given a form of property rights with respect to their own personal data. He says, "[i]nformation is people in disguise, and people ought to be paid for the value that they contribute that can be sent or stored on a digital network" (2013, p. 245). In Lanier's vision of a "humanistic information economy", the data you upload—whether it is your online posts, data about the videos you watch, or other usage data—would be connected to you. Lanier introduces a concept called "provenance", to describe the recording of your personal data's origin. In Lanier's view then, when you share your data online, its provenance (the record connecting the data to you), would also be uploaded. In this information economy, provenance records would be connected to you and give you certain rights.[9] How exactly one would manage their own data in this new data economy would be challenging, but it could certainly help to give users compensation for sharing their data. However, we would still need to be mindful that people are not exploited or coerced into providing consent for their data to be shared, if Lanier's proposal was to ever be implemented.

3.4 Practical Application: The Case of Cookies

I have identified three main problems that arise in contemporary personal data collection practices. It may be possible to introduce other categories, but these seem to be the central ones. My hope is that this framework provides us with a way of evaluating consent procedures. For example, suppose a company is seeking to get informed consent by providing users with a 200-page privacy policy. We can ask whether doing so would truly make data collection and use practices transparent to users, given that there is a small chance that they will understand and read it all. We might also question the choices a company offers users in the policy—that is, is it a take-it-or-leave-it agreement, or can users negotiate the terms of conditions? And, users should clearly understand what is happening in the future with their data. They should be assured that if their data are to be re-purposed in ways that exceed their original consent, their consent will be sought again. I thus propose three conditions to help assess online consent procedures.

[1] Be *transparent* to data subjects;
[2] Do not *re-purpose* personal data without informed consent from data subjects;
[3] Provide *meaningful alternatives* to data subjects.

How one interprets these in different contexts will, of course, be likely to generate controversy, as we may disagree on what constitutes a "transparent" procedure or whether an option is "genuinely meaningful". But this gives us a starting point. Let us consider a test case.

In the last few years, websites have started to give you options about which "cookies" you would like to share. No doubt you have noticed the pop-up windows while browsing online. Cookies are an important part of the internet and work by storing information on your computer from the websites you visit. As Francis and Francis put it, they are "small bits of code installed on your computer by a website you visit so that the website will recognise you" (2017, p. 215). For example, if you go to Amazon and add items to your basket, or log into a website, the website can remember your actions when you progress to different parts of the site. Cookies allow this to occur by storing information on your local device. There are different types of cookies, of course. Some cookies may be required for the website to function, while others might make your experience on a website easier if allowed. Other cookies, such as third-party cookies, pertain to advertising, and can be stored on your device too.

That users have a choice about what cookies they would like to allow, such as selecting to accept only the "necessary to function" ones, or to allow all cookies, is a step in the right direction in terms of informed consent. Pop-up windows seem transparent too, as they are often one of the first things you see when visiting a website, and often explain how the cookies will function.[10] Furthermore, much of the time, you appear to have meaningful alternatives, as you often do not have to allow the use of all cookies. In some cases, you have the option to disallow third-party cookies, giving you control over whether your personal data will be collected for advertising purposes or even re-purposed later.

While pop-up windows that allow you to manage your cookie choices are a positive sign, their use is far from optimal. One problem has to do with their practicality. You may be motivated to complete them the first few times you see them, but for many people, it will not take long for "consent fatigue" to kick in. In a *Wired* interview, Lou Montulli, who invented cookies, voiced his dissatisfaction with the current way that people are required to manage their use. He said, "I'm just like everybody else . . . I want that pop-up to go away as soon as possible. The idea of asking people about permissions every single time they go to a website is annoying" (as cited in Olds, 2022). As a result, Montulli calls such a way of self-managing cookie use "a really silly idea" (Olds, 2022).

If there were only two or three sites that used cookies, these pop-ups would be a good idea. But since most websites use cookies, the reality is that such ways of managing consent become burdensome to users—so much so they risk undermining the extent to which they provide *meaningful alternatives* to users. Montulli (as cited in Olds, 2022) suggests that a better idea would be that you would only need to make your choice once, instead of every time you visit a new site. In Chapter 6, I consider the possibility of automated consent, which may be able to facilitate such an idea.

We might also be concerned with how transparent these pop-up window choices really are. As Dorri Olds suggests there is still a "lack of transparency about how cookies work and who manages the data collected from them" (2022). Thus, someone who carefully manages their cookies through these pop-ups might still not be able to provide informed consent because websites are not transparent about what is done with the personal data collected.[11] So even if pop-up alerts are a positive sign that consent is starting to be taken more seriously, they are, according to the framework developed here flawed.

3.5 Conclusion

In this chapter, I have outlined three of the main types of impediments that prevent us from providing informed consent online: the Transparency Problem, the Re-purposed Data Problem, and the Meaningful Alternatives Problem. To assess the viability of new solutions for the providing and obtaining of informed consent, it will be helpful to keep these problems in mind as we progress. Over the next four chapters, I begin exploring ways to address these impediments. The next chapter starts by examining how the law can assist, while at the same time outlining some of its limitations. This discussion will lead us to look beyond the law for ways to improve consent practices.

Notes

1 This chapter develops and expands upon a framework that I first introduced in Andreotta et al. (2022).
2 As we also saw in Chapter 1, this has not always been the case in the medical context. In the "Doctor Knows Best" paradigm, transparency was not always

practiced if a medical practitioner believed there were benefits of withholding information from patients.

3 See Allhoff (2003) for a reconsideration of Carr's view. Allhoff suggests that some business bluffing is "morally permissible" and a "practice that should be endorsed by all rational negotiators" (2003, p. 283).

4 See Mejias and Couldry (2024, pp. 222–228), for a discussion about how we can work "within the system" to bring about change with respect to inequitable data collection and use practises. One of their suggestions is to work with local governments to enact social change.

5 These quotes also feature in a recent report by Manwaring et al. (2021), about how Australians are uninformed about how their personal data are used.

6 The issue could arise in medical ethics, for example, if an AI algorithm recommends a medical treatment and it is not clear why it has done so (see Xu & Shuttleworth, 2024).

7 See Tsamados et al. (2022) for a discussion of some of the key ethical problems and solutions related to the use of AI algorithms. The authors address issues of transparency and discuss Explainable AI.

8 The European survey that Nguyen and Solomon (2018) refer to is found in Custers et al. (2014).

9 See Lanier's (2018) book, *Ten Arguments for Deleting Your Social Media Accounts Right Now*. In Chapter 1 of his book, he addresses the concern of behavioural manipulation and how social media undermines your "free will". The option to delete your social media is an *option* if you are worried about this issue, but it is unclear whether this is a meaningful alternative for everyone, given that some may rely on social media for their business, or to connect with family, for example.

10 Cf. Stewart (2019).

11 In general, we might also worry how the "default" settings are configured online. Véliz, for example, points out that settings for products and services, like websites and applications, are often *privacy-unfriendly* by "default" (2021, p. 228). She also suggests that it can be hard to change the settings sometimes.

4 The Limits of the Law and Soft Governance Approaches

In the preceding chapter, we explored three types of impediments, or challenges, related to providing and obtaining informed consent on the internet. In the remainder of the book, I examine ways in which these problems might be solved or at least minimised. I begin here by looking at the extent to which the law can provide recourse. While the law undoubtedly plays a crucial role in protecting privacy rights and ensuring ethical practices, it is by no means a panacea. In this chapter, I will discuss how the law has helped to impose necessary constraints on companies' attempts to collect and use our personal data. Simultaneously, I will also sketch some limits of the law. This latter discussion will lay the groundwork for my proposal about the efficacy of "soft governance" approaches, and how they might complement legal measures.[1]

I consider this book a work of applied moral philosophy rather than a work of legal interpretation, so my analysis of the legal aspects will not go into the level of detail a legal scholar would. This does not mean that I take there to be a disconnection between the legal and the moral domains, however. Morality *ought* to inform the law, and the law, in turn, can help us to understand the practical application of moral thought.[2] In Section 4.1, I look at some recent fines which have been issued to companies for failing to obtain informed consent from data subjects. In Section 4.2, I offer a brief discussion of some of the limits of the law. And then in Section 4.3, I discuss the details of a "soft governance" approach, which draws inspiration from ethics review committees in the research context.

4.1 The Law and Its Limits

The introduction of the General Data Protection Regulation (GDPR) has made a significant impact on the way that businesses operate in the data economy in Europe. Adopted in 2016 by the European Union, and made effective as of 2018, the GDPR has done much to protect the privacy rights of those whose data are collected by companies operating in the region.[3]

DOI: 10.4324/9781032626048-4

Like any legislation, however, there are important things to be said about its potential shortcomings and limitations.[4] Before addressing such concerns, I want to begin by looking at how the GDPR offers a way of addressing two of the impediments to informed consent that were examined in the previous chapter, namely, the Transparency Problem and the Re-purposed Data Problem. In Chapter 2 (Articles 5–11) of the GDPR, for example, we see a section called "Principles", which states that personal data are to be "processed lawfully, fairly and in a *transparent* manner" (European Union, 2016, Article 5.1.a, my emphasis); and also "collected for specified, explicit and legitimate purposes and not *further processed* in a manner that is incompatible with those purposes specified" (European Union, 2016, Article 5.1.b, my emphasis). The GDPR also has something to say about consent in general. In Article 4, "Definitions", it is stated that consent must be "freely given, informed, and unambiguous" (European Union, 2016).

The GDPR offers protection to EU citizens from the companies operating in the region (regardless of a company's country of origin). We also see positive signs, with respect to privacy legislation, in other jurisdictions. The Federal Communications Commission (FCC) in the United States have penalised companies for failing to get proper informed consent from data subjects before using their data; and in Australia, the Australian Competition and Consumer Commission (ACCC) has been active in issuing large fines to companies too, as we explore below.[5] If the law has been able to place limits on companies, and there is legislation that specifically mentions informed consent, why look to other solutions?[6]

The answer that I propose here is as follows: while the law is effective in restricting the most egregious personal data collection techniques, it is less effective when it comes to the actual process of providing detailed and context-specific guidance. For example, as Lundgren (2020a) points out, while it is good that the GDPR requires companies to be "transparent", it is hardly effective if a company's method of adhering to transparency is to provide users with a lengthy privacy policy that they are unlikely to read. Therefore, in Lundgren's view, there is a practical problem with the GDPR (a point I will return to in Chapter 6). Or consider the notion of "informed consent" itself as a concept. While the GDPR is effective in looking at cases where consent did not occur, as will be shown in the discussion below, the legislation is less clear about providing a more philosophical conceptual analysis of what constitutes informed consent in the first place.

4.1.1 Amazon

One of the largest fines under the GDPR (at the time of this writing) involves Amazon.[7] In 2021, the company announced that they had been issued a €746 million ($887 million USD) fine by the Luxembourg data protection regulator (Telford, 2021). The fine stemmed from a complaint lodged in 2018 by La Quadrature du Net—a French advocacy group that promotes digital rights on the internet (La Quadrature du Net, 2021). The group accused Amazon of engaging in problematic personal data collection and use practices related to targeted advertising. As La Quadrature puts it, "the targeted ad system that Amazon forces onto us is not based on free consent" (La Quadrature du Net, 2021). They claim, as a result, that Amazon's practices violated GDPR requirements.

What exactly was wrong with Amazon's targeted advertising system—that is, was the personal data they used to facilitate the targeted advertising acquired without securing proper informed consent or did consent failed to be secured at all? As the case is still ongoing as of 2024, we do not have all of the answers yet. In early 2024, an Amazon spokesperson suggested that they still intended to challenge the fine, by saying that the accusations stemmed from "subjective interpretations of the law" (as cited in Asokan, 2024). That the case has been ongoing for a long time has not escaped the attention of some commentators, as it raises issues about the lack of transparency about the details of the case. As far back as 2021, Matt Burgess, a writer at *Wired*, said "Despite the headline-grabbing fine, little is really known about the details of what Amazon has been fined for" (2021). This was further complicated by Amazon's claims that they had done nothing wrong. A spokesman in 2021, for example, told CNBC that "[t]here has been no data breach, and no customer data has been exposed to any third party" (see Shead, 2021). This claim is quite ambiguous, however. As we saw in Chapter 2, the Facebook-Cambridge Analytica scandal was not a "data breach", even though personal data were clearly collected and used without valid consent.

A year later in 2022, Neil Hodge, of *Compliance Week*, said that the "details about the decision—as well as the actual complaint—remain sketchy" (2022). As of the time of this writing (early 2024), the case is not finalised. The fact that legal cases, such as this one, can drag on for years is a problem. For one reason, as Burgess (2021) notes, appeal processes can sometimes bring fines down. So it may be that after several years of appeals, Amazon will end up paying a much smaller fine. Nevertheless, Burgess still thinks that the case is important as it shows the *power* of the GDPR, and describes it as "arguably the most important GDPR decision issued" (2021). The large amount of the initial fine may motivate other companies to attend to their consent-gathering practices more closely.

While the amount of money involved is significant, and certainly sends a powerful message to other companies, there are problems that can arise with such delays. One is that it prevents a clear message from being sent to other companies about what was specifically wrong with Amazon's data collection process. Is there something unique about how Amazon sought consent, or did they use processes that are widely adopted elsewhere? The Amazon case is not unique in that it has taken time to achieve a verdict, of course. As Saqr (2022) notes, there is an increasing number of GDPR-related filings that remain unresolved. He cites reasons such as "restrained resources, number of filings, case complexities, and the GDPR law itself that experts and regulators are finding difficult to apply" (Saqr, 2022, p. 2). The slow pace of enforcement can be contrasted with the "breakneck speed", as Burgess (2022) puts it, that the information economy moves at. Of course, we would think that it is important to get the details right, but the timeliness concern does mean that there are delays in lessons learned. And so, by the time a result is given, the technology used may have been adapted and newer issues may have arisen.

Another example involving Amazon also highlights what I will call a "minimum standards" problem that arises when companies align their ethical standards with what is required of the law, without taking measures to go far beyond it. In 2019, for example, Burin (2019) reported in the *ABC News* in Australia on the conditions of Amazon's recently opened fulfilment centre, located on the outskirts of Melbourne. The article, which interviewed workers at the fulfilment centre, noted that there was a "culture of fear" that existed there; that there was an expectation to work at "Amazon pace", which was described as being between jogging and walking; that there existed high-pressure targets that workers were expected to meet, which made some feel they could not use the bathroom, or had to compromise safety; and some workers had general feelings of anxiety about when they would get another shift (Burin, 2019). What is particularly noteworthy in Burin's article is the quote from associate professor Sarah Kaine who says, "I think [Amazon] probably examined the laws in detail and they're doing what they can to stay just within those laws" (as cited in Burin, 2019). Kaine says that this provides a "perfect storm for vulnerability" (as cited in Burin, 2019). Analogously with our concerns about informed consent: the awareness that some companies have of the laws and their efforts not to break them is only a starting point. There still needs to be a concerted effort to work on ethical practices that may not be required from a legal perspective but are necessary from a moral perspective.

4.1.2 Bounty

The case of Bounty—the parenting club which we examined in Chapter 2—provides us with a more straightforward example of how the law can restrict certain data collection and use practices. Recall that in 2019, Bounty was fined, £400,000 by the Information Commissioner's Office (ISO) for sharing personal data without users' consent. While the fine was significant, it could have been much larger if not for the fact that Bounty had stopped its personal data collection and sharing before the GDPR was enacted. The fine, as such, was brought about under the Data Protection Act 1998 (DPA), and as a result capped at £500,000 (Hern, 2019). Ben Wolford, for example, notes that the GDPR fine for similar behaviour could have "reached £17 million (€20 million)" (n.d.-b). As we discussed in Chapter 2, Bounty failed to get proper informed consent when it collected and used its members' data; they were not transparent about how the data were used; and did not help to protect its "vulnerable" members, some of whom were new mothers, from harms.[8]

The ICO notice to Bounty, which provides the key details of the case, makes direct reference to informed consent in several places. For example, the notice states that "any 'consent' provided by data subjects was not informed, nor could data subjects have foreseen that their data would be shared with those organisations" (ISO, 2019, p. 10). This statement directly addresses the Transparency Problem and also the Re-purposed Data Problem that we discussed in Chapter 3, and demonstrates how the law can help overcome these issues, as evidenced by the fact that the fine put an end to such practices. As the ISO notice states: "[o]n 30 April 2018 Bounty ceased its practice of sharing data with third parties for direct marketing purposes" (ISO, 2019, p. 10).

The fine would have also sent a clear message to other companies whose data collection and use practices were not associated with the informed consent of data subjects. Large fines can draw a lot of attention from the media, and this can provide a powerful deterrent to other companies. As Ben Wolford of GDPR.EU suggests, the law can inform us "what not to do" (n.d.-b). In the Bounty case, there are two clear lessons, according to Wolford, one is to "[b]e clear about your intentions" and the second is "[y]ou must have a lawful basis" (n.d.-b). We can clearly see that Bounty's actions are in conflict with, for instance, Article 7 of the GDPR which states "the [data] controller shall be able to demonstrate that the data subject has consented to processing of his or her personal data" (European Union, 2016).

Following the GDPR guidelines, we might say that Bounty ought to have secured informed consent. How should they have gone about this? Recall that in Chapter 2, there were several key issues with Bounty's consent-gathering procedures: [1] in the opt-in policy Bounty used for offline registrations, there was a *lack of choice* about data sharing; [2] the offline registrants did not have access to Bounty's privacy policy. And [3], those who made online registrations were not informed that large broker companies might have access to their data. Some of these issues appear to be easier to fix than others, as Bounty could simply give users a choice about what happens to their data and make sure they have access to a privacy policy. But would this be enough for informed consent?

The ISO report also stated that Bounty operated a data broking scheme, and until April 30, 2018, "supplied data to third parties for the purpose of electronic direct marketing" (ISO, 2019, p. 5). The scale of the collection and use was clearly something that should have been communicated to users. According to the ISO report, Bounty received consent during the "member registration process" (ISO, 2019, p. 6) and it

> [S]hared a total of 35,027,373 personal data records with Acxiom (a marketing and profiling agency), Equifax (a credit reference agency), Indicia (a marketing agency) and Sky (a telecommunications company) for the purposes of direct electronic marketing.
>
> (ISO, 2019, pp. 6–7)

How Bounty should have ensured that its users actually *understood* that this was occurring is hard to say. The GDPR states that consent needs to be "freely given, informed, and unambiguous" (European Union, 2016). However, as we know, informed consent is not guaranteed even if data subjects are given a privacy policy. One might think that from a legal perspective, all Bounty needed to have done here was provided such a policy and then it would have been up to users to facilitate informed consent. But the problems highlighted in the previous chapter showed the flaws with such an approach. If informed consent is more than just information transfer, as was argued in Chapter 1, then simply providing a data subject with a lengthy privacy policy, that they are unlikely to read, may not be the best way to facilitate informed consent.

Bounty continues to operate as a company today, and now features references to "informed consent" in their current privacy policy. The policy on their website boasts that "[a]t Bounty, we are 100% committed to protecting the privacy and security of our Bounty Members" (Bounty, 2023). In a section on user rights, the company also states that users have "[t]he right to be informed about how your personal information is being used (like this notice!)" (Bounty, 2023). The fact that the law played a causal role in bringing about this change speaks to its importance. However, to truly meet ethical standards in obtaining informed consent, we will need to go beyond legal requirements.

4.1.3 Google and the ACCC

Even though the GDPR's jurisdiction is limited to Europe and stakeholders within its domain, it is of course true that other countries have laws protecting privacy rights, although they may not offer the same level of protection. I will now turn to cases from Australia involving Google and the ACCC (Australian Competition and Consumer Commission).

4.1.3.1 Google and Informed Consent About Location Data

In 2022, The Federal Court of Australia ordered Google LLC to pay $60 million AUD (about 40 million USD) in penalties due to the way it allegedly misled Android phone users about how their personal data were being collected between 2017 and 2018 (ACCC, 2022a). The type of personal data in question was "location data", which is, broadly speaking, information about the geographical location of a device (i.e., where it is currently located or where it has been).

How did Google mislead customers about how these data were being used? In the Federal Court's view, Google misled some users by causing them to think that their personal data were not being collected, when in fact they were (Byrne, 2022). This was because there was more than one setting that needed to be turned off in order for this type of personal data not to be collected. Even when users had their "Location History" turned off, Google could still collect location data if "Web and App Activity" (which saves a user's searches and activities from sites and apps that use Google services) was on (Byrne, 2022). Google's data collection practices were found to be misleading because some users may have thought that turning off "Location History" (clicking "Don't save my Location History in my Google Account") was a sufficient step to take in order for their location data not to be shared.

The case provides us with another example of how the law can restrict certain data collection practices. However, the case is particularly noteworthy in that it focuses on what data subjects would have likely believed. This is reflected in the ACCC's claim that Google's actions were "misleading" (ACCC, 2022a). Perhaps someone with the requisite knowledge could have known about the multiple settings, and then provided informed consent, but the Federal Court took into account how the average user would interpret this setting. After all, it was not as if Google made it impossible for the data not to be shared, or that it lied to users. What Google did not do, in the Court's view, was take into consideration how some people might think that if one setting was off, then the data would not be collected (again a completely reasonable belief). If we think about how consent works in the medical setting, doctors can ask patients to explain to them their own understanding of a procedure. This encourages doctors or physicians to reflect upon the ways in which they inform patients. One problem with obtaining online consent is that it can be hard to know the extent to which data subjects understand what they are consenting to, as companies do not often need to check to see what data subjects believe. A lot of the time, all they need to do is check to see if consent has been given.

Now, I am of course not suggesting that Google needs to hire consultants to help its users comprehend how they process personal data. What I am suggesting is that "informed consent" cannot simply be thought of as a process that involves the clicking of an "agree" button, which does not take into account the psychology of the consenter. For this reason, the Federal Court's decision sends a clear message to companies, namely, that some thought must go into how people actually experience companies' consent procedures. Recall that this was a core component of our discussion about informed consent in Chapter 1. As the ACCC Chair Gina Cass-Gottlieb said, the size of the fine "sends a strong message to digital platforms and other businesses, large and small, that they must *not mislead consumers* about how their data is being collected and used" (as cited in ACCC, 2022a, my emphasis). As of late 2018, the practice was no longer used by Google.

4.1.3.2 Google and Informed Consent About Data Combination

Now, while the law can play a significant role in ending unethical practices, the process does not always go smoothly. Companies can of course challenge fines, as there is room for different interpretations of the law. In a different case, also involving personal data collection, the Federal Court of Australia rejected the ACCC's claim against Google, which also involved an accusation that Australian Consumers were misled. Unlike the first case, this one went in Google's favour. In 2022, the Federal Court actually dismissed the case (see ACCC, 2022b). This case involved the privacy policy that Google employed.

In 2016, Google published on-screen notifications to Australian users indicating that it had changed its privacy policy, such that the scope of the data it collected and used was increased (ACCC, 2022b). The original complaint by the ACCC was that this notification was "misleading" (see ACCC, 2020). Why did they think so? If a user clicked "I agree" on an on-screen notification, then Google was able to combine personal data from users' Google accounts (e.g., Google Maps, Gmail, YouTube), with personal data from non-Google sites that users visit. The personal data collected from these two types of sources was then used to "improve Google's advertising business" (ACCC, 2022b). As we have seen, the more personal data a company has, the better it will be able to target ads.

We may ask, though, what is morally objectionable about this, since Google appears to have notified users? Here is what Rod Simms, the ACCC Chair, said in 2020:

> We are taking this action because we consider Google misled Australian consumers about what it planned to do with large amounts of their personal information, including internet activity on websites not connected to Google.
>
> (as cited in ACCC, 2020)

The Federal Court, in 2022, dismissed the case, however. It claimed that Google did technically inform users. The court found that Google "did not mislead Australian consumers when it published an on-screen notification to Australian users, and changed its privacy policy to expand the scope of its use and collection of personal data" (ACCC, 2022b).

In terms of informed consent, however, we might ask how well Google did to help their users understand *how* to manage their data, even though they were found, from a legal perspective, not to have misled them—they may have met a minimal legal standard, as discussed above. We know, for instance, that people do not read privacy policies, and we also know that many do not understand how their data are being used even when they provide consent for data to be shared. So, while sending data subjects to privacy policies (that companies know few are likely to read and understand) might succeed in meeting certain legal standards, it will be unlikely to represent the best way to ensure that informed consent is given. The Federal Court's ruling seems to suggest that as long as companies meet some minimum standard, that is—they do not deceive data subjects—then they will not be fined. But clearly, as we have seen, this is only a starting point when it comes to informed consent.[9]

4.2 Limits of the Law

We have examined several examples involving large companies being fined for their data collection practices from Europe and Australia. These cases show how the law can help to address the three problems identified in the previous chapter. For example, in both the Bounty and Google cases, there was a lack of *transparency* regarding the use of personal data, leading to data collection without informed consent. The law played an important role in ending such practices, and thereby sent a powerful message to other companies.[10] However, as we also saw, not all cases proceed smoothly. One problem has to do with the time it can take to process cases, as evidenced in the Amazon case, which can sometimes drag on for years. While the fines can be substantial, it is debatable how much of a deterrent they provide to giant companies, as they might just be viewed as the "cost of doing business". Moreover, these fines can be challenged, as the laws can be difficult to apply in certain contexts.

A second problem had to do with interpretations of the law. In the second Google case we examined, it might seem like the company attempted to do all it could to provide users with a chance to provide informed consent, in some very basic sense, as they provided information to users. The Federal Court found after all that they did inform users, so it was not correct to say that Google deceived users. However, reasonable people might of course disagree about the nature of "deception". And even if Google were not found to be deceptive, it does not follow that they provided users with the best chance of providing informed consent in any kind of robust ethical sense.

If it is a psychological fact about human beings that we suffer from "consent fatigue" after clicking through large amounts of privacy policies, then that is something that companies should take into account when designing consent-gaining procedures. Ideally, we want informed consent practices for humans, not for some perfectly rational being with endless time and resources. The law can point out problems, but we also need to go beyond the law if we are to fulfil the purpose of informed consent.[11]

4.3 On Soft Governance

The introduction of the GDPR, as well as other data privacy regulations from around the world, provide a powerful incentive for companies to prioritise informed consent. However, as our short survey has shown, while the law can effectively restrict and protect against certain egregious actions, it has limitations guiding future practices. In this section, I will focus on the so-called "soft governance" approaches and discuss their utility. In using the terms "soft governance" and "hard governance", I am following Maggetti (2015), who says, "[h]ard' governance in the EU is operated through rules that arise from treaties, directives and regulations, while 'soft' governance involves the use of non-binding rules that are nevertheless expected to produce effects in practice" (p. 252).

Some of the limitations of hard governance approaches are nicely articulated by Floridi (2018) in his commentary on the GDPR, which takes place within a broader discussion of "soft ethics", which may be thought of in parallel to "soft governance". With respect to the 99 Articles of the GDPR, he says:

> As it is often the case with complex legislation, the Articles do not cover everything, leave grey areas of normative uncertainty even about topics that they do cover, are subject to interpretations and may require updating when applied to new circumstances, especially in a technological context where innovation develops so quickly and radically; think for example of face recognition software, or so-called deep fake software.
>
> (2018, p. 6)

I take Floridi's main point about the GDPR, of course, to generalise to other regulatory frameworks around the world. Furthermore, his comments are relevant to some of the concerns that we have examined in this chapter. Complex legislation cannot cover something as specific as an opt-in policy that Google produces or specify the details about how a social media site can verify that a user has actually understood a privacy policy, as this can vary significantly in different contexts, depending on what is at stake and the mechanisms used. Moreover, there may be debate over what "deceptive" or "transparent" processes look like, as these notions may be hard to define in a legal context.

The concept of "soft ethics", (which I take to address the same concerns as "soft governance") as Floridi explains, covers the same "normative ground as hard ethics" (2018, p. 6), such as the ethics of gaining informed consent. Soft ethics is distinct, however, in that it is concerned with "what ought and ought not to be done over and above the existing regulation, not against it, or despite its scope, or to change it, or to by-pass it (e.g., in terms of self-regulation)" (2018, p. 6). In this sense, soft ethics, and analogously, soft governance, can be thought of as "*post-compliance ethics*" (2018, p. 6 emphasis in original). Such a focus can be seen as addressing the kinds of questions that have arisen above, *after* a company has met the minimum legal requirements.

Suppose the law says that you cannot deceive data subjects into consenting, or that data subjects must be provided with a privacy policy. A soft ethics, or soft governance, approach could prompt one to ask, "what's next", to ensure ethical standards are met, in a way that works alongside the existing legislation, as Floridi mentions above. A good example in the medical context is the Declaration of Helsinki, which as we saw played an important role in transforming informed consent practices. While not legally binding under international law, it provides "ethical guidelines for physicians and other participants in medical research" (Carlson et al., 2004, p. 695); and has been called "the most widely recognized source of ethical guidance for biomedical research" (Macklin, 2003). In our attempt to extract lessons from the medical context, the idea of developing ethical guidelines for the use of personal data holds promise. In what follows, I will sketch the basics of a soft-governance approach that I began developing in an earlier paper. My aims here are, of course, far more modest than those offered in the Declaration of Helsinki.[12]

4.3.1 Looking to HRECs in Australia

In 2021, my colleagues Nin Kirkham and Marco Rizzi and I published a paper in the journal *AI and Society* (Andreotta et al., 2022) that put forward some ideas about how we might improve online consent practices. One idea we briefly discussed involved the possibility of companies subjecting their data collection and use practices to an ethics approval process. We did not envision such a process as being a legal requirement, but rather one inspired by the ethics approval processes that university researchers are subjected to when they undertake studies involving human participants. In this way, we thought the collection and use of personal data, for commercial and administrative purposes, could be subject to a "soft governance" ethical regulation (Andreotta et al., 2022)

In order to understand our proposal, let us take a closer look at how ethics approval works in the research context.[13] Suppose you are employed at a university and are curious about how incivility in the workplace affects staff retention rates. After you have reviewed the extant literature and identified gaps, you might consider planning a research project. This involves deciding whom would be best to interview (e.g., employees, CEOs, managers) and what questions should be asked of them. However, before commencing the interviews, you would first need to get ethics approval. Depending on what country you live in, this could be a legal requirement, but in others it might not be. In Australia, for example, ethics approval is overseen by Human Research Ethics Committees (HRECs), which review proposals to ensure compliance with the National *Statement on Ethical Conduct in Human Research* (hereafter, 'National Statement'). Unlike certain countries, an HREC review of research is not mandated under legislation in Australia (Eckstein et al., 2022), although there are some exceptions to this norm.

How does this work in practice? Once an individual researcher, or team, is ready, they would submit their application to get reviewed. It might include participant information forms, participant consent forms, information about the kinds of data that will be collected, risk assessments, and other required documentation. If the researcher has failed to include anything, such as information about how the interviews will be performed, an appropriately detailed consent form, and so on, the HREC may require that a revision be performed. The HREC will also require that you do not start any data collection (so in our example, data from interviewees) until approval is granted, and that retroactive approval will not be given to research already done.[14] This may seem like a laborious process to go through just to know what people's work experiences are like, but it ensures that a certain level of protection is given to interview subjects helping to maintain a certain standard for research.

What happens if you do not get ethics approval in Australia? Depending on what it is you intend to do with your findings, there may not be much that the law can do. Suppose you do not bother to get HREC approval, and you decide to talk to your friends about how they find their respective workplaces and how it impacts them. There are unlikely to be any legal consequences you will have to face by doing this; however, without ethics approval, there are several things you might not be able to do.

First, you will have difficulty publishing in a *reputable* journal, as they typically require ethics approval for work that involves human subjects.[15] This is because, as Newson and Lipworth (2015) point out, ethics approval ensures that a basic standard is maintained, something that helps maintain a journal's reputation. The authors, additionally, give four key reasons why health promotion research, to pick one example of research involving humans, should not be published without ethics approval. Ethics approval, in their view can

(i) enhance the legitimacy of the research, which in turn helps to establish public trust;
(ii) it ensures that the research project is well designed;
(iii) it can help investigators see "aspects of their planned activity that may give rise to risk"; and
(iv) it gives "due respect for persons".

(2015, pp. 173–174)

Another reason that ethics approval is important, as my colleagues and I (Andreotta et al., 2022) discussed in our paper, has to do with the consequences of not publishing your research—that is, if your study is not published, then there is a good chance it will be ignored or not taken seriously by other academics.

Furthermore, if you do work for a university and are looking to publish, then your institution will require that you receive ethical approval. As Eckstien et al. point out, "[c]ompliance with the National Statement for all research involving humans is a precondition for institutions to receive research grants from major Australian funding bodies" (2022, p. 200). Universities clearly have an interest in ensuring that researchers meet this standard. So, while anyone can do research without ethics approval, there are some important reasons why people should get it, even if those reasons are not legal in the country you find yourself in.

4.3.2 *Ethics Committees and Online Informed Consent*

Essentially, our aim was to draw inspiration from the ways that HRECs work in Australia and apply the concept to the online personal data collection context, more broadly. How might this work in theory? Simply put, our idea was that before companies (e.g., Google or Facebook) sought to obtain personal data, they would need to first apply for approval from ethics committees. In putting together an application, companies would then detail what personal data collection would occur, and also explain how they would gain informed consent from data subjects. Companies wanting to make changes to their data collection practice—say when new types of personal data were sought, or new third parties wanted to collect these data—could then reapply for ethical approval, depending on how significant the change was.

How might this work in practice? Let's take the case of Google in Australia we discussed above, where they published on-screen notifications to Australian users indicating that they had changed their privacy policy, such that they sought to collect more types of personal data so that they could combine data from users' Google account (e.g., Google Maps, Gmail, YouTube), with personal data from non-Google sites. An ethics committee that reviewed this data collection procedure might advise Google that while their practices may not violate any legal requirements, they are nonetheless not conducive to informed consent. They might explain their decisions to Google based on the fact that people generally struggle to understand procedures of this nature. The ethics committee might then also make suggestions about how to better communicate such changes to users. For example, they could recommend a more engaging, and less misleading, notification process, so that users are effectively informed that such changes have occurred (recall the ACCCC accused Google of misleading Australian consumers).

Consider, further, a recent case involving Facebook and its practice of "scraping" data from users on its platform. According to *ABC News* in Australia, Facebook admitted, in an inquiry, that it was scraping the "public photos, posts and other data" (Evans, 2024) from Australian adults on its platform so that it could train its AI models. Problematically, there was no "opt-out option" offered to Australian users. This was in contrast to what was offered to European users, who *were* given an opt-out option (Evans, 2024). The presence of the GDPR in Europe likely motivated Facebook to give European users such a choice. Facebook, thus, took advantage of the weaker privacy laws in Australia and collected such data for its own benefit. An ethics committee reviewing such a practice would surely not approve of depriving Australians of an opt-out option, just because the laws in the country did not require them to provide one. They may have recommended that users be presented with meaningful alternatives (as discussed in Chapter 3). Ethics committees could not only help ensure ethical standards are met, but also potentially prevent legal cases, as problematic consent procedures could be identified and addressed before companies begin to collect personal data. Committees, depending on their composition, could support decisions with empirical findings from research too. For instance, studies showing the relevance of certain human biases or conditions where "consent fatigue" is likely to arise, say when navigating lengthy privacy policies, could inform these decisions.

In the case of Bounty, as examined above, an ethics committee might have pointed out that Bounty should not share customer data with third parties for advertising purposes until they have first developed a *transparent* way of informing customers about what they plan to do, and then second, actually worked out how to verify that data subjects really have understood what is occurring with their data. If privacy experts were on the committee, they may emphasise the fact that information about mothers and babies is sensitive, and therefore, it is crucial to ensure that such data are only shared after valid consent. They might also make recommendations based on successful approaches adopted by other companies attempting similar practices, to ensure decisions are not purely negative.

Why could companies not just do this themselves? The GDPR, for example, has a checklist on its website that is designed for data controllers, so why could not companies simply follow this.[16] One concern with companies handling ethical analyses themselves has to do with the problem of objectivity. Just as researchers do not approve their own research, it may be difficult for companies to scrutinise their own consent-gathering practices in an objective way. Even excellent researchers, for example, have biases that can be hard to overcome. Or a conflict of interest may also arise. Furthermore, those associated with a company will likely have a desire for the company to move forward as quickly as possible, without delays. Self-imposing non-legal restraints could be difficult. Another reason is that ethics committees could offer expertise that individuals at certain companies do not possess. If the ethics committees review many proposals, they then will be able to build up a body of knowledge and develop expertise.

Before anything like a system of ethics committees could be established in the online personal data collection context, several problems with current HRECs, in the research context, would need to be addressed. One issue is that they can cause delays to projects. It can take time for researchers to revise their proposals if an ethics committee requires multiple revisions. Companies who are not used to subjecting their processes to such reviews may be dissuaded to use them if they will cause lengthy delays. Additionally, the possibility of backlogs could cost companies financially (see Mehta et al., 2023).

There would also need to be a focus on how decisions are made, so that mechanisms for challenging decisions could be sought. For instance, Hawe et al. (2022) describe how their "citizen science pilot project", which involved the topic of breastfeeding in the workplace, was undermined by the ethics review process. The authors note that the HREC objected to some of the language used in their proposal, and also required participants to obtain consent from their employers, which led to a loss of participants in their study. Hawe et al. (2022) note that "ethics requirements worked contrary to our purpose and possibly acted to reinforce the powerlessness some women experience at work" (Hawe et al., 2022, p. 194). If companies like Google or Facebook were met with similar decisions or delays from ethics committees, it is easy to imagine that this might deter them and other companies from pursuing them—especially if there were not a legal mandate. If an ethics committee fails to approve a data collection or use procedure, for example, then it would be crucial to ensure that substantive reasons are given to justify the decision, so decisions are not seen as arbitrary. This is an issue for HRECs, of course, but it will be important to get right in the online context, especially since many will need to be convinced of the benefits of the idea first.

Eckstein et al. (2022) offer a suggestion that is also relevant to the application of ethics approval online. They say that

> HRECs could provide reasons for their decisions, to be deposited in a database available to other HRECs, thereby encouraging consistency and improving the quality of decision-making. More radically, HRECs could be subject to judicial review, meaning their decisions could be reviewed by administrative decisions tribunals, broadly on the grounds that decisions were beyond power, procedurally unfair, or irrational.
>
> (p. 202)

This would obviously be very important to get right in the online context as well. Judicial reviews would provide a way to maintain consistency and ensure that companies do not perceive the review process as unjust or arbitrary. Furthermore, the more transparency that is offered through suggestions and case studies, the more companies could feel as if they were working with an ethics committee, rather than against it. For example, suppose a parking app company's ethics approval application for its new app is rejected due to a misleading privacy policy and a difficult-to-find method for turning off non-compulsory data sharing. An ethics committee that rejected their application would need to be clear about the reasons why they arrived at this decision, and possibly point to other apps or websites that attempted the same process, and how they were able to modify their consent-gaining practices. For example, an ethics committee could point to examples in a database, as Eckstein et al. (2022) suggest, to illustrate the reasons why similar parking apps, or even different social media apps, were not given ethics approval because of a similar issue. This documentation would help establish norms and establish a more collaborative relationship with companies.

Although speculative, I believe drawing inspiration from HRECs, while imperfect, has some advantages over other suggestions that have been made. This is because HRECs and ethics review processes, in general, have been in place for some time, and thus have established methodologies to draw from. Consider an idea of Shane Green's—former CEO of private data-sharing platform digi.me—who stated in *Vox* that websites could have rating systems. Green suggests that websites could have "some seal of approval or ratings system that would signal to users that a website follows good privacy practices" (as cited in Stewart, 2019).[17] According to this idea, data subjects could evaluate websites based on their privacy concerns and the necessary approvals or ratings. This would give them more control over who has access to their data compared to the current system, where they are in a poor epistemic position regarding the workings of the website or app. Green himself acknowledges that his proposal raises several issues. Who would set the standards for example? Would it be up to the private or public sector? It will be hard to find a consensus, for example, on any number of issues such as whether a certain consent procedure is misleading, to questions about whether a consent procedure is transparent enough to users.

It is, however, important to note that this problem faces the proposal of ethics committees too. The question of how they would be set up is also a difficult one. To address these issues, though, we could look to existing HRECs and analyse the way that they have been designed. Although the research context is quite distinct from the online personal data collection context, there would no doubt be valuable lessons to extract. In Australia, for instance, HRECs require a minimum membership of eight people, as stipulated by the National Statement. These members must include the following:

> (a) a chairperson with suitable experience . . . (b) two people who bring a broader community or consumer perspective and who have no paid affiliation with the institution . . . (c) a person with knowledge of, and current experience in, the professional care or treatment of people . . . (d) a person who performs a pastoral care role in a community . . . (e) a qualified lawyer . . . and (f) two people with current research experience that is relevant to research proposals to be considered at the meetings they attend.
>
> (National Health and Medical Research Council, Australian Research Council and Universities Australia, 2023, p. 90)

How ethics committees would be formed to handle online consent processes is a question that needs much further careful consideration. It's not clear for example, from the outset, what size an online ethics committee should be or who should be included in it. Still, the work that has gone into determining how HRECs should be constituted would no doubt instruct such investigations.

For example, it would be beneficial to include individuals with no affiliation to the institution in question. Someone affiliated with Google might be biased, perceive the process as an obstacle, or simply be so familiar with their own systems that they find it difficult to imagine how an average data subject could fail to understand how it works. It would seem sensible to have at least one member who has knowledge and experience in creating online consent procedures, whether they are researchers or professionals in related fields. Qualified lawyers would be useful to ensure that consent practices comply with legislation. And of course, ethicists and others who study similar cases could contribute too. Certainly, there is room for debate about how ethics committees, in the online data collection and use context, would be formed and maintained.

4.3.3 The Motivation Objection

An objection might have occurred to you while reading the previous section. You might question why companies like Google, Facebook, or Spotify would subject their procedures for collecting and using personal data to external ethics committees, especially when they are under no legal obligations to do so. It may be hard to imagine a company like Amazon, for example, transparently outlining how it collects personal data, where it sends it to, and the procedures it will put in place to ensure "informed consent" is gained from its customers. All of this, I confess, may seem fanciful.

My co-authors and I (Andreotta et al., 2022) were certainly aware of this problem when we first put forward the idea of ethics approval in our paper, and we did not pretend that it could be easily solved. However, we did see some reasons for optimism. One thing to note is that privacy has gained importance in the last few years, and some companies have embraced it. For instance, as discussed in Chapter 3, Apple recently launched a privacy feature, "App Tracking Transparency", which allowed users to click "Ask App Not to Track" if they did not want their personal data shared. Apple accompanied the update with an advertising campaign that likely appealed to privacy-conscious users, emphasising the control they could have over their personal data if they used an Apple product.[18]

Privacy is one thing, but ethics review committees are quite another, of course. With no companies currently subjecting their practices to ethics approval and the public not currently demanding it, companies might find it hard to market the idea to users. One idea my colleagues and I proposed is that since it is extremely *unlikely* that big tech companies would voluntarily sign up to this idea, other sectors, such as universities or educational institutions more broadly, would make better pioneers.

Our proposal was that universities could play a leadership role by initiating and promoting these efforts. Universities, after all, typically see themselves as having noble aims and ambitions related to shaping students' characters. For example, in his book, *Towards the Virtuous University*, Jon Nixon (2008) argues that "[i]n a rapidly changing world, universities have a vital leadership role to play not only in gauging and mapping change, but also in grasping its full implications" (p. 15). If the potential harms of personal data collection are as significant as many have pointed out, then a case can be made for why universities ought to lead by example.

Once we have examples of data collection practices going through ethics approval, we could move beyond theory. In Chapter 1, I discussed the concept of "paradigm shifts" and emphasised the importance, as suggested by Baker (2019), of observing alternative ways of acquiring consent in practice, not just in theory. This is important as Baker points out because "[o]ur intellectual natures abhor conceptual vacuums, preferring an established albeit problematic paradigm to none at all" (2019, p. 173). He goes on to suggest that while the "intelligentsia" may offer criticisms about existing practices, it is not until someone "invents an alternative paradigm" (2019, p. 173) that can address these problems will we give up on current paradigms. Baker is making a point about the medical paradigm, but I think his central argument generalises to our concerns—that is, I think we must go beyond mere criticism of online consent practices; viable alternatives must also be proposed. If people could observe institutions subjecting their consent practices to ethical review, and if such practices were seen to be effective, we might witness the beginning of a paradigm shift.

Since universities already deal with ethics review processes—and indeed, some mandate ethics review for researchers—it would not require them to invest in a wholly novel process; it would require only a shift of focus. Furthermore, there are important reasons for them to do so, independent of inspiring others, namely, the fact that they collect a lot of personal data about their students, such as demographic information like age and economic status, as well as academic data such as grades and student progress.

As Russell et al. (2018) note, there exists a commercial marketplace for personal information about students. If that is the case, we may ask how *transparent* the data collection practices are and scrutinise the role of consent in the collection and use of these data in universities. We might ask how well-informed students are about the use of their data, whether their data are sold to data brokers, and whether they have the capacity to opt out of sharing their personal data, if they wish. Russell et al. (2018) suggest that parents, students, and the public ought to know "(i) the identities of student data brokers, (ii) what lists and selects they are selling, and (iii) where the data for student lists and selects derives" (2018, p. ii).[19] If universities were to subject their student data collection and use practices to ethics review, this would ensure that universities were upholding their ethical obligations to students, and at the same time show that the idea of ethics review in the data collection context is possible. As this practice becomes normalised, private companies could then adopt it.

It is one thing to expect educational institutions to subject their data collection and use practices to ethics approval, but why should we think that large companies like Amazon, Google, or Spotify would follow suit? A positive sign that they might do so comes from widespread focus on the United Nations Sustainable Development Goals (SDGs) over the last few years. The SDGs were established in 2015 as part of the larger UN 2030 Agenda for Sustainable Development (Filho et al., 2020) and have been embraced not only by governments but also by large companies, such as those discussed in this book, like Google and Meta.[20]

There are 17 SDGs in total. Each goal focuses on a global issue, such as eradicating poverty, providing clean water, promoting clean energy, preserving the oceans and seas, as well as many more. Each goal has specific targets. For example, the goal of reducing inequality within and among countries (SDG 10), has a target to "empower and promote the social, economic and political inclusion of all, irrespective of age, sex, disability, race, ethnicity, origin, religion or economic or other status", by the year 2030.[21] One notable thing about the SDGs has been the readiness of companies to adopt them. Search the website of any major company you are familiar with, and it is highly likely that you will see evidence of the company's engagement, say by the presence of a sustainability report. Similarly, educational institutions, like universities, now report on how they are helping to achieve the SDGs. The University of New South Wales (UNSW) website, for example, explains how it contributes to each of the 17 goals.[22] And Western Sydney University has been recognised as a world leader, from 2022–2024, by the Times Higher Education (THE) University Impact Ranking, for its contributions to the goals.[23]

What are the implications of all of this for our discussion about informed consent? The prominence of the SDGs, I believe, shows that companies can be incentivised to focus on significant ethical issues that go beyond what is required by law.[24] The challenge, of course, is to determine what *would* motivate companies to improve *consent practices* further, in the same way that companies were motivated to care about SDGs. What would motivate them to subject their consent practices to ethics review for example? Whether economic, political, or public pressure ends up becoming the motivating force is something that is hard to predict. What is important to point out, in my view, is that the SDGs did not emerge in isolation—there is a history of movements addressing environmental issues, global poverty, gender equality, and more. It seems plausible that a similar consciousness-raising movement on the importance of privacy will need to accompany such efforts to make ethics approval something that would actually be demanded by data subjects. This task might appear particularly challenging since in the case of the SDGs, issues like gender discrimination, environmental degradation, and poverty are widely discussed and visible to millions of people. One concern here is that personal data collection and use practices are comparably hidden.

On the other hand, there is a growing emphasis on the importance of protecting privacy and why privacy matters more generally, due to there being a greater awareness of the harms that can arise from neglecting it (see Richards, 2021). If the act of providing informed consent could be seen as a practical way of self-managing one's privacy, and if the importance of privacy became more widely appreciated, then data subjects may start to choose to use websites and apps that used effective consent procedures while avoiding or deleting the ones that lack them. How exactly sites would let users know their consent-gathering practices have been given ethics approval is, of course, an open question.

One final challenge to mention pertains to the advice or suggestions that companies might be given. Just as with the SDGs, finding solutions will be difficult. It is one thing to aim to end poverty, but accomplishing the goal is a difficult task. Similarly, in the case of informed consent: even if companies want to become more transparent in their consent-gathering procedures, how would they do it? Is transparency even the kind of thing that could be "improved" like in the case of the SDGs? Could consent targets realistically be set? Some of these challenges will be easier to tackle than others. For example, ensuring that a company places an opt-out button in a prominent or visible location on their website, rather than hiding it, is a straightforward improvement that could indicate a measurable enhancement of transparency. How a 10,000-word privacy policy could be made more transparent or comprehensible, on the other hand, is obviously far more challenging.

4.4 Conclusion

The law has played, and will continue to play, an important role in preventing the misuse of personal data. The large fines issued under the GDPR, for example, send powerful messages to companies operating in the data economy about the importance of securing informed consent. As we have seen, there are limits to the law, however. Technology can move so quickly that the law can sometimes lag behind, fines can be challenged, and cases can drag on for years. Alongside the legal framework, however, there exists a softer approach to governance that is also promising. Drawing inspiration from the way HRECs work in Australia, and the ethical processes researchers undertake before performing studies involving human subjects, I suggested that ethics review processes could help ensure that informed consent is provided.

However, what should the recommendations of such ethics reviewers be? An ethics committee, for example, might examine a 10,000-word privacy policy and determine it will not help data subjects to provide informed consent. In the next two chapters, I explore possible ways to improve consent procedures. In Chapter 5, I examine the prospects of adding visuals to consent procedures to improve engagement; and then in Chapter 6, I explore the idea of automated consent. While these changes may not represent the groundbreaking shifts envisioned by some (see the Preface for a summary) they do align with the book's central thesis of the efficacy of incremental change. I will argue that these small changes can lead to substantial positive outcomes that help facilitate informed consent.

Notes

1 See Cohen's (2019) book *Between Truth and Power*, which looks at informational capitalism through a legal lens.
2 See Paulo (2016), for a discussion of some of the similarities between morality and the law. He argues that "there are striking similarities between ethics and law, especially between applied ethics and law" (p. 11). He also challenges the view that law and ethics are entirely different practices.
3 See Warren and Brandeis (1890) for a highly influential essay on the right to privacy.
4 See Wachter et al. (2017), who argue that "a meaningful right to explanation is not legally mandated by the GDPR" (p. 96). See Saqr (2022) for a discussion of some of the general issues with the GDPR. These issues include the lag time between the filing of a complaint and the ruling, and how the "GDPR has proven hard and oftentimes intricate to apply in real-life" (2022, p. 1).
5 In 2016, for example, the FCC fined Verizon Wireless $1.35 million USD for its use of "supercookies" (tracking cookies which are not stored on users' devices, making them hard to detect or delete) which were used to facilitate targeted advertising without users' consent (see Kang, 2016).
6 See Solove (2021) for a discussion on how regulation can address such privacy concerns. He notes that "regulation can also regulate to make certain types of personal data transfers impermissible or more difficult to undertake. Additionally, privacy regulation can control downstream transfers and uses of personal data, protecting the data as it flows from an initial transfer to other organizations down the line" (p. 50).
7 At the time of writing, there was a larger fine, namely, the €1.2 billion fine that was given to Meta for "mishandling" user data (Milmo & O'Carroll, 2023).
8 The ISO report also notes that "[t]he data subjects were not only potentially vulnerable new mothers/mothers-to-be, but also very young children" (ISO, 2019, p. 15).
9 Google is no stranger to legal controversies. In late 2023, the company agreed to settle a $5 billion lawsuit that claimed it misled users about how its "incognito" mode worked on their browsers. Contrary to what many believed, the mode did track users (see Reuters, 2023).
10 The GDPR has already issued several large penalties to major companies, including TikTok, WhatsApp, H&M, and British Airways.
11 See Citron's (2022) book, *The Fight for Privacy*, Chapter 5: "Law's Inadequacy", for further examples of how the law has failed, in recent years, to protect people's privacy.
12 See Brandsen et al. (2006) for a discussion of a problem with soft governance approaches, namely, that in certain contexts, guidelines that lack legal status can, in practice, take on the character of "formal regulation".

13 We focused on HRECs because all three of us worked at Australian universities and were familiar with the process. However, we were optimistic that this approach could be applied more broadly.
14 Visit any Australian university website and you will see evidence of this. Charles Sturt University's website states, "if you are doing research involving humans in Australia and overseas you will need to apply for ethics approval in most circumstances" (Charles Sturt University n.d.). And Deakin University's website states: "Deakin staff, students and external associates and visitors who intend to conduct human research must comply with the National Statement, all other relevant national guidelines, Commonwealth, State and international Statutory Regulations and where applicable, with any other specialised ethics guidelines and codes of practice" (Deakin University, 2021, Section 5, "Procedure").
15 As Newson and Lipworth (2015) point out, there are indeed researchers who fail to obtain ethics approval. They note that "journals continue to receive submissions from authors who have failed to obtain such approval" (p. 170).
16 The checklist can be found on their website: https://gdpr.eu/checklist/.
17 Another interesting idea is the "privacy scoring framework" which is explored in Kim et al. (2023).
18 As Sara Morrison states in *Vox*, "The end result, however, is roughly the same: You're being targeted with ads" (2022).
19 There are also concerns about how the data are being stored, given the risk of data breaches. In 2023, the University of Sydney was involved in a data breach (see Hollingworth, 2023).
20 Meta, for example, discusses how it is engaging with several of the SDGs (e.g., Climate Action and Gender Equality) on their website: https://about.fb.com/sdg/.
21 See https://sdgs.un.org/goals/goal10#targets_and_indicators.
22 See, for example, https://www.edi.unsw.edu.au/sustainability-matters.
23 More information can be found on the Western Sydney University website: https://www.westernsydney.edu.au/sustainable-development.
24 See Filho et al. (2020) for a discussion of eight different barriers to the implementation of the SDGs. These include the vagueness of the goals, financial constraints, and collective action problems.

5 On Comics and Consent

As discussed in the previous chapters, many of the privacy policies or terms and conditions encountered online are long and can be difficult to understand. Few of us, as a result, read all the "online agreements" that apply to us, and thus many of us do not fully understand how our personal data are being collected and used. The consent that we do provide online often fails to be *informed*. In this chapter, I will consider one specific way in which online consent practices could be simplified and made more engaging, namely, by drawing inspiration from the so-called "comic" or "visual" contracts. These have been used recently in contract law to establish legally binding agreements, and they have also been used to explain terms and conditions in several interesting contexts. In what follows, I consider their potential application to the websites and apps that regular internet users encounter on a daily basis.

In Section 5.1, I discuss some of the barriers that prevent us from reading and understanding all of the privacy policies and terms and conditions that apply to us. In Section 5.2, I briefly discuss some of the different contexts in which comic contracts have been used. In Section 5.3, I consider empirical data which show the efficacy of these kinds of contracts, and then in Section 5.4, I provide examples of how visual consent procedures might work in the online context. There I introduce two of my own examples involving Spotify and Meta. In the last two sections of the chapter, I deal with the objection of what would motivate companies to embrace the technology (Section 5.5) especially if they are not legally required to do so, and then in Section 5.6, I look at the concept of two-way consent, showing its relevance to the use of comic contracts.[1]

5.1 On Text Based Privacy Policies and Terms and Conditions

In the Preface, we looked at survey data which painted a picture of how people interact with online privacy policies. One study, for example, suggested that 94% of Australians did not read *all* of the privacy policies

DOI: 10.4324/9781032626048-5

and terms and conditions that they encountered online in the year surveyed (Nguyen & Solomon, 2018)[2]; and an EU study found that 33% of respondents *do not* read the terms and conditions when using online services, compared to the 22% who *always* read them (FRA, 2020, p. 9). To someone who has never read a privacy policy or terms and conditions before, a plausible explanation as to why this behaviour arises might be that people do not care about protecting their privacy or that they are simply lazy. To the average internet user, however, these statistics should not be surprising. Think about your own case, for example. What percentage of the terms and conditions, or privacy policies, that you encounter online can you say that you read and fully understand? If your answer is "all of them", you must have a lot of free time on your hands. Recall that a 2008 study said that it would take an average of 244 hours to read all of the privacy policies you encounter in a year (McDonald & Cranor, 2008). If we look at websites on the internet today, *The New York Times* website features a "Company Privacy Policy" document (last updated on July 1, 2024) that is over 10,000 words.[3] In a more extreme example, from 2017, Amazon Kindle's terms and conditions document was called "unreasonable" because it was estimated that it would take 9 hours to read all 73,198 words of it (Hunt, 2017).

In addition to there being a *volume problem*, there is also a *comprehension problem*. Supposing that you could read a percentage of the privacy policies you encounter online, would you also be able to fully understand them? Some privacy policies are written in a way that makes them difficult to understand for the average internet user. If we *ought* to be reading these privacy policies, then it should be actually possible for us to do so. As Immanuel Kant famously reasoned, *ought implies* can. If it's not possible for most of us to actually complete such a task, then we cannot be blamed for not doing so. Furthermore, if we do not understand what is happening with our personal data, then it's hard to see how we can give informed consent.[4]

If we are serious about addressing this issue, one idea would be to simplify the text in online privacy policies. If you need a legal degree to understand what companies are doing with your personal data, then very few of us are going to be able to give informed consent. With respect to this problem, in the context of research studies, Hadden et al. (2017) note that while consent forms are often recommended to be at sixth to eighth-grade reading level or lower, they claim: "most research-related consent forms are written at a level much higher than participants' reading skill levels" (2017, p. 362). Grant (2021) furthermore adds that the eighth-grade reading level or lower for consent forms "may be too generous a standard" (2021, p. 2). Generalising from this context, then, might simplifying the text found in online privacy policies be one way in which to elevate comprehension levels?

Recently, Geier et al. (2021) conducted a study with over 500 participants about how they interacted with research-based ethics consent forms. They gave participants one out of six versions of the same consent form. Each of the forms outlined the same risks, benefits and purpose of the experiment. The forms differed in the way that the text was spaced out, the reading level difficulties, and the way in which the participants were encouraged to interact with the consent forms. Perhaps unsurprisingly, their results showed that subjects in the highly interactive group had a greater understanding of what was occurring compared to those subjects in the low interaction group. The researchers stated it made a "difference in terms of comprehension" (Geier et al., 2021, p. 162). By "interaction", the researchers meant participants could "interact with the content rather than simply read it" (Geier et al., 2021, p. 155). For example, this included testing the participants after they had read a certain part of the consent form or using multimedia in the consent form to draw their attention to a particular feature.

While it is perhaps unsurprising that the more interactive version of the consent form was found to facilitate greater levels of comprehension, such results are still important because they provide us with evidence that making changes to the way that consent is acquired could actually make a difference to informed consent. The findings also give rise to a question that is relevant to our current focus, namely, "would interactive privacy policies or terms and conditions agreements make informed consent online easier?" In order to start addressing this question, it is worth noting some further qualitative results from the Geier et al. (2021) study. First, Geier et al. note that only 13.9% of the participants read the entire consent form (Geier et al., 2021, p. 159). When participants were asked why they did not read the whole thing, they gave some familiar reasons: 7% noted that they did not want to, were lazy, or careless. A sample response was: "[i]t was long and I got lazy" (Geier et al., 2021, p. 159). And 20% did not due to a belief that consent forms were all the same. A sample response was: "[t]hey usually all contain the same information" (Geier et al., 2021, p. 159). These are by now familiar responses that are also given by data subjects in the online context, and they highlight the problem of consent fatigue (cf. Schermer et al., 2014; Choi et al., 2018).

Interestingly, the study also asked the participants about how consent forms could be improved upon. The most popular response pertained to their length. One participant, for example, said that "[t]he length itself makes me not want to read the whole thing. If possible, shorten the amount of words" (Geier et al., 2021, p. 160). Another popular response was about the format of the consent forms. For example, one participant said that "[n]obody wants to read paragraphs, bullet points would be more effective" (Geier et al., 2021, p. 160). Not every participant appeared willing to change their behaviour, however, with 2.8% of participants saying that nothing could be done to make them fully read the consent form. A sample of this type of response was: "[n]o improvement will ever make anyone want to fully read a consent form" (Geier et al., 2021, p. 160). Such responses suggest that making consent forms more engaging will not motivate everyone to change. However, if we could *improve* engagement rates, that would still be significant. Finally, the study also asked participants about what it would take to make consent forms more engaging. One participant said that "adding pictures could make them more interesting" (Geier et al., 2021, p. 160). While only 2.5% of participants gave this answer, it does raise an interesting question about whether adding visuals could actually facilitate informed consent online.

Studies like these suggest—while they do not prove—that data subjects may not be averse to consent forms, or in the online context: privacy policies and terms and conditions, entirely. Perhaps if online consent processes could be more engaging, shorter and understandable, then data subjects might actually engage with them. To be sure, this would not solve the volume problem, since a large number of consent agreements would still apply to us, but it could be a start. If people felt they had a chance of understanding the online agreements they receive, they might be more motivated to engage with them, and thus give informed consent. This is a question that I think needs to be settled empirically. That being said, I think there are positive signs that do suggest that adding visuals to online consent agreements could be effective. And given the problems with online consent agreements that we have looked at, it is thus important to explore alternatives to the current paradigm. As the researchers point out, one risk of not reading a consent form associated with a research study is that you "may not understand the potential benefits, risks, or details of the study before participating" (Geier et al., 2021, p. 154). This issue relates to the providing of consent in the medical context as well as the online context.

If the act of drawing people's attention to certain types of information can make a difference in their capacity to understand something, then we might ask how online consent procedures could be simplified, made shorter, and if possible, be made more engaging. I now look at how adding visuals to online consent agreements might facilitate this. First, though, I look at some other contexts where they have been employed.

5.2 On Comic Contracts

In Chapter 3, we examined the Transparency Problem. This problem revolves around the challenges companies face with respect to communicating the ways in which they will use our personal data, and also the challenge that we face, as data subjects, in becoming informed about how companies are using our personal data. Sometimes, of course, companies are not motivated to be transparent, such as when doing so might cost the company money. However, in other cases, we do see companies at least attempt to be transparent, in that they present information about how they will use our personal data, say by providing users with the details of how they operate in their privacy policy. The problem is of course that many of us just don't read them. This raises questions about the responsibilities companies have in addressing this matter. Suppose a company aims to enhance the readability or comprehensiveness of their privacy policy by taking into account common struggles such as its length or reading level difficulty. Should they be expected to do it, or does the responsibility fall on individuals to try harder? Before scrutinising the moral obligations of companies in this regard, I will first present some options that are already available to them.

One emerging piece of technology that has featured recently in contract law is the so-called "Comic Book Contract" (hereafter, simply "comic contract"). One of the leading researchers on this topic is Law Professor Camilla Baasch Andersen, from the University of Western Australia, who has not only designed several of them, but is the creator of them (see Andersen (2020), for an overview of how she became involved). Comic book contracts, she says, "include a set of pictures with some text, designed to drive behaviour and encourage better access to justice so that disputes do not arise" (as cited in UWA Research Impact, 2020). In the last few years, she has played a key role in creating several successful comic contracts for some large companies in Australia, some of which I will examine below. One of her key claims is that "complex contracts" (UWA Research Impact, 2020) have to stop. Andersen notes that: comic contracts could help with "engagement, comprehension, and perception" (UWA Research Impact, 2020).[5]

To understand how comic contracts could help in the context of online personal data collection, let us first consider one of their earliest uses—i.e., a contract that Robert de Rooy, from Creative Contracts, created in South Africa in 2016. This case involved South African fruit pickers and was created for Indigo Fruit (Pty) Ltd, a farming company in Limpopo in South Africa. The contract was given to over 200 fruit pickers and can be seen if you do a web search for "ClemenGold Comic Contract".[6] Perhaps the first thing you will notice about the contract is that it is very light on text. The contract itself is only a few pages and yet is able to convey key ideas about payment, probation, work hours and sick leave through the use of cartoon-like images. Yet despite the brevity of the fruit-picking comic contract, it ended up having a positive impact on the onboarding processes. According to Creative Contracts, the contract had an impact on *induction time*—bringing it down from 4 hours to 40 minutes (see De Rooy, 2019); furthermore, the contract was able to be understood by those without high literary skills. As noted on their website, comic contracts are not contracts written for lawyers (see https://creative-contracts.com/). Comic contracts, thus, hold promise for reducing reading time and improving comprehension with respect to current online consent-giving and -receiving practices.

Comic contracts have also been used in Australia, in two very different contexts which are worth exploring. The first involves an engineering consultation company called Aurecon which was able to transform its employment contract from a standard text-based one to a comic-based one. According to the team responsible for the contract, Aurecon's "original employment contract was dense, unapproachable, and in need of an update" (Comic Book Contracts, n.d.). Andersen, and her team from UWA, worked with Aurecon to produce a visually *engaging* employment contract, which was able to replace a substantial amount of dense text with comic book style pictures. Impressively, the revised contract was able to eliminate 4000 words (UWA Research Impact, 2020). Aurecon became the first company in Australia to use visual contracts when they launched it in 2018 and were able to communicate their values, code of conduct, and health and safety guidelines, in their onboarding processes to its new employees. In addition, the comic contract featured images which helped to explain employee expectations and rights. (See McGuire & Andersen, (2019) for a lengthier description of the contract.)[7] In the following image (Figure 5.1), we see an example of the "avatars" used, and the concept of "cultural fit" being conveyed by two characters as puzzle pieces fitting together.

Figure 5.1 Excerpt from Aurecon's Employment Contract.

Source: Reprinted with permission from Camilla Baasch Andersen. The Aurecon Visual Contract was developed by UWA Comic Book Contracts (Prof Camilla Andersen) and Aurecon. Illustrations are by Gemma Young.[8]

A second use case involves Bankwest—a bank (one of the biggest in Australia) based in Perth, Western Australia. In 2021, they worked with Camilla Andersen, and her team from UWA, to introduce a comic-style terms and conditions document in what was described as an "Australia-first innovation" (Bankwest, 2021). The problem of facilitating engagement with terms and conditions documents is not limited to online consent practices, after all. The purpose of adding comics was to improve engagement. In an interview published in The *Australian*, Andersen said "[o]ur research has shown that people are far more likely to engage with the comic contracts than the text-based terms, and research in psychology shows that images help people to associate and remember things better" (see Cockburn, 2021).[9]

Bankwest was able to transform its "Bankwest Easy Transaction Account product schedule" (Bankwest, 2021) into a visual style terms and conditions document, as shown in Figure 5.2. As with the Aurecon Employment contract, we can see that images do not replace text—there is still a need for text. The images help to draw attention to the text that may otherwise have been hard to conceptualise. Bankwest claims that the visuals encourage users to engage with its products in a more "simple, friendly and engaging way" (Bankwest, 2021). An example from their visualised terms and conditions can be seen in the following:

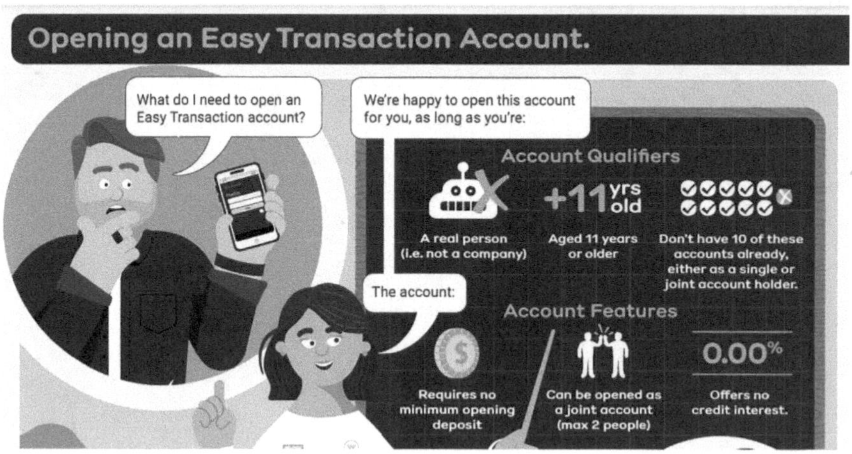

Figure 5.2 Excerpt from Bankwest: "Opening an Easy Transition Account" visual T&Cs.

Source: Reprinted with permission from Camilla Baasch Andersen. The Bankwest Visual Contract was developed by UWA Comic Book Contracts (Prof Camilla Andersen) and Bankwest. Illustrations by Bankwest/Louis Silvestro.[10]

I have mentioned three different examples of comic-styled visuals being added to contracts and terms and conditions (Figures 5.1 and 5.2 show actual examples). In all three examples, there is promise that transparency and engagement will be improved. The question I now turn to is whether online privacy policies and terms and conditions could also benefit from them. To answer this question, we will first consider some of the empirical evidence that exists which relates to the effectiveness of the Aurecon and Bankwest contracts, in order to assess their general practical application.

5.3 The Viability of Comic Contracts

Our short discussion above has shown that there are already alternatives to standard text-based terms and conditions out there that are worth exploring. The broader question is, how effective are they? We have already seen, in Section 5.1, that comic contracts hold much promise, with respect to making consent forms, employment contracts, terms and conditions, and so on, more *engaging* and *comprehensible*. But is there any direct evidence to show that adding *visuals* actually achieves this? In their research, Bobek and Tversky (2016) show that visual explanations can be more effective than verbal explanations when it comes to learning. This is because, as they note, visual explanations help with provide checks for "completeness and coherence" (Bobek & Tversky, 2016, p. 1), and thus they conclude that "[c]reating a visual explanation is an excellent way to learn and master complex systems" (Bobek & Tversky, 2016, p. 13). While our focus here is on online consent practices, and not on verbal explanations, or the learnings of difficult scientific concepts, such results still hold relevance. If visuals can help students learn difficult topics in science, for example, then they may be worth trying in the online context. There they could help to explain concepts like targeted advertising or how cookies work to data subjects, in a way that is more effective than their text-based counterparts.

The use of comic contracts, or visual terms and conditions, is relatively recent, and while they hold promise, what empirical evidence is there that they are effective? We have seen that they can cut down text, as the above examples show, but are they actually more effective in improving understanding? In a recent study, Zan et al. (2023) sought to address this question by analysing data from both the Aurecon Employment Contract and the Bankwest visual terms and conditions.[11] They did so by measuring *comprehension* (how people understood the visual contract), *engagement* (the extent to which people actually read it), and *perception* (the extent to which the visual contract had an effect on them). The authors employed a Transaction Cost Economics (TCE) approach, because this approach focuses on "seeking efficient contracting based on a cost-benefit ratio" (Zan et al., 2023, p. 4713), which is essentially a way to assess in an *objective way* whether comic contracts are indeed more "effective" than text-based ones.[12] Their data set analysed the experiences of over 450 participants who used the Aurecon contract and the Bankwest terms and conditions.

The experimenters asked participants how they *enjoyed* the comic contract, whether the *format* of the contract made them feel *valuable*, and whether the contract helped them to *understand* the content of the contract. Based on the participants' responses to these questions, Zan et al. (2023) found, in the data from both contracts, that the visual contracts can "significantly reduce transaction costs" (p. 4723), and hence they concluded that there is evidence to suggest that visual contracts can be seen as more *efficient* than text-based contracts.[13] While these results were encouraging, the researchers recognised some important limitations of their study. One issue had to do with diversity. The authors note that there were "no data collected about the attributes of the users in terms of disability or neurotypicality" (Zan et al., 2023, p. 4723). A second issue with this study, especially for our concerns about informed consent, concerns the nature of the questions asked—specifically, how some of the questions were about how people felt and not so much on whether they actually were informed.

This is an issue that the authors were aware of, but it is one that should require us to exercise some caution with the results. This is because the questions in the study were about how well the participants felt they understood. While these subjective reports are important, they should ideally be corroborated with objective measures of understanding. For example, consider feeling confident that you understand how a heart operation will go or that you did well in a mathematics test. You might be completely justified in your confidence, but evidence of whether you understand what will occur during the operation, or how well you did perform in the test, must be found elsewhere. The phenomenon of overconfidence is a common one. None of this is to say that the results are unimportant of course. On the contrary, often our first-person reports about how well we understand something can be a guide to how well we do actually understand (e.g., when someone realises that they have no idea about how a process works); and it is also important to state that these introspective feelings of understanding relate in an important way to how the subjects feel towards the organisation using the comic contract. Feeling valued, for example, is a type of self-knowledge best procured from the first-person perspective, and as we saw in Chapter 1, ought to play an important role in the informed consent process.

A final issue (or "limitation", in the author's words) with Zan et al.'s (2023) study pertains to the generalisability of the results. The authors state that "these results cannot be generalized beyond the standard-form contracting situation—involving terms and conditions–and additional research is to be required to assess the use of visual methods in negotiated contracts" (2023, p. 4724). This final point requires us to be somewhat cautious and circumspect in our approach moving forward. For this reason, the ideas I present in the next section should be viewed as hypotheses in need of further testing, even though I believe they hold much promise.

5.4 Visuals in Online Consent Procedures

In 2017, the American artist Robert Sikoryak (2017) released a graphic novel called *Terms and Conditions* which consisted entirely of Apple's then 20,669-word terms and conditions contract for iTunes.[14] The text of the book was accompanied with Sikoryak's own comic-styled images. For example, in one of the pages from the book, we see a comic strip style image of a man who looks shocked against a red background with black lines, indicating that the man is undergoing an intense emotion, such as fear or anxiety. The image of the man is accompanied with Apple's subscription policies, namely, information that subscriptions are non-refundable and will automatically renew for one-year periods. In another comic strip, we see several images of the Simpsons family, with Homer being drawn to resemble Steve Jobs. They are accompanied with text from the section of Apple's *Terms and Conditions* document which relates to cover art and copyright.

For certain readers of Sikoryak's book, this may have been the first time that they actually read Apple's terms and conditions, even if they had been using iTunes for years. I confess that this describes my own case. What Sikoryak was able to do, intentionally or not, was to make Apple's previously dry 20,000-word terms and conditions actually *engaging*. In doing so, people (again some for the first time) were motivated to actually see what was in the terms and conditions document. Now, while it is unlikely that Apple would be calling Sikoryak to illustrate their future terms and conditions, as perhaps not all of his images flatter Apple, his book does raise a serious question about whether other online consent-gathering practices such as the ones employed by Google, Spotify or Facebook could benefit from the use of visuals (whether cartoon or otherwise) to make them more engaging. If comic or visual contracts can make employment agreements simpler, or explain banking processes to customers, then might they work in the online commercial collection and use of personal data context? In what follows, below, I provide two examples of how visuals could be added to online consent procedures involving Spotify and Meta.

5.4.1 Spotify

First let us consider Spotify, one of the biggest music streaming platforms on the planet. At the time of this writing, Spotify claims to have over

615 million users. Given that Spotify is known to collect large amounts of personal data, it is a good case for us to consider, with respect to the question of whether online consent practices could be improved upon by adding visuals. One of the concerns with Spotify's practices, that is identified by Evan Greer from Fight for the Future (a digital rights advocacy group), relates to their advertising model. He notes that "Spotify uses the same surveillance capitalist business model as Facebook and YouTube: they harvest your data and sell access to it to advertisers who think they can use that data to manipulate you into buying their products and services" (as cited in Morse, 2022). As there is a growing need to scrutinise such companies' data collection process and see if consent-gathering practices can be improved upon, it thus presents us with an important test case.

First, what personal data do Spotify collect? As their privacy policy tells us, in order to run their service, they collect personal information such as a user's profile name, email address, phone number, date of birth, and country (Spotify, 2023). Additionally, Spotify collects other personal data that can be classified as "usage data"—the kind of data that may worry some users (though, of course, the collection of the first type of personal data may worry users too). Usage data includes search queries, streaming history, playlists you create, browsing history, your interactions with Spotify users, and use of third-party services connected with Spotify (Spotify, 2023). To Spotify's credit, all of this information is stated in their privacy policy, and they have also published a video titled "Personal Data at Spotify" which states that they collect information about the music users like, so that they can recommend playlists or other music.[15] In this video, Spotify notes that usage data are collected in order to improve Spotify's service, and suggest new music or podcasts. The video also mentions that it uses "tailored ads" that can be "controlled" in users' privacy settings.

If all of this information is given to users, in the form of a privacy policy and video, then might it already be the case that Spotify has done enough to facilitate informed consent? I think the answer here is no. For one reason, while Spotify makes this information available, they do not, just like many other companies, provide any mechanism for checking that people *understand* how they use personal data. At the time of this writing, Spotify's privacy video has 60,000 views on YouTube—a small percentage of its 615 million users. Further, as we saw, privacy policies are not read by a large percentage of users. Above we saw that only a small percentage of data subjects actually read privacy policies. Morse (2022), for example, cites a Pew Research Center report which found that 36% of American adults "never read a privacy policy before agreeing to it" (see Auxier et al., 2019). This behaviour is consistent with other findings from across the world. We may wonder what percentage of Spotify users actually give informed consent to Spotify to collect and use their data in the ways described in their privacy policy. Spotify should assume that a vast percentage do not provide informed consent.

Another issue concerns the advertising methods that Spotify use and how well users understand them. As Morse points out, Spotify users who pay a subscription fee may not be subjected to the same ads that are given to those who use the service for free, but it is "not advertiser free" (2022). At present, if you want to find out about what occurs with respect to your service, you can go and read the privacy policy. Again, to their credit, Spotify not only informs users about what "tailored ads" are but also explains how they are used. Their policy states "[a]n example of tailored advertising is when an advertising partner has information suggesting you like cars. This could enable us to show you ads about cars" (Spotify, 2023). However, given that it is uncommon for data subjects to read all of the policies that apply to them, we might wonder how many actually give informed consent here. Furthermore, for those data subjects who want to know which advertisers, or third parties, are involved in the use of their personal data, they will have a difficult time becoming informed about it. The Spotify privacy policy states that usage data are sent to "advertising and marketing partners" (Spotify, 2023), but users might be curious about how that is done, and what companies get the data.

Personalised or "tailored" advertisements seem to me like an important place to start thinking about how visual contracts could help with informed consent online, since they are so widespread. I think we could draw upon visual contracts in order to explain key concepts and show users what choices they have. Consider the following example I have put together with the help of the Western Australian artist Jordan Andreotta.

In a very simple way, Figure 5.3 helps to convey the idea of how targeted advertising works in the context of Spotify. I have opted to depict the data collection process as one involving "faceless observers" who collect data in the shadows, since the data collection process occurs on Spotify in the background without users being aware. This may strike some as suggesting that the process is "intrusive", and perhaps companies would not approve of such depictions of their product. On the other hand, there is a sense in which this is what actually occurs. And if companies are interested in being transparent, then it may simply be something that they have to live with. If the process, depicted in visual form, makes someone perceive the data collection and use as intrusive, it might make them reflect upon whether they are okay with it. And in this way, it encourages them to engage with the overall process of sharing data.

Of course, this is only one example, and it remains a difficult question about how Spotify would integrate visuals into their privacy policy and

Figure 5.3 How Targeted Advertising Works.

how they would bring the images to their users' attention. However, I think it shows that it could be quite easy to depict key concepts with the help of visuals. I say "help" here, as there are many details the visual images leave out here. One thing that is not explained are the risks involved in allowing one's personal data to be collected, and it does not tell us about which companies are involved. On the other hand, there seems to be no reason in principle why these concepts could not be explained by further visuals. Using visuals could, furthermore, cut down the length of Spotify's privacy policy and, in doing so, encourage people to engage with it. Think about how much time it took you to look at Figure 5.3 and grasp what was occurring—possibly only a few seconds. Spotify's current policy (Spotify, 2023) is over 6000 words.

The use of visuals could also help explain to data subjects their options with data sharing. As Morse points out, "those concerned with how their listening habits might be weaponized against them have more options than just 'delete your account'" (2022). He notes that at present, there are some options that users have to manage their privacy—one of which is to *turn off tailored ads*. That such an option exists relates to a requirement for informed consent that we looked at in Chapter 3, namely, that, ideally, meaningful alternatives should be provided for those giving consent. However, one worry relates to what percentage of users actually know how to manage their personal data on the site. In Morse's article, he explains how to do this. He suggests that one just needs to go into one's profile, then into one's account, and then to the privacy settings. Once in the section on tailored ads, one just needs to make sure that the "Process my personal data for tailored ads" button is toggled to the "off" setting (Morse, 2022). While this process is only a few steps, there is a concern here about how many users actually know about them. Visuals could be quite useful here. Possibly when first setting up their account, and providing Spotify with consent, a visual step-by-step guide could be provided to users so they are aware of what they need to do.

Visual images are unlikely to solve all of the problems we have outlined, but they might help encourage engagement. Even if they can do this, however, the difficult task of determining how they should be used in a privacy policy would remain. As suggested above, the point of comic contracts is not to replace all of the text in a text-based contract. Decisions would need to be made about which concepts might be best explained with visuals and which ones as text.

5.4.2 Meta

In Chapter 3, we looked at the case of Onavo Protect, a free app, which provided a VPN service that was promoted as an application that would help keep user data safe. As we also saw, Meta, the parent company of the app, was fined 20 million (AUD) dollars after it was revealed that the app was monetising users' data. This was contrary to how the app was advertised. The ACCC noted that Onavo did so by using privacy-friendly language such as the following: "Use a free, fast and secure VPN to protect personal information" and that the app "Helps Keep You and Your Data Safe" (Cass-Gottlieb, 2023). In reality, however, users' personal data were shared with the app's parent company, Meta (Cass-Gottlieb, 2023). As we also discussed in Chapter 3, a significant amount of people downloaded the app. It was installed more than 270,000 times by Australian users between February 2016 and October 2017 (Kaye, 2023)

How could the use of visuals have helped here? It might be worth thinking about how Meta could have done better in securing informed consent. According to the ACCC, data subjects were "not clearly told that, in downloading and using this app, they were actually facilitating the use of their data for Meta's commercial benefit" (Cass-Gottlieb, 2023). So, one thing visuals could do is help explain that this was occurring. You might think it would have been easier to simply tell users, say in the privacy policy, but the problem with doing so in this context is the fact that the app was marketed as protecting users' data, so users might simply have assumed it would not take their personal data. For these reasons, it is hard to imagine that an ethics committee, as described in the last chapter, would have given ethical approval to Meta's consent-gathering procedures, given the way that the app was marketed. They may have pointed out that if people are told that an app offers privacy protection, people might form the (reasonable) belief that the app would not monetise their personal data. For this reason, an ethics review committee might have suggested that burying this important fact in a privacy policy may not have been the best thing to do, from a transparency perspective.

What would have been a better way to inform people then? Here is where I think adding visuals to privacy policies—or an onboarding screen or welcome screen—could be useful. Perhaps the idea that the app still extracts personal data is something that might work better in the form of a picture, since it might not be the easiest concept for users to understand. One reason for this is that the word "protect" has several uses in this context, and people who read that the app protects users might have a certain sense in mind. A VPN might "protect" your data from hackers, it might protect you from certain types of ads, and certain cyber-attacks—so yes, the VPN can certainly "protect" in that sense. On the other hand, some might want to be "protected" from data brokers, or targeted advertising in general.

The benefit of using visuals in such a case is that they could help to clarify the different senses of "protection" in an easy-to-understand way.

Figure 5.4 How Protection Works.

While offering protection from hackers, Meta also collected: "anonymised and aggregated data about users' internet and app activity, such as records of every app they accessed and time they spent using those apps. This data was used to support Meta's market research activities" (Cass-Gottlieb, 2023). One way that the company could have tried to explain how they were "protecting" data subjects, and at the same time "sharing" personal data, could have been explained via an image like the one I created with the help of Jordan Andreotta.

In Figure 5.4, there are a couple of important elements. First, the image demonstrates how "private data" are "protected" by the VPN, namely, by preventing criminals from accessing it, as illustrated by the criminal character familiar to many. However, since Meta would still be able to collect some data, the giant cat's large presence tries to *draw attention* to the fact that it is also giving "internet and app activity" to Meta. In a recent study, Karegar et al. (2018) showed that interactivity can be higher when attention is drawn to information. And that is exactly what is done in the image—attention is drawn to the dual aspects of "protection". Employing a comic-style consent procedure could have made the process interactive and engaging in a way that would be hard to achieve with a lengthy text-based counterpart.

5.5 The Motivation Problem

Even if it could be demonstrated that Spotify or Meta could improve their online consent practices by incorporating visual elements, you might be sceptical that they actually would be motivated to do so, especially if they were not legally required to do so. (This is, by now, a familiar objection that has come up multiple times in the book.) One way to respond to this objection is to point out that legislation has been introduced around the world that does emphasise a need for consent. In Australia, after all, Meta was fined for the way that they failed to get proper consent. While it is unclear where there would ever be a legal requirement to use visuals, it is clear that companies should be concerned with avoiding such fines. In the case of Meta, for example, visuals or comics could have helped them avoid a legal fine. There are thus economic reasons to avoid "misleading" customers.

On the other hand, visual contracts, as they are not legally binding, seem to exceed the bare minimum. Perhaps there are ways for Meta or Spotify to fulfil the legal requirements without utilising them. What would incentivise them to surpass legal mandates? I confess, it is challenging to envision how such companies could be motivated, unless, of course, the market demands it. An important point that Zan et al. (2023) make, after all, is that the effectiveness of visual contracts relies on companies' desires to remain transparent. They claim their study was based on the "assumption that entities such as banks and employers would wish the users of their contracts to understand them, and to read them" (Zan et al., 2023, p. 4724). If a company does not want their users to understand their data collection practices, and do not make a genuine attempt to secure informed online consent, then of course, we would not expect them to embrace them. In the so-called "age of surveillance capitalism" as Zuboff (2019) has put it, it may be economically advantageous to remain opaque in some contexts. Recall, for example, that in Chapter 3, we looked at the so-called "hiding strategy" that was employed in the early days of Google.

Even though one can point to these trends and become pessimistic, there are also indications from other companies, such as Apple, who are actually leveraging their privacy benefits as a notable selling point (see Chapter 3). It is possible that companies who use visual-based contracts could been seen as prioritising transparency to its users and thus build trust. Consider the way Bankwest has marketed the fact that they use visual terms and conditions on their website, for example. They state: "Bankwest has reinvented terms and conditions in an Australia-first innovation" (Bankwest, 2021). They also state that they have "developed its Visual T&Cs with the aim to reimagine and deliver key product information to customers in a more engaging style and manner than the traditional text formats often provided" (Bankwest, 2021). Customers may be impressed with the fact that the bank has pioneered such an approach, and this may translate into customer trust.

Analogously for consent online. If people believe that a certain news website, or social media page, has actually tried to explain how they collect personal data, then people may be more likely to trust them. This is clearly something that could entice companies to gain trust, especially for brands like Meta who have been involved in several "privacy scandals" as of late and have paid large amounts of monetary fines, and in the process have suffered some reputational damage. However, if Zan et al. is right that "consumers and other users of contracts increasingly demand that they be presented in a comprehensible, accessible manner" (2023, p. 4724), then companies may look to use visual contracts to help them to gain trust.

5.6 Two-Way Consent

In an unpublished manuscript with my colleagues from UWA, Camilla Andersen and Nin Kirkham, we have explored the idea of extending the use of comic contracts into other contexts. In earlier work, Kirkham and Andersen (2020) for example have argued that visual aids could be incorporated into the context of medical consent forms, and so we thought there was an important research question to ask about what it would take to introduce them into a new context. In an attempt to answer this question, we focused on a concept we called "two-way consent", the term we gave to consent processes which sees both the consenter and the person wanting to get consent working together to facilitate meaningful consent. In our view, this is a necessary *condition* for comic contracts, or visual-based consent agreements, to be effective. A company that views consent as merely something to check off a list, or something only for lawyers, does not exercise two-way consent.

Given that it is not common to see two-way consent in the commercial use of personal data collection and use online, might the prospects of visual-based consent procedures be doomed to fail? Not necessarily. Even if two-way consent is not commonly seen with respect to online consent agreements now, a cultural change is not out of the question. An example that shows that change is possible in a short amount of time comes from the Banking Sector in Australia. From 2017 to 2019, there was a "Royal Commission into Misconduct in the Banking, Superannuation and Financial Services Industry", which was set up by the Australian Government to report on misconduct in the banking sector in Australia. As Penny Crofts, points out, the commission "presented evidence of malfeasance, malpractice, and unethical and criminal behaviour by the banks" (2020).

In the five years since the completion of the Royal Commission, several have pointed out that significant changes have occurred in the sector, even though there is still much work to do. As Ziffer (2024) points out in his article in *ABC News*, millions of dollars have been returned to customers, there have been court cases showing wrongdoings, and also new laws introduced. One thing Ziffer's article also notes is that the culture has changed in the banking sector. He cites the deputy chair of the corporate watchdog

ASIC, Sarah Court, who claimed that "[w]e've seen a change in culture, and a change in the way that banks treat their customers" (as cited in Ziffer, 2024). Until we see a similar change in culture from big tech companies, or other companies using our personal data, we are unlikely to see two-way consent, and thus unlikely to see them adopt visual-based contracts.

Given this context, it is perhaps more understandable why Bankwest sought to improve its terms and conditions, given that this change happened only a few years after the Royal Commission, and thus customer trust was low. Bankwest claim that "[t]he Visual T&Cs project has allowed us to reimagine how we present critical information to customers in a far more simple, friendly and engaging way to support them in improving their financial wellbeing" (Bankwest, 2021). Even if one thinks that Bankwest did this just to improve its public image, we can draw parallels with online consent on the internet too, and how companies may wish to gain trust. Just as there have been lawsuits and fines in the banking sector, there have been large fines issued to companies who have failed to get informed consent from data subjects before using their data. Trust in online companies may be low, just like in the banking sector. If companies like Meta wish to repair their brand image after disasters like the Facebook-Cambridge Analytica Scandal, and others mentioned in this book, then one way they could do so is attempt to foster two-way consent.

This will be increasingly necessary when companies start to collect new types of personal data. As Till (2023) points out, Spotify have "recently made various interventions" into areas such as health, exercise and wellness. He says, "Spotify seek to monitor, analyse and package the rhythm of their users' lives by identifying the times of the year when they are most passionate about exercise" (Till, 2023, p. 6). The potential for more detailed types of targeted advertising is significant here. The more Spotify knows about the psychological and emotional experiences of its users, the greater its ability to persuade them to take certain actions (Till, 2023, p. 9). Till goes on to say that these newer types of personal data collection are also quite sensitive since they reflect "crucial aspects of individuals' and groups' sense of self, self-expression, identity and broadly corporeal being in the world" (Till, 2023, p. 9). Thus, as the capabilities to collect these data grow, it will be increasingly important that users are informed about how they are collected (e.g., through smart devices), the choices they have about controlling their use (e.g., whether they can prevent their collection), and the risks associated with their collection.

Here, visuals could help explain their use and risks to data subjects. For example, a picture of someone exercising, associated with a graphic of having their exercise-related data captured by a team of "faceless observers" like the image in Section 5.4.1, could help to explain to data subjects the implications of such data collection. Similarly, if these data were ever combined with personal data captured from other apps—such as data from the exercise app Strava, which partnered with Spotify in 2023—and then sent to Spotify, an illustration of a heartbeat alongside an image depicting the transfer could help to draw attention to the issue.[16] Visuals might do a better job of explaining the reality of such types of data collection and use over, say, 10,000-word privacy policies, which as discussed here can be difficult to navigate

5.7 Conclusion

This chapter has looked at one way to improve current online consent practices. I have attempted to draw inspiration from the so-called comic or visual contracts, which have been used to help explain terms and conditions, and employment contracts, and argued that they may help companies secure more meaningful consent online. However, I do not claim that the introduction of visuals into consent-gaining practices online will fix all the problems we have looked at. My more modest claim has only been that they hold much promise and have been shown to be effective in relevant domains. I believe, then, that we should attempt to integrate them online, since they will not only help to cut down words from privacy policies, and terms and conditions, but they are also relatively simple in principle to produce. The chapter can be thought of as an empirical hypothesis, so these ideas need to be tested, and their efficacy demonstrated. How people react to visual terms and conditions, or privacy policies, online will be important to measure.

Furthermore, there is a real risk that even if they are initially successful online, people may grow tired of them. The comic artist Robert Sikoryak's book *Terms and Conditions*, for instance, encouraged many people (myself included) to read the iTunes terms and conditions for the first time. However, this book was over 100 pages long. It would be naive to think that we can convert all existing terms and conditions into comics and people will suddenly make time to go through them all. Even if that could be done, we would be left with the problem of reviewing hundreds of visual-based privacy policies or terms and conditions. We already have a problem with "pop-up fatigue" and the issue of "habituation", as Bravo-Lillo et al. (2014) call it. Nevertheless, there are several compelling reasons to think that visual-based consent agreements can play an important role in facilitating online informed consent.

Notes

1 This is one of the suggestions for improving online consent practices that my colleagues and I briefly discuss in an earlier article (see Andreotta et al., 2022).

2 A more recent CPRC report (CPRC, 2020) found the same results—that is, only 6% of Australians read all of the privacy policies or terms and conditions that apply to them when signing up for a service.
3 *The New York Times* Company Privacy Policy can be viewed online here: https://help.nytimes.com/hc/en-us/articles/10940941449492-The-New-York-Times-Company-Privacy-Policy.
4 Understanding how our personal data are being used is an important part of what it means to give "informed consent", but it is not the only thing that matters, as discussed in Chapter 1.
5 For more on this topic, see: https://researchimpact.uwa.edu.au/research-impact-stories/comic-book-contracts/.
6 Alternatively, you can see their website: https://creative-contracts.com/clemengold/.
7 The contract can be viewed online here: https://www.comicbookcontracts.com/aurecon-contract.
8 The entire contract can be found here: https://www.comicbookcontracts.com/aurecon-contract.
9 More information can be found on their website: https://www.bankwest.com.au/about-us/media-centre/news/pictures-make-a-thousand-words-in-visual-style-australia-first.
10 The entire contract can be found in Bankwest (2021).
11 See Passera (2017) for an earlier study. Zan et al. (2023) point out that one limitation of Passera's study was that it was not conducted in a real-world setting, unlike the Bankwest and Aurecon cases.
12 For an overview and history of Transaction-Cost Economics, see Gibbons (2010).
13 As Zan et al. (2023) point out, the implementation of comic contracts does not simply involve: "replacing text with images" and nor does it "involve transferring existing text into a new format alongside images", but rather a "redesign" of the contract (p. 4714).
14 The book is based on the iTunes contract published in 2015. Apple reduced their terms and conditions to 7,000 in 2017 (see Cain, 2017).
15 The video in question can be found here: https://www.youtube.com/watch?v=FhnwTljFiaM.
16 See Spotify's website for more information on the partnership they have with Strava: https://newsroom.spotify.com/2023-04-12/spotify-strava-integration-stream-track-workout/.

6 On Automated Consent

So far, we have explored some of the ethical shortcomings with contemporary consent practices on the internet. In Chapter 5, we looked at one way in which these practices could be improved upon, namely, by adding visuals into them. We reviewed evidence to suggest that doing so can help with *comprehension*, *transparency*, *trust*, and even save data subjects time. In looking to address the three main problems with contemporary consent practices that we looked at (Chapter 3), drawing inspiration from comic contracts seems like a promising approach. However, I also stressed that adding visuals to consent procedures will *not* solve all of the problems we have looked at. Even if doing so would reduce the length of many of the "consent agreements" we encounter online, problems would still face us. First, users may still have to go through thousands of them. As more and more of our personal devices connect to the internet, the burden will only get heavier as time progresses. Furthermore, there is a risk that the novelty of visual-based consent agreements could wear off over time—that is, there is a risk that people may revert to previous behaviours such as not reading privacy policies or terms and conditions, and thus resulting in a failure to provide informed consent.

This chapter looks at another potential solution that is capable of working alongside some of the others we have examined (rather than rival them). Specifically, I consider how consent could be automated. The basic idea is that browsers, programs, and apps—in some cases powered by AI—might be configured to provide consent for us in ways that do not require us to read through and click "accept" to lengthy consent agreements. I do so by drawing upon a recently published collaboration I have had with Björn Lundgren, a philosopher who researches the ethics of AI. In our work (see Andreotta & Lundgren, 2024), we have explored some of the normative implications of *bypassing* consent procedures altogether.

This chapter presents the basic idea of automated consent and then introduces some normative issues that I believe need scholarly attention before automated consent is widely implemented. In Section 6.1, I outline a practical problem with requiring companies to get informed consent from

DOI: 10.4324/9781032626048-6

data subjects. In Section 6.2, I present the basic idea of automated consent. In Section 6.3, I present three different ways in which automated consent might be realised. I then consider various issues with automated consent: first, whether it *undermines* informed consent (Section 6.4); second, the risk that personal information about how users configure their automated consent applications could be re-purposed or misused (Section 6.5); third, the problem of what would motivate companies to take up the idea (Section 6.6); and then finally the problem of what happens when automated consent makes *mistakes* (Section 6.7).

6.1 Practical Problems With Privacy Legislation

As discussed in previous chapters, the GDPR represents an important step forward in terms of protecting privacy rights and human rights more broadly. The legislation places special emphasis on the importance of securing consent, which is defined in Article 4 as follows: "consent means any freely given, specific, informed and unambiguous indication of the data subject's wishes by which he or she, by a statement or by a clear affirmative action, signifies agreement to the processing of personal data relating to him or her" (European Union, 2016). Importantly, as is made clear here, the consent obtained needs to be "informed". If you do not properly inform a data subject about how exactly you intend to use their personal data, the fact that they gave express consent, say by clicking agree on a consent agreement, is insufficient.

One consequence of the GDPR's requirement that informed consent ought to be secured is that it places a fairly significant burden on data subjects. Consider the multiple pop-up requests one receives to "accept cookies" whenever one logs onto a website. As Lundgren points out, it is hardly convenient to navigate a "pop-up spam festival" (2020a, p. 759). So, while it is certainly a good thing that the GDPR emphasises the importance of informed consent, data subjects are left with the practical problem of how they are supposed to go through all of the consent agreements that they encounter online. Lundgren (2020a) has thus described this as a "practical flaw" in the GDPR.

The same problem also arises in a recent piece of legislation called the Data Governance Act (DGA), which is part of the larger framework of data protection in Europe. The legislation was approved by the European Commission in 2022 and went into force in late 2023 (Ruohonen & Mickelsson, 2023). The purpose of the DGA is to provide a framework in which the data economy can operate in Europe. As Ruohonen and Mickelsson point out, there is an emphasis on small- and medium-sized enterprises, as well as start-ups, to innovate (Ruohonen & Mickelsson, 2023). In their recent review of the act, Ruohonen and Mickelsson (2023) discuss two core tenets. One is that the DGA attempts to help provide a framework for the reuse of data held by public sectors; and second, the DGA introduces a new concept called *data altruism*. The latter concept is important because it seeks to facilitate the further sharing of personal data as part of the "data economy", by "European public sector bodies" as the authors put it (Ruohonen & Mickelsson, 2023) The term "data altruism" is defined in the second article "Definitions" (no. 16) of the DGA as follows:

> [T]he voluntary sharing of data on *the basis of the consent of data subjects* to process personal data pertaining to them, or permissions of data holders to allow the use of their non-personal data without seeking or receiving a reward that goes beyond compensation related to the costs that they incur where they make their data available for objectives of general interest as provided for in national law, where applicable, such as healthcare, combating climate change, improving mobility, facilitating the development, production and dissemination of official statistics, improving the provision of public services, public policy-making or scientific research purposes in the general interest.
>
> (European Commission, 2022, my emphasis)

The definition of "data altruism" is one that is conducive to the gaining of informed consent, as it provides guidance on how personal data ought to be shared. The definition is also interesting in that it highlights the mutual benefits of sharing data. This is made clear by its mention of scientific research, for example.

Again, however, an important question arises about how data subjects are supposed to provide informed consent. The DGA thus seems to face the same "practical problem" as the one facing the GDPR, as Lundgren (2020a) puts it. It remains difficult to see, then, how one can "voluntarily share" their data if they have little idea about what is being done with it. As Ruohonen and Mickelsson (2023) note, the DGA, for all its benefits, would still seem to allow the same problematic "20,000 word bulletproof legalese documents" (2023, p. 10) that we have examined in the book. Furthermore, the DGA appears to be subject to the Re-purposed Data Problem that we looked at in Chapter 3, since, as the authors note, it would be hard "to specify the purpose of processing personal data at the time of initial data collection in a context that involves further processing" (2023, p. 10). Adding visuals might help simplify these procedures for data subjects, but fundamental issues regarding the number of privacy policies one would have to review, and the problem of data re-purposing, could still persist. The introduction of new legislation requiring data controllers to obtain consent is clearly beneficial and draws attention to the concept of consent itself. However, questions remain about how informed consent is supposed to be effectively secured, from a practical perspective (cf. Ruohonen, 2021).

6.2 On Automated Consent

When I first started to think about, and then research, ways in which to improve informed consent practices online I came across a short two-page paper by Björn Lundgren (2020a) published in *AI and Society* which discussed the role that software developers could play in helping data subjects self-manage their privacy. I referred to this paper in earlier work (Andreotta et al., 2022) noting that Lundgren's idea of configuring browsers to "remember" our privacy choices could save us a lot of time. In his view, web browsers could "be utilized to save the ideal of these consent-agreements, by providing functionality that allows users to give pre-set responses to these types of request" (2020a, p. 759). This would seem to offer the best of both worlds—that is, we would be in control of our privacy, and we would not have to give our consent every few minutes online.

When I started to think about expanding the ideas in my earlier paper, I contacted Dr. Lundgren, primarily interested in discussing the prospects of automated consent being adopted on a large scale. What emerged from a series of discussions on the topic was a shared concern for how automated consent ought to be instantiated, and a greater appreciation of the different ways in which it could be realised (see Andreotta & Lundgren, 2024 for an overview). In what follows, I will go into some of the details. First, let's get clear on the concept.

What is automated consent? The basic idea is that software handles the consenting process for you. To illustrate, consider a simple example involving a pop-up window that asks you to accept the use of cookies on a website. The basic idea of automated consent is that software could recognise and manage this process, and similar ones, for you. For instance, if you always want to reject the use of cookies, the software could automatically do so. That's the core idea. The question of how complex it could become remains open for researchers to explore, as I mention below. Some types of automated consent are rather simple, others more complex. In Andreotta and Lundgren (2024), we provided an overview of three different ways in which automated consent could materialise. While we both agreed that automated consent could play an important role in managing our privacy, we also agreed that we will need to grapple with several important ethical issues before the technology is implemented.

6.3 Three Different Approaches to Automated Consent

6.3.1 *The Minimalist (Reject All) Option*

The first option that Lundgren and I proposed in our paper was an approach we called the "minimalist (reject all) option". According to this option, a browser or app could be equipped with a function that allows users to block all attempts by companies to collect their personal data. Suppose you never wish to give consent for a company to collect and share your IP address, phone number, browsing history, or any other type of personal data. With the reject-all approach, you could simply enable a setting in your browser to block all such collection attempts. This approach could be straightforward to set up and manage, requiring users to toggle just one setting; and this would save users time, as they wouldn't need to read through numerous privacy policies or make individual "reject" clicks every time a website or app requests their data. No sophisticated AI algorithms would be necessary, making it easier for data subjects to understand and control how their data are used.

In our paper, we mentioned how this technology already exists in some form. For example, The Onion Router (TOR) enables users to browse the internet anonymously (cf. Goldschlag et al., 1999). For those who do not wish to share their IP address or their location, or have third-party trackers and ads targeted towards them, all they need to do is download the TOR browser onto their device and make sure to conduct their internet use on it. Some privacy friendly browsers such as Brave, furthermore, even have TOR functionality now.

If this technology already exists, then why not advocate the wide-scale adoption of it? The reason is that while TOR browsing has its place—for example, for those wanting to use the internet in a country which censors online activities, or for journalists looking to hide their identity—many of the websites that we use require us to log in, and give away personal information as part of a registration process (cf. Lundgren, 2020b).[1] Some apps, furthermore, require the collection of some personal data to actually function. If you use a parking app on your smartphone, for example, you might not have a choice to withhold your licence plate number or credit card details for payment purposes. Or if you use Spotify, and have a paid subscription, your credit card details, and billing address will need to be collected. And when you are logged onto Facebook, and interact with your friends, Meta can begin to collect data about you from your interactions. If you use your real name, it can find out who you are, what you have clicked on, which friends you have interacted with, and so on. Once Facebook has all of these data, they can be used to predict sexual orientation, political views or religious affiliations (Kosinski et al., 2013), and we are back to the original problem. Anonymous browsing thus has its limits. One could always choose not to use social media in general or pay for anything online, but this is an option few of us would be willing to accept, given how much of our lives are spent online.

If one cannot escape the collection of such data, then might the "reject all" option fail to offer much protection? Lungren and I did not think so.

While some sites necessitate data sharing, this does not render the reject all option useless; in fact, that is precisely where its utility lies. Consider the ubiquitous requests for cookies on many different websites. While it would be tedious to individually reject each request, a reject all function could streamline this process via a single setting that would automatically choose "minimal options" every time. If a website offers users a choice, with respect to the collection of some type of personal data collection, a browser equipped with a reject all option could automatically decline such requests, thus saving the data subject from having to click "reject" in each instance. Essential data sharing might be unavoidable, say for sites or applications to function; but any user-facing choices could be identified and rejected. For instance, if Facebook mandates data sharing for likes without consent, users have little recourse. The more choices a site gives users, however, the more types of personal data collection could be rejected.

Here are two different examples. Consider first *The New York Times* website which features a privacy policy that states: "[i]f your browser doesn't accept our cookies or similar technologies, you can't access certain parts of our websites (e.g., your account on nytimes.com)" (New York Times, 2024). Users with software that implements the "reject all" option would not have much of a choice here, if they wanted to use the site. In other cases, where a website offers an opt-out option, the "reject all" function could identify and reject such requests. Take, for example, Bounty, the company we looked at in Chapters 2 and 4. On their website, they note that they, and their partners, process data to provide

> precise geolocation data. Actively scan device characteristics for identification. Store and/or access information on a device. Personalised advertising and content, advertising and content measurement, audience research and services development.
>
> (Bounty, 2024)

To manage one's "consent preferences" on the site, users are presented with a pop-up window which lists the cookies that are used on the website. The different cookie types each have a button that allows them to be enabled or disabled. This includes targeting cookies, functional cookies, and geolocation data, for example. "Strictly Necessary Cookies" are shown to be "always active" and described as being *required* for the site to function. That Bounty give users the option to disable certain types of cookies is beneficial and helps to address the Meaningful Alternatives Problem we looked at in Chapter 3. However, it does require the user to spend a lot of time going through the settings if they visit many sites on the web (as discussed in Chapter 3). This is where the minimalist option could be helpful, as it could automatically disable all non-necessary cookies.

One objection to this view—that was put to me and Lundgren—was that the reject all option does not seem to have anything to do with consent, let alone *informed consent*. By having a "reject all" option turned on, users may not know anything about what personal data they are sharing (e.g., the necessary types of personal data) and what they are rejecting if it is done without their conscious act of consenting (though if the option had some way to intervene in exceptions there would be some).

It is hard to deny this. Someone who activates an automated consent function would not seem to put oneself in a good position to understand how a certain site uses their data. It thus seems difficult to see how they can provide informed consent to the company operating the site. On the other hand, it is important to appreciate that a key part of the concept of privacy has to do with control. As Borg et al. (2024) point out, "privacy is about the *control of information*" (p. 99, my emphasis). And one can certainly be in control of their personal information if they choose to never give it away. The reject all option does not, however, offer users much granularity.

6.3.2 *The Semi-Automated Option*

The second approach that Lundgren and I outlined in our paper is the "semi-automated option". The main idea behind this approach is that users could configure different rules in browsers, apps, or even operating systems that would allow them to manage the types of personal data that are collected about them. Like the reject all option, the semi-automated option would allow users to bypass the need to click many of the same privacy choices for different sites (e.g., only accept the necessary cookies), but it would also have more of a say in how this occurs. Users could still choose to simply deny all non-necessary data sharing; however, the semi-automated option would provide users with the ability to customise their privacy choices. This would offer them much more granularity and scope than the minimalist option. Lundgren gave a basic idea of this in his earlier paper. He says, "by providing functionality that allows users to give pre-set responses to these types of [cookie] requests; effectively solving the problem of click-through agreements" (2020a, p. 759). He adds that "it should be possible for any user to adapt these changes as she sees fit (e.g., on websites of type x, allow for sharing y1, . . ., yn, under conditions z1, . . ., zn)" (2020a, p. 759).

Once a user sets up the rules, that user could browse online with the confidence that certain types of data would not be shared, or that only certain sites would be able to have access to their personal data. In our paper, we envisioned several possible ways that this could occur. For example, when you first open your browser, you might encounter a series of options for configuration. Your choices here would guide the browser's behaviour.

If you prefer not to be tracked across websites, then such an option can be turned on in much the same way that the *reject all* function is realised in the minimalist option. If you are happy for certain sites, but not others, to make recommendations to you based upon your personal data, then such a rule could be enabled too. Furthermore, you could specify the websites that are allowed to collect and share your personal data and the ones that are not. In principle, the rules could become as customisable as the user prefers, or as general as they prefer too.

There are many ways that the semi-automated option could be realised. One idea would be that users could customise their rules on a dashboard on a web browser, where they could see an overview of their active rules, allowing them quick and easy access to modify and change them. But there are other ways in which this might be done. Gomer et al. (2014) have outlined the concept of "semi-autonomous consent", in a short paper, which involves the three following steps. First, you set your preferences, perhaps in the way that Lundgren describes. Second, there is a consent phase, where the automated consent function "responds to consent requests on behalf of the user" (2014, p. 656), and third, there is a review stage where you can review the decisions that have been made on your behalf. This final step enables you to refine your preferences. If you see that the rules or preferences that have been set up do not really reflect your privacy preferences, then they can be refined.

One benefit of the semi-automated option, over the reject all option, is that users would have more confidence that their choices are being met, as they have more oversight over the process. On the reject all option, everything is rejected in the background, and the user does not have much awareness of what is going on. The semi-automated approach, on the other hand, would enable data subjects to enjoy the benefits of data sharing (e.g., product recommendations) while retaining control over their privacy.

There are, however, challenges with the semi-automated option. One significant issue, that Lundgren and I discussed in our paper, is that setting up the rules could be *time-consuming*. Currently, people often do not read the privacy policies that apply to them online, so it is unclear whether they would take the time to set up rules. Furthermore, one of the consequences of many people not reading privacy policies, or terms and conditions, is that many may be unaware of what personal data are being collected and what the associated risks of such data collections are. This means that some people might set up the rules or preferences in a context that they are unfamiliar with. For instance, if a user sets up a rule to allow certain apps to track them, such as a supermarket app, they may be doing so *without* an understanding of what the implications of setting up such a rule would be. And if users are not adequately informed when they set up rules, then they may put themselves at risk without even knowing they have done so. If users do not really understand how the rules are working, it's hard to see how they can help provide informed consent on behalf of the user.

With respect to these difficulties, one solution is that data subjects could be helped to set up their privacy preferences from experts. In a recent paper, Mario Pascalev has outlined the idea of "Privacy exchange authorities" (PEAs) (2017, p. 39). The PEAs would be "public, private or non-profit service providers of privacy services" and they would be there to "to assist individuals with defining their privacy terms and provide technical support in delivering these privacy terms to big data companies" (2017, p. 43). Pascalev's basic idea is that PEAs would be responsible for standardising and codifying certain privacy options (e.g., settings about whom to share personal data with or which types of personal data should not be shared). Then the user would be able to select one of the PEAs' privacy options, based on which one accords with their values. Finally, the PEAs would generate a record of the user's choices, which could be used for websites and services that the user encounters in the future. So, as Pascalev states, "instead of reading and accepting the company's privacy policy, the individual user will present their own terms" (2017, p. 43).

Pascalev suggests the possibility of having different profile options that could be available to choose from, eliminating the need for users to spend time determining which one best suits their needs; PEAs could, furthermore, assist data subjects in selecting one. PEAs could replicate the role of tax professionals whom individuals consult for tax advice. Moreover, this could mirror the consultation process used by doctors who take time to explain meaningful alternatives to users, and make sure they understand what they are consenting to (in this case, the PEAs would be able to help data subjects understand the rules they are putting in place).

One benefit of Pascalev's proposal is that it could help facilitate transparency. If the PEAs could help data subjects understand the risks of choosing certain rules, or which ones suit their preferences, then informed consent could become part of the process. While it is true that one would not be providing consent each time one visits a website or uses an app, it does not follow, as shown, that informed consent is wholly absent from the process. If you understood what each of the rules did, your selection of the rules would be guided by informed consent. For example, PEAs could explain how an opt-in function works, or explain the risks of allowing certain websites to collect personal data. PEAs could then recommend packages from level 1 data sharing, which allows all kinds of personal data sharing, to a level 10 "near complete anonymity" (Pascalev, 2017, p. 45). This is an excellent idea, but there are worries about how it would work. After all, PEAs are not widespread now, and there are numerous questions about their economic feasibility. How expensive would the services PEAs offer be? Would it be equitable, or would only the wealthy be able to afford it? Pascalev says that users "could receive assistance from volunteer or for-fee privacy advisors, similar to getting tax advice" (2017, p. 45) but many questions remain about how this would work in practice, even though I think it's a promising idea.

There are further issues with the semi-automated approach, however, which relates to the way that data collection and use can change; and also, how data can be re-purposed over time. Throughout this book, we have examined how such issues can make it difficult for data subjects to stay updated about how their personal data are *currently* being used. Some have argued these kinds of issues make the giving of informed consent very difficult or impossible (as we will see in Chapter 8). A semi-automated option could certainly simplify the self-management of this issue, since users would only need to adjust their rules from time to time. However, depending on how significant these changes are, a significant burden could still be placed upon users. One of the benefits of using PEAs, as Pascalev claims, is that users would just "need to set their privacy preferences once, and they could then spend sufficient time and resources to understand and select their options" (2017, p. 46). In reality, however, they may need to set and modify their privacy preferences more regularly.

For example, as we will see in the next chapter, once emotional AI becomes more widespread, we may start to see requests to collect biometric data. Privacy rules may then need to be revised, if they are not sufficiently updated to cover such use cases. If the risks associated with certain types of data collection change, as they certainly might as new stakeholders become interested in collecting personal data, then rules would need regular review. For instance, rules governing cookie permissions might become outdated if more advanced super cookies start being used by a company. Users may find themselves needing to spend a significant amount of time setting up these rules regularly, whether with PEAs or by themselves. While some might be motivated to manage their rules initially, many might find the task of privacy self-management difficult, if it becomes a constant task that requires help from PEAs. I now turn to a third option capable of addressing such problems.

6.3.3 *The Fully Automated Option*

The third type of automated consent that Lundgren and I discussed in our paper was the "fully automated option". Arguably, this is the most exciting of the three, yet potentially the most challenging from a moral and legal perspective. The basic idea of this approach is that automated consent would be guided by artificial intelligence and machine learning. It would not only make decisions based on pre-selected rules and preferences but also infer consent on your behalf for novel matters based on your previous decisions. For example, Jones et al. say, "AI may be able to technically grant consent as an agent of the data subject by predicting what a particular user finds unobjectionable" (2018, p. 69).

At first glance, this approach seems to have all the benefits of the previous two, without any of the drawbacks. Not only would it be able to provide consent on your behalf—freeing you from reading privacy policies or terms and conditions—but it would also offer granularity, if personal data collection or use were to change. If biometric data were requested to be collected, for example, and the user had never set up a rule about how to handle such data, a fully automated consent system could infer what you would have decided from your previous options. A fully automated consent function might decide to block such a type of data collection because you have previously been cautious about sharing your personal data online. Furthermore, it is easy to imagine that the fully automated approach may even be able to handle the problem of initially setting up the rules, which was one of the difficulties with the semi-automated option. It is hard to see how PEAs could help millions, or billions, of people configure their rules. A fully automated, AI powered, system or agent, on the other hand, could in principle be utilised by a large number of people.

How would such a system be set up or trained? This is a technical question that would need to be addressed in a fully worked-out version, but it is not hard to imagine possible ways in which it might be done. For example, users might set up a fully automatic consent mechanism in the same way they set up or train recommendation algorithms on platforms like Netflix when they first sign up. Users might, for example, fill in a questionnaire or answer some questions, and the algorithm would then start to get a picture of the kind of user you are. The more choices you make, the more it can learn about your profile and refine its suggestions based on your past choices. Once you have provided sufficient "training data", the software would be ready to consent for you. Instead of merely recommending privacy settings or suggesting which sites to avoid, the software would autonomously share or restrict the collection of your personal data, depending on which site requested its collection, or depending on what type of data in question is being sought. Once users have made their initial selections (which could be edited later), the browser would assume control and implement these choices.

In the last few years, this space has seen several developments. Jones et al. (2018) discuss an example of an AI agent already in development: the "Personalized Privacy Assistant Project", which they note is part of the Usable Privacy Project (the site can be viewed here: www.privacyassistant.org).[2] According to the company's website, it is "impractical for people to keep up with the many different ways in which their data can potentially be collected and processed" (Personalized Privacy Assistant Project, 2019). Their project has thus sought to solve this problem through the use of "personalised privacy assistants" to help users make these choices. Their website notes that these privacy assistants could "learn" user preferences and even "nudge" users to reconsider the implications of their decisions. These personalised privacy assistants may be better thought of as "almost" fully autonomous, as the developers see a role for users to stay involved in the privacy self-management process. The trick will be, of course, to get the balance right, namely, just the right amount of intervention: not all the time and not too far apart (cf. Carter, 2022). Though it is easy to imagine that when more learning takes place, the model could be thought of as fully autonomous for practical purposes, even if from time to time, nudges or reminders are sent.

With all of this in mind, is the fully autonomous option the most preferable? This is hard to say. There are certainly advantages to all of the accounts, and disadvantages too. While the reject all option does not offer much granularity, it is easy to set up. The fully automated option, in principle, may also be easy to set up, run, and continue, but it raises the most concerns from an informed consent perspective. This is because it has the potential to consent on your behalf, even in novel situations that you have not thought of before. Could we really trust such a system to get it right? The semi-automated option, despite its faults, would at least involve users more directly. Therefore, users may place the greatest amount of trust in it. It is not my aim, however, here to say which one is better. My aim here is to lay out some of the normative issues and some of the implications of each option. It may turn out that each option is better suited for certain people or needs. But we should not forget that informed consent is what we are focused on addressing here. There is also the risk that automated consent may actually undermine informed consent.

6.4 Does "Automated Consent" Undermine Informed Consent?

We have examined three different ways in which automated consent may be realised. One objection, facing all three options, is that automated consent undermines informed consent rather than helping to facilitate it. Recall our discussion from Chapter 1. There we discussed four conditions that are required in order to facilitate informed consent. These include the Autonomy/Respect for Persons Condition, the Harm Condition, the Communication Condition, and the Knowledge Condition. While it seems that automated consent could help with the Harm Condition, since it could block certain kinds of personal data collection, it is hard to see how it could help assist with autonomy, communication, or knowledge—that is, it is hard to see how you can give informed consent for a type of personal data collection if you do not know the details of that collection or do not have knowledge that you have even provided consent.

Consider a thought experiment. Imagine you have just installed a fully automated consent system, say a "Consent Assistant", onto your smartphone or operating system. Suppose your consent assistant is so adept at detecting your privacy preferences that you never see a pop-up notification asking for consent to use cookies, nor are you ever prompted to agree to any type of personal data sharing. Suppose you use this system for several years. Can we truly say that during this period you have given companies *informed consent*, or even *express consent*, to collect and use your personal data if you know nothing about the consent processes that you have been involved in during this period, or know what specific companies have your personal data or what they are doing with it?

The real question is: does automated consent undermine informed consent? At first glance, it might appear that it does. One might reason as follows: It's called "informed consent" because subjects are required to have at least some information, deliberate, and ultimately make a decision. One issue, after all, with merely giving "express" consent without reading a privacy policy is that people often have little idea about what they are consenting to. Does not automated consent leave us with the same problem? Consider the psychology of two people: one who gives automated consent without reading a privacy policy, and the other who simply gives regular express consent by clicking "I agree", also without reading the associated privacy policy. Both seem to fail to give informed consent. While I agree that the psychology is similar, I would argue it is not identical. Someone using automated consent may lack knowledge of what is happening at any one moment with their personal data, but could understand, and be in control of, the rules governing how their data are being used. In fact, automated consent could potentially motivate users to care about their privacy settings. A data subject, for example, may have knowledge that third-party cookies are not tracking them online, since they have set up rules to prohibit such data sharing. Thus, it is not automatically correct to say that automated consent undermines informed consent.

One reason informed consent is important is that it allows us to manage risks. Automated consent can facilitate this. Consider the semi-automated option, for example. Suppose you are consulting with a PEA and are discussing the benefits and risks of setting up certain rules. You may express a desire to share a certain type of personal information, but the PEA may advise against doing so due to the associated risks. In this case, the setting up of an automated consent system can facilitate a kind of informed consent.

It may be objected that such a data subject would still be ignorant of much, such as the specific details of the data collection and use that is occurring. However, in response, it is not clear if this would be required to provide informed consent. It may be useful to compare this process with one that occurs in the medical context. Suppose your physician informs you about a procedure you are about to undergo. They may explain the duration of the process, the associated risks, and other relevant details. But as discussed in Chapter 1, they will not disclose everything. Not only would this take a lot of time, but it may also require years of specialised study to understand. Yet, informed consent is still given without such knowledge. Similarly, if you understand the reason why you have made certain privacy choices, such as sharing cookies under specific circumstances, it is not accurate to equate your psychology with someone who simply clicks "yes" and gives express consent. You have provided informed consent on a more general level. Of course, the difference is that the consent given in the medical setting, say for an operation to occur, applies only for that one act, i.e., the operation. Automated consent could in principle operate indefinitely.

A fully automated option that left you completely out of the process might be undesirable then. Even a system that consistently "gets it right" without any input from you would not leave you with knowledge. A fully automated system powered by AI that would occasionally require interventions, on the other hand, could do this. These interventions would need to be selective to avoid "notice fatigue" (cf. Carter, 2022) and to uphold the purpose of automated consent. Consider the following example: suppose you are using fully automated consent software. You can browse the internet with confidence knowing that your privacy preferences will be respected. Cookies will be used as you prefer, your data will not be re-purposed in ways you do not approve, and your settings regarding shared information will be honoured. However, from time to time, you may receive a notification informing you of recent changes to several privacy policies. Your automated consent has made the decision not to share your data, but the system has informed you or perhaps it would like a confirmation just to make sure. Occasionally, notifications with explanations may be provided to keep you informed. This process would keep you engaged, even though you are not explicitly consenting to every website's request for data. These explanations, if paired with visuals as discussed in Chapter 5, could enhance transparency, and help to facilitate informed consent.

Still, might there be something fundamentally wrong with automating such an important process? In Carissa Véliz's (2021) book *Privacy Is Power*, she discusses a related idea of César Hidalgo's which is that we could have "digital avatars that vote on our behalf" (p. 100). In her view, this is a "bad idea" (Véliz, 2021, p. 100). She claims that we "should look out for claims by tech that your gadgets can interpret your will and vote for you" (Véliz, 2021, p. 100) In Véliz's view, then, there are grave dangers associated with giving avatars the capacity to vote on your behalf. Véliz is concerned that voting is an important part of liberal democracy, and we would risk much by giving it up. Might there be similar kinds of risks associated with automated consent? Does it risk removing a critical safeguard of democratic life and, in the process, enable us to be controlled by big tech companies?

Lundgren and I (see Andreotta & Lundgren, 2024) considered such an objection in our paper but felt that automating consent differs from automating a political vote. When it comes to politics, it is important that each of us exercise our right to vote on often deeply personal issues. Yet, in our view, voting is not really the same as providing consent online. When faced with hundreds of requests to collect your personal data, such as IP addresses or location data, or to track you, the benefits of providing consent each time for these repetitive requests remain unclear—assuming it is even possible for one person to provide informed consent each time. Being active in politics requires awareness of the process itself, the options available to you, and consequences of electing a certain politician. If there are no good candidates, you can protest, raise awareness about it, or not vote. I agree with Véliz that withdrawing oneself from this important process is not something we should try to achieve.

So why isn't the same true of automated consent? As Lundgren and I observed in our paper, politics is deeply personal, whereas online interactions can be repetitive: such as the repeated requests for cookie use, or IP address tracking across multiple websites. What one would need to show, for such an argument against automated consent to work, is that there is intrinsic value in clicking hundreds of cookie requests for example, in the same way that being a part of the democratic process is intrinsically valuable. But before one can do that, one would also need to demonstrate that it is actually possible to read through all the privacy policies one receives, or properly investigate the implications of accepting or denying all cookie requests one receives. As shown in this book, achieving this is not feasible. Therefore, the comparison is between an automated consent mechanism with risks, versus a system where users are unable to read or understand the policies that apply to them at all. Democratic involvement might be challenging, but there are benefits from being involved in the process.[3] It is not clear that the same kinds of benefits are present with respect to providing consent online.

What about the automated consent settings themselves? Could they be manipulated by companies to take advantage of us? While this is a risk, I think that if users played a role in setting up the rules, whether by manual procedure or by machine learning, and they had some oversight over the process, it could empower them rather than manipulate them. For such a reason, we may need to exercise a degree of caution with fully automated approaches that lack any intervention or communicate to users what is being done with their data. As long as we can guide automated consent, say by assistance from PEAs, or through machine learning and AI, it will give us a chance to self-manage our privacy.

In some cases, automated consent could actually give us *more* protection from big tech. For example, consider how in 2021, Fitbit was acquired by Google. Unless you follow the news closely, you might not have realised this, and thus like many, you may not be aware that the data preferences or risks associated with your Fitbit may have changed. Automated consent would be well suited to handle such changes. As soon as such a change occurred (i.e., the data controller or processor changes), a user could be notified, or data sharing could be temporarily blocked until a user manually intervenes. An automated consent function might alert you that Google platforms share data with each other, and thus you may face new risks that were not present before. The average user, without such a function, may not even realise such a change has occurred, or understand the risks associated with such a change. This illustrates how automated consent could actually assist users in making informed choices, compared to say manually monitoring all these changes yourself.

6.5 Re-Purposing Privacy Preferences

In Chapter 3, I examined the Re-purposed Data Problem. This refers to the problem of data being used in ways that go beyond its original purpose. If consent was only given for a specific type of personal data use, then further uses of that data would require informed consent to be secured again. One of the benefits of automated consent is that it could help users track these further requests for collection and use. If companies were required by law to obtain consent for re-purposing data, in ways that went beyond what was specified when the original consent was secured, automated consent would allow us some control over whether we approve of such reuse. Of course, if automated consent worked as intended, we might not even need to become aware of these new uses. If each of our automated consent applications were set up to match our preferences, it could be that the data would not be used in ways that we would disapprove of. At present, getting data subjects to give consent to each new use places a large burden upon them.

An additional issue that is important to recognise here is that the data required to power this kind of automated decision-making would itself be a form of personal data—specifically, information about our preferences, the privacy rules we wish to uphold, and other relevant details. In the case of the semi-automated approach, a copy of our privacy preferences would need to be stored so that consent could be given in a way that adheres to them. In a more complicated fully automated consent system, a substantial amount of data may need to be collected—that is, the rules we set up, our search history, keystrokes, online interactions, and so on. These data may need to form part of the data set that a fully automated system uses to determine our preferences. The reject all option may be the simplest, and therefore would not require as much personal data to function, but it could still require sensitive personal data for its operation, that some people would want to keep private.

Several key questions arise here: who would have access to these data, and what are the implications if they were to be exposed? It might be thought that not much could be done with such data, but as demonstrated by the Netflix competition data set, or the data set containing mobile phone pings (see Chapter 3) such data can be combined with other data sets to reveal information about us. While this risk would be minimal with the reject all option (though still important to recognise), it would be much greater if the fully autonomous option were used—especially if machine learning applications were making inferences about what your preferences were over an extended period, with the result of each decision stored in a database. Furthermore, if data brokers were to purchase these data, it could become valuable for targeted advertising purposes, even in cases where users blocked certain types of personal data collection. For instance, if you knew the privacy preferences of certain users, you would know how best to target them—for example, through specific sites which users have permitted data sharing, or via other vulnerabilities.

Lundgren and I were aware of this problem and noted that such personal data could be valuable to data brokers and others operating in the data economy (see Andreotta & Lundgren, 2024). Thus, we claimed that it would be important to secure these data. But while there are risks that personal data required to run automated consent mechanisms itself could be re-purposed, the point that Lundgren and I made in our paper was that we cannot look at these risks in isolation. In our view, we need to compare these risks with the risks associated with current data-sharing practices. There are good reasons to think that while automated consent has its fair share of concerns (as I explore in more detail below), they are not as significant as the ones associated with current personal data collection practices. If businesses could make money by helping people set up their automated consent software, or if the companies who create privacy assistants could charge small subscription fees for users to employ them, then it is possible that an economy built around automated consent could emerge. Of course, one risk that may arise is in the case of "free" privacy assistant services that provide you with an AI privacy assistant but use your data as a form of payment, similar to how Google offers you a "free" service where you "pay" with your personal data.

6.6 The Motivation Problem

An issue that has repeatably arisen throughout this book is the problem of what would motivate companies to change. Even if there exist viable solutions to some of the problems surrounding informed consent, it does not follow that companies will necessarily be interested in implementing them. In Chapter 4, for example, we saw that it was hard to see, at least initially, how companies would be motivated to subject their consent practices to ethical review. And in Chapter 5, I questioned whether companies would be interested in adding visuals to privacy policies or terms and conditions even if doing so would help with transparency and engagement. Might companies be equally as cautious with automated consent?

The first thing to point out is that automated consent is slightly different from these other approaches because it would not immediately require companies to fundamentally change—though of course, widespread adoption of the technology would likely cause companies to make adjustments. For example, Google would not need to take immediate action. The work would be done by app and software developers to create automated consent technologies. And as I said earlier, the process is already underway (see, e.g., www.privacyassistant.org). The real question is whether such approaches could be widely adopted and easy enough to use for the average internet user.

One positive sign to consider is that beliefs about privacy are changing. As we have seen, survey data show that privacy is a major concern for people. Companies are starting to make it a priority too, and eventually, we might even see these automated consent functionalities built into operating systems. For example, in 2021 a small but notable change occurred when Apple updated its operating system (iOS 14.5), which we have discussed in previous chapters. Notably, they gave users a choice about whether to allow apps to track them. For instance, if you installed and opened Instagram, a notification would appear stating that the app "would like permission to track you across apps and websites owned by other companies". Apple was able to feature this in their advertising campaign, appealing to people who care about privacy. Integrating a minimalist option into an operating system (like Apple's OS)—which allows users to select an option that "always blocks" apps from tracking—would be quite feasible.

However, one thing to take into account with such changes, is that they do not please all stakeholders. In 2020, for example, when Apple announced its planned changes, Facebook criticised Apple for their decision, saying that it would be harmful to small businesses, for example. As Rebecca Bellan from Forbes said:

> Facebook has an advertising system called Audience Network, where third-party app developers turn to sell marketing spots and earn income, using Facebook's trove of user information to target the ads. Audience Network gets a slice of whatever revenue developers get. So if Facebook stops getting user data, it won't be able to target ads as well inside apps and may actually shut down Audience Network for Apple users when the new software is launched.
>
> (2020)

Some companies would certainly risk losing money as a result of this change, and thus may be opposed to it. As others have noted, Google and Facebook have expressed concerns that many users would opt not to share such data (O'Flaherty, 2021). However, as more data subjects demand the ability to choose, and buy products which have such options, there may not be much large companies can do. One consequence of such changes, of course, may be that sites may start charging its users, to make up for the loss in revenue. As Kate O'Flaherty says, in *Forbes*, a loss in advertising revenue could "mean apps and services will have to fund their businesses in other ways" (2021). This may not be a bad thing for consumers, as it may ensure that they are given an actual choice about how their data are used, even though there may still be concerns associated with such decisions.

Another positive sign, as I mentioned above, has been the emergence of privacy-friendly browsers like Brave in the last few years. Their website notes that it is a "free and open-source web browser" which "blocks privacy-invasive ads & trackers. It blocks third-party data storage. It protects from browser fingerprinting. It upgrades every webpage possible to secure https connections. And it does all this by default" (Brave, 2024). As mentioned above, Brave offers TOR functionality, which as mentioned offers similar functionality to the minimalist option. It is possible that in the future, browsers like Brave could become more sophisticated and actually implement data-sharing rules (as articulated by Lundgren, 2020a), which they can then advertise to attract new users. Furthermore, if Pascalev's idea about PEAs could be realised, an economy around privacy could emerge. PEAs could be paid for their services to help users select their privacy settings. And once more users start to see the benefits from using automated consent software, companies may be forced to change too, as they would no longer get away with "hiding" information in long privacy policies or including hard to find "opt-out" settings. While these could be hidden from users, automated consent would be better suited to identify and manage them.

6.7 Automated Consent Gone Awry

I will finish this chapter with a brief discussion about what happens when automated consent goes wrong—that is, when a program or browser grants consent on behalf of a user that conflicts with the user's preferences (or what they would have chosen themselves). For example, imagine that you have implemented a fully automated consent program to manage your online privacy. You do not want cookies to track you across websites, nor do you want your personal data shared with third-party advertisers. However, to your surprise, this has actually occurred: the automated consent system has failed to obtain consent in a manner that you would agree with.

The problem is not unique to automated consent, of course. You may have heard about cases where AI does not perform as expected, such as in incidents involving driverless cars that crash. In 2018, for example, an Uber self-driving car killed Elaine Herzberg in Arizona while she was riding her bike. The operator of the car was not paying attention to the road and was instead watching television while the car hit Herzberg (Wolmar, 2023). One question that arises in such tragic cases is: who is to blame? If you are a passenger in an autonomous car that kills someone, are you to blame, should you have been ready to intervene? Or would it be the software developers, the car manufacturers, the algorithm guiding the car itself, or any number of other people that played a causal role in the process, such as the regulators (i.e., the State of Arizona) as Coeckelbergh (2020, p. 2056) points out.[4] Even if only humans can be assigned responsibility, and thus it would be mistaken to hold the "AI" or the "algorithm" responsible (Coeckelbergh, 2020), we still have the problem of determining where to place the blame.[5] Coeckelbergh calls this the "many hands problem", which is the problem that is "difficult if not impossible" (Coeckelbergh, 2020) to find who is to blame, if indeed is right to talk of there being one person to blame in cases where AI does something unexpected.

We should expect to encounter similar issues with automated consent. If you use a fully automated consent application and it consents to something contrary to your preferences, who should bear responsibility? Should you be accountable for using automated consent initially? Was there an error in how it was trained, or was it the result of a software bug? These questions are difficult to answer, and the kind of errors will differ with the type of automated consent in question. One issue that makes such questions even more difficult is the fact that the mistakes made by automated consent software may not be easy to see. In the case of driverless cars, crashes are obviously visible. But would the analogous "crashes" be so easy to see online—that is, would it be obvious that your personal data started to be used and collected in ways you do not approve of, or might it take a while for you to notice? The consequences may not lead to immediate death, as in the case of driverless cars, but the risks could still be significant.

Lundgren and I were aware of the risks associated with automated consent potentially making errors, and we suggested that great care would need to be taken in mitigating these risks before widespread adoption. One response to the problem of "mistakes" which we discussed, comes from Le Métayer and Monteleone (2009), who argue that if our automated "privacy agents" consent in ways that conflict with our preferences and errors occur, data subjects could simply object to any further processing of their data and seek compensation from the responsible "privacy agent" (Le Métayer & Monteleone, 2009, p. 139). This is a sensible solution, but it overlooks some key issues. As mentioned above, one might not even realise when it fails. Unlike a car crash, which is visible to anyone who witnesses it, mistakes in automated consent might go unnoticed until a substantial amount of personal data has been collected and utilised—or errors might never be noticed at all. After all, many people remain unaware of the extent to which their personal data are collected and used today, and the effects such data use has on their behaviour.

Of course, since there are multiple fully automated options, each of them would not carry the same risks. A fully automated consent mechanism, which requires no user involvement, may be risky and not advisable for privacy-conscious individuals who are not prepared to monitor their automated consent applications. A reject all option, while the least robust, faces the lowest risk of generating errors in contrast. Although it could malfunction, for example, through a bug, its simplicity could also be its strength. The semi-automated option, with predefined rules, would presumably be in the middle, with respect to its propensity to malfunction, especially if it cannot make inferences based on a user's previous consent choices. If users were in control of setting and managing the rule set, then it could be better controlled. However, mistakes could still occur, and unforeseen loopholes could exist. Of course, these are risks, and may not necessarily occur. AI could assist in setting up one's initial online profile, and a fully automated approach might always be accurate if fed the correct information. If inaccurate answers are provided, however, the AI might misunderstand preferences—as the famous maxim goes, "garbage in, garbage out".

A final concern here is about unintended consequences that arise from a company's failure to adhere to their own policies. These would not be strictly speaking a failure of automated consent, but they are still important to address. A company that fails to do what it promises in its privacy policy or terms and conditions will be able to take advantage of fully automated consent. Consider, for example, the case of Better Help, an online counselling service which offers therapy to its users. In 2023, they were fined $7.8 million US Dollars by the FTC for disclosing personal information about its users (Clark, 2023). After promising users that it would not disclose personal health data, they passed on these data to other companies.

The FTC said "BetterHelp used and revealed consumers' email addresses, IP addresses, and health questionnaire information to Facebook, Snapchat, Criteo, and Pinterest for advertising purposes" (FTC, 2023). Automated consent mechanisms would obviously not be able to protect such data sharing. If a site says that it will only store your data, and not use your data for advertising purposes, and your automated consent grants consent (on your behalf) for the site to have access to your personal data, but the site sells the data anyway, that is not the fault of the automated consent mechanism. It is important, however, to remember that a manual consent function would not have helped either. With such large fines being issued for these behaviours, we will hopefully see fewer of these cases in the future, and thus fewer examples of such consent failures.

6.8 Conclusion

This chapter has explored the possibility of automated consent. In looking to address the *volume problem*—the issue that there are too many privacy policies and terms and conditions that apply to us on the internet for us to read and understand—automated consent offers much promise. I examined three different ways in which it may be implemented: the minimalist option, the semi-automated option, and the fully automated option. Before widespread adoption, of course, there will be much to consider, including whether the benefits of automated consent outweigh the risks.

In suggesting that automated consent holds much promise, I do not mean to suggest that it cannot work with other solutions examined in the book. In setting up rules for automated consent, visuals could help users see the implications of consenting to certain types of personal data collection. And neither do I mean to set the three options of automated consent as rivals. Each of them could represent different choices for different privacy needs. Some may feel uncomfortable with consent being *fully* automated—that is, they might find the idea of a "privacy agent" consenting on their behalf "creepy". Others may not have a problem with it. And others still may prefer a rule-based system where they can make choices and spend time understanding the rules, rather than examining long and repetitive privacy policies.

Notes

1 Of course, the fact that TOR hides a user's IP address makes it appealing to those who want to engage in criminal activities online, such as online fraud or scams.
2 See Carter (2022) for a discussion of the different types of personalised privacy assistants (PPAs) currently being developed at Carnegie Mellon University.

3 See Brennan (2016) for a critical analysis of democratic forms of government, where everyone has a right to vote. One of the claims he defends is that becoming informed regarding basic facts about how politics works can be very challenging. As a result, he argues, voters often lack basic knowledge that is pertinent to their voting decisions.
4 See Taddeo and Floridi (2018) for a related discussion on AI delegation and responsibility. They claim that "[r]obust procedures for human oversight are needed to minimize such unintended consequences and redress any unfair impacts of AI" (2018, p. 751).
5 See Andreotta (2021) for a related discussion on AI rights.

7 Looking into the Future of Informed Consent

In the last three chapters, we considered different ways in which informed consent might be more meaningfully secured online. The potential solutions included the establishment of ethics committees, the incorporation of visual elements into online consent procedures, and the implementation of automated consent. As technological advances progress over the next few years, it remains uncertain how well these solutions will be able to facilitate meaningful consent online, even if it turns out that they can help us with some of our current issues. Despite this uncertainty, this chapter looks at some new and emerging technologies that present us with novel challenges, as well as opportunities, for the gaining of informed consent. In Section 7.1, I examine emotional AI and raise concerns about the personal data collection required for its operation. In Section 7.2, I discuss deepfakes, which are already beginning to proliferate online. In Section 7.3, I examine Generative AI and the complex issues it raises concerning informed consent. In Section 7.4, I discuss Bluetooth trackers, and then finally in Section 7.5, I consider blockchain technologies.

7.1 Emotional AI and Informed Consent

Our emotional self-expressions play an important role in our interpersonal communications. When one clenches their teeth and furrows their brows, they can convey anger. Similarly, smiling and tilting one's head in a certain way expresses happiness. Of course, we guard our emotions too. One may wish to hide their feelings of anguish, or sadness, about a private matter while they are in the workplace, for example. In recent years, as AI has become more sophisticated, these kinds of emotional reactions have become yet another type of personal data that are able to be collected and used. The technology in question here is called emotional AI (hereafter, "E-AI") and goes beyond facial recognition technology, which has been used for several years. E-AI "detects" human emotions by applying algorithms and machine learning to biometric data. While this technology

DOI: 10.4324/9781032626048-7

has some important use cases, it also raises some serious issues regarding informed consent that require careful consideration. Some of these issues will be familiar to us, as obviously E-AI requires the collection of personal data to function. However, it introduces some novel issues, as the technology promises to provide a direct way of gaining access to people's emotions without needing to infer them from extensive data sets.

To understand some of the current applications of this technology, consider one of the companies in this space, Zenus, who asserts on their website that they can "obtain behavioural insights with 95% accuracy without collecting personal data" (Zenus, n.d.-a). In one of their use cases (featured in a promotional video that is uploaded to YouTube, titled "Zenus AI: Promo video"), we see footage of four shoppers walking around a small clothing store, looking at different items, with various analytics superimposed on each of them (see Zenus AI, 2021). The analytics purport to show the level of *enjoyment* or *engagement* a person is having while in the store; and also, a percentage figure called "purchase likelihood" which is superimposed on the shoppers. One screen shows two women, one is given an 88% purchase likelihood, and the other is given a 47%. While the methodology used to determine these percentages is not fully disclosed, it is not hard to imagine many finding this technology useful (assuming the figures are accurate). In typical circumstances, a shop assistant would have no knowledge of these details unless they communicate directly with shoppers. Zenus claims on their website to "Protect people's privacy", "Practice radical honesty", and "Do things right" (Zenus, n.d.-b). The claim that the company protects people's privacy may seem to conflict with their surveillance technologies. However, Zenus claims that they do not collect data; they can view everything in real-time, so information about people is not collected.[1]

Another company, Realeyes, has developed AI-E-enabled software that allows them to monitor students in online classes, which could, if properly managed, enhance teaching practices. In one of their promotional videos on YouTube titled "Realeyes—Education Use Case", the company shows how they measure "engagement" in an online classroom (Realeyes, 2022).[2] If students lose attention or become distracted, nudges can be sent to them (such as increasing the volume or by sending prompts/alerts to the screen). A third company in this space is Affectiva (which was recently acquired by Swedish company Smart Eye). One of the use cases involves sending alerts in cars when drivers are experiencing fatigue. On their website, they suggest that biometric data, in combination with E-AI technology, could detect levels of "driver fatigue" and "driver distraction", so that AI could take measures to assist drivers—such as adjusting the radio volume, or playing lively music, to draw driver's attention to the road; or making recommendations to drivers to pull over and get some coffee (Affectiva, 2024). Given that several thousand people die annually in the United States due to crashes caused by driving while drowsy or fatigued, this technology has the potential to save lives.[3]

Advertisers, of course, stand to benefit from E-AI too. Frank Rose (2021), in his book *The Sea We Swim In*, notes that Coca-Cola and Nestlé have teamed up with Realeyes to learn how people feel about marketing campaigns as opposed to how they say they feel, since some people may lack self-knowledge. If people express genuine excitement about a product through their emotions but do not communicate this overtly, then traditional techniques like asking customers could be inaccurate and time-consuming. All of these different use cases illustrate how valuable E-AI will be to companies operating in the data economy. But they also raise a number of ethical issues pertaining to informed consent, especially in cases where we "give away" our emotions unconsciously.

If you have made it this far in the book, you might think that there is nothing new about E-AI. Personal data analytics from the web or smartphone app use can be collected for the same purposes, surely, you might reason. Is this not just another example? While there is truth to this, E-AI is, in another sense, distinct from other forms of personal data collection, as emotions are so central to our lives and closely relate to the way we see ourselves.[4]

If we look to the recent literature on the topic, we encounter various concerns. For instance, Andrew McStay (2020) conducted over 100 interviews with stakeholders who have a particular interest in the technology. These included "privacy-oriented NGOs, policymakers, legal actors and diverse industrial and service sectors interested in data about emotions" (2020, p. 2). The results from this (qualitative) survey are particularly instructive, as they raise common concerns about how the technology will be used. One interviewee from a global technology firm noted "the reason why emotion detection has not scaled as quickly as expected has less to do with the technology itself, but reticence of clients and their desire to avoid a PR backlash" (2020, p. 7). However, another interviewee suggested that what was crucial was how the technology was being used. They said, "if you're aware that machines are tracking your emotions to make interactions better, that's OK" (2020, p. 8). For example, they added, "[i]f my smartphone understands that I'm angry and can provide a response that calms me down, that's OK" (2020). Clearly, it will be important to manage how informed consent is sought with such technology, as there may be some use cases that are considered acceptable while others may make people quite uncomfortable. McStay also notes from his interviews with the stakeholders that there was consensus regarding a "creepy factor" associated with the technology that would need to be addressed for the technology to be successfully scaled (2020, p. 9).

McStay also conducted a "demographically representative' UK nationwide survey in 2015 and found that over half of the 2,000 participants were "not okay" with emotion detection (2020, p. 9). And in a more recent study (also involving McStay), Bakir et al. (2023) asked UK participants whether they would be willing to *sell* certain forms of personal data (anonymised, identified, or at all). They found similar results—that is, many participants opposed the use of such data in certain contexts. Only 41% of participants were willing to sell data about their emotions, moods and mental states to advertising and marketing companies; and only 38% were willing to sell these data to social media companies (Bakir et al., 2023). Given that a significant number of people will likely be opposed to the collection of their emotions, it will be crucial to manage consent carefully. That is, it will be important for companies to ensure that data subjects are aware that the personal data they wish to collect includes emotional data, and not just another type of personal data. Even if some individuals may give informed consent to having their emotions captured, especially if it enhances app functionality such as calming them down or improving car safety, survey data show that there will be a significant number of people opposed to it.

One problem that reemerges here is the Re-purposed Data Problem (as explored in Chapter 3). Consider the use of E-AI in online classrooms as an example. Students may consent to have their camera on during a session and their data collected, but they may not fully appreciate the implications of having their emotions "captured" and used for other purposes. If E-AI can derive insights from the camera feed, we need to exercise caution. Given the numerous opportunities for our cameras to be active and the many chances for emotional data collection, automated consent procedures may prove useful here, as one would not need to manually examine the various requests for collection.

Semi-automated consent functionalities could enable data subjects to self-manage the collection and use of these data (see Chapter 6). A rule could be set up, for example, to never share emotional data. Or a rule could be set up to only share emotional data with certain companies. This could make people feel more secure about using the technology if websites or apps begin to collect this type of personal data. Furthermore, ethics committees could play a crucial role in ensuring that privacy policies are not misleading or obscure the use of the technology (see Chapter 4). And visuals could help users to understand the implications of sharing emotional data (see Chapter 5). For example, an image could help explain to users that emotions will also be collected for marketing purposes and not just for immediate use, say, for monitoring awareness while driving.

Of course, the efficacy of these approaches changes a bit when we factor in one worry: our emotions, unlike our online activities, can be captured in real time. While automated consent might be useful in blocking attempts to capture biometric data when integrated into a car's operating system or online, such as when one is on their computer, it is hard to see how it can safeguard data if a person walks into a clothing store. In public locations like stores, companies may collect biometric data without people's awareness.

Zenus claims that their technologies give rise to anonymous data collection—so that someone can be detected as engaged in real-time. However, even without providing your name, the vast amount of personal data currently being collected could still potentially compromise anonymity, especially if it can be correlated with data from Facebook or Instagram (given that your images may already be online) or other personal data repositories. An "anonymous shopper" who happens to be engaged with certain items of clothing could be de-anonymised quite easily depending on what information is freely available about them online.

These fears are not unfounded. In 2020, a real estate company called Cadillac Fairview embedded cameras in kiosks at 12 shopping malls across Canada and in doing so captured images of the people that were passing by (Tunney, 2020). The Privacy Commissioner of Canada, Daniel Therrien, in his commentary of the event, actually made specific reference to "consent". He said, "[t]he lack of meaningful consent was particularly concerning given the sensitivity of biometric data, which is a unique and permanent characteristic of our body and a key to our identity" (Office of the Privacy Commission of Canada, 2020). It is not hard to imagine a world where department stores are able to capture video content of shoppers and combine it with personal data they may already have available online, such as data from social media platforms. Alternatively, there is the risk that such data could be sold to data brokers. It will be imperative for legislation to be created to place restrictions on the use of these data without consent.

Of course, it should be noted that these concerns also apply to current personal data collection practices, as we have seen in this book. However, our emotions can be visible and immediate, revealing significant aspects of ourselves, as the Canadian Privacy Commissioner alludes to. When we enter a store or attend a class, we may inadvertently reveal information that speaks volumes about our preferences and behaviours. While it is true that current personal data collection practices, such as those involving Facebook likes or browsing behaviour, can accumulate over time and reveal much about us, we can often take measures to conceal our actions or self-manage our data. Emotions, on the other hand, can be challenging to conceal—they are often "given away" in our daily interactions. E-AI has the potential to provide companies with valuable engagement and attitudinal data. Whether these data prove to be more valuable to companies than the personal data currently being collected, as I am suggesting, is an empirical prediction that could prove incorrect. Nevertheless, emotional data could potentially offer insights that are absent from current personal data collections. Legislators will thus have an important role in ensuring that this space is regulated effectively.

A final concern here is the accuracy of E-AI itself. The discussion thus far has scrutinised E-AI under the assumption that it will be accurate. Is that the case? Some have suggested that there are limitations to the technology. In a recent article, Pragya Agarwal offers a critical perspective and says, "the majority of emotional AI is based on flawed science" (2022). In her view, while "algorithms can recognize and report that a person is crying, it is not always possible to accurately deduce the reason and meaning behind the tears" (2022). There is a difference between tears of joy and tears of sadness of course. A similar perspective is evident in a recent study by Cabitza et al. (2022), who sought to test the reliability of automated facial emotion recognition by putting some of its various assumptions to the test. Essentially the experimenters sought to test whether human observers are in agreement "regarding the emotions they sense in static facial expressions" (2022, p. 2). These questions bear importance for the accuracy of E-AI, as we seem to require agreement about what anger is, versus sadness, anxiety, and so on. If everyone disagrees about what anger is, how would an AI system be trained to recognise it?

The authors found significant variability in the emotions different people attributed to the same "static pictures" of individuals expressing emotions (2022). However, the experimenters also noted that emotion recognition was "improved" (defined as "reduced disagreement") when participants were provided with contextual information about the faces (for example, the video footage that the still images were taken from) (2022, p. 13). The experimenters acknowledged the problem of ground truth, which is as they note "a problem with the reliability of the data used to train . . . classification systems" and concluded that "*we cannot speak of accuracy for facial expression and emotion recognition technology*: in fact, no reference can be reliably established against which to compute meaningful error rate" (2022, p. 14, emphasis in original). This research suggests that E-AI's current capacity to detect emotions may be lacking until a solution to this problem is found.

However, there are some further scientific reasons to think it could be difficult to detect emotions, if we look at some recent work on the nature of emotions. Lisa Feldman Barrett (2017), in her book *How Emotions are Made*, has suggested that we "construct" our emotions, and that it may not even be possible to talk about "getting it right", with respect to what emotion we are undergoing, from a scientific point of view. Consider the following account of her attributing an emotion to herself that she does not possess, when she was on a date, and *thought* she was undergoing a romantic emotion.

> As we sat together in a coffee shop, to my surprise, I felt my face flush several times as we spoke. My stomach fluttered and I started having trouble concentrating. Okay, I realized, I was wrong. I am clearly attracted to him. We parted an hour later—after I agreed to go out with him again—and I headed home, intrigued. I walked into my apartment, dropped my keys on the floor, threw up, and spent the next seven days in bed with the flu.
>
> (2017, p. 30)

Anyone observing Barrett on her date (or even E-AI technology detecting what emotion she had), and even Barrett herself, it would seem, might think that all the evidence points to her experiencing certain emotions that she does not actually have. It is not until she goes home and throws up that she realises she has misinterpreted the emotional state she is in. Yet Barrett goes further; she suggests that "[i]nstances of emotion have no objective fingerprints in the face, body, and brain, so "accuracy" has no scientific meaning" (2017, p. 40), only social meaning. In Barrett's view, an "emotion is your brain's *creation* of what your bodily sensations mean, in relation to what is going on around you in the world" (2017, p. 30, emphasis in original). What does this mean for E-AI software? One implication is that E-AI might have made the same mistake. Indeed, objective fingerprints in the face and body are the very things that, presumably, E-AI would be looking at. If emotions have no objective "fingerprints" in the face or body, we might wonder how well E-AI will do in terms of accuracy.

However, one need not agree with Barrett's conclusion about accuracy having no meaning to fully appreciate her main point (see Andreotta, 2023). It could be that we can not only talk about mistakes when it comes to emotional attributions, but that we can also talk about getting it right. It may just be that additional contextual information is required. Problematically for E-AI, however, this is something that will be hard to get from biometric data even when combined with AI and machine learning; what is needed is additional contextual information about the person and the circumstances surrounding their emotional self-expression.

Now, it is one thing if advertisers make mistakes in detecting the emotions you are experiencing and advertise the wrong product to you (e.g., E-AI mistakenly thinks a shopper is excited about a new TV), but it could be dangerous in cases of driving or education. Still, as the technology progresses, might the accuracy problem be lessened with technical advancements involving machine learning and more sophisticated algorithms?

Possibly. A larger concern is whether companies will be motivated to fill in context, which may require users of emotional AI to combine it with other types of personal data in order to fill the gaps left by a lack of context.

If anger is expressed in different ways by certain people, or if people show excitement in different ways, there still might be consistency or "ground truths" within certain groups—you might express your own anger in a consistent way too. This would make emotion detection much harder, as not only would you need personal data about individuals, but you would also need data about the context in which the emotions have arisen. Such personal data might not be gleaned from E-AI, but could be gathered from elsewhere, such as from hundreds of other types of personal data we provide from Fitbits, smartwatches, movie reviews, and so on.[5] Data subjects would, of course, still need to provide informed consent for these other data to be used for this purpose, of course. This is where automated consent could be valuable. While it may be challenging for data subjects to keep track of such uses, automated consent could potentially block such data sharing, if that is what data subjects wanted, and provide a way for users to actually self-manage this complicated space.

7.2 Deepfakes and Informed Consent

The term "deepfakes" refers to the audio, image, or video files which portray individuals saying, or doing things, they have not said or done. Given the ubiquity of deepfakes, chances are you have encountered them online, such as the clips featuring Arnold Schwarzenegger "inserted" into movies like *Titanic*, *Ace Ventura*, *Crocodile Dundee*, and *Napoleon Dynamite*. While some modern-day deepfakes are technically impressive, they can often be easy to spot, since they are not only labelled as deepfakes, but they are often created in ways that are comical and thus not trying to deceive you. For example, even if you have never watched the movie *Titanic* before, you are unlikely to think that James Cameron made a strange casting choice by including Arnold Schwarzenegger as Jack's love interest—you would recognise it as a deepfake.

Others are not so easy to spot. In 2021, Cadbury released an advertisement to support local businesses titled "Supporting Local Retailers This Diwali | Not Just A Cadbury Ad" featuring the Indian Bollywood actor Shah Rukh Khan.[6] As the advertisement progresses, however, the innovative feature of the ad is revealed, namely that the advertisement used machine learning to recreate Shah Rukh Khan's likeness (his face and voice). This enabled viewers within a certain area code to see advertisements for businesses close to them advertised by Shah Rukh Khan, one of the biggest movie stars on the planet. Furthermore, since machine learning was employed to create the advertisements, there would be no need to get the actor to record hundreds of variations.

Unlike the Schwarzenegger deepfake, the Cadbury deepfake is very realistic. If the advertisement did not reveal how it was produced, it no doubt would have led many to believe that the actor was really involved. We may see more of these advertisements in the future, as they allow advertisers to use the likeness of recognisable public figures to promote local coffee shops or hardware stores to people who live near them, even if the actor in question has never heard of a certain business or product. According to Kshetri et al. (2024), the Cadbury advertisement was quite successful. As they note, "[a]bout 130,000 ads were reported to be created that featured 2000 stores" (Kshetri et al., 2024, p. 6). The authors also note that as of mid-August 2023, the advertisements have "been viewed 94 million times on YouTube and Facebook" (Kshetri et al., 2024, p. 6).

The advertisement is impressive from a technical point of view, and is no doubt a clever ad campaign. However, the technology does raise serious ethical concerns that reveal themselves in other cases. For example, in October of 2023, an Australian TV and radio host, Hamish Blake, was "deepfaked"—that is, his likeness and voice were used to advertise weight loss gummies without his knowledge or consent. The quality of the deepfake, which included video, was good enough to fool some who had listened to Blake over the years into thinking that it really was him (though the quality of the deepfake was of a poorer quality than others). In an interview on an Australian radio station, 2GB Sydney, Blake confirmed that it was indeed not him doing the advertisement and said that while the deepfake did not cause him too much harm, it was concerning to think about what it would be like when the technology improves (see Fordham, 2023).

An important point that Blake also raised was that since he had been on radio and TV for two decades, there were hours and hours of examples of his voice. However, what was concerning was that his consent was not sought to use these data to help create a deepfake. Those with public profiles, or those with audio and video recordings of themselves online, may be at risk of this happening to them in the future. A case of a different kind occurred in 2024, which involved OpenAI and one of its ChatGPT voices, Sky, which according to some resembled the actor Scarlett Johansson. Upon hearing the voice, Johansson said that it "sounded so eerily similar to mine that my closest friends and news outlets could not tell the difference" (as cited in Robins-Early, 2024). OpenAI had originally approached her to do a voice for them, but she declined. Johansson was reported as saying that she was "shocked, angered and in disbelief" (as cited in Englezos, 2024) over the existence of the voice. OpenAI has denied the claim that they based the voice on her, however.

Might there be something *intrinsically* unethical about deepfakes? I agree with Adrienne de Ruiter (2021) that there is not. In some contexts, their use seems entirely appropriate. How to distinguish then, the ethically appropriate uses of deepfakes from the unethical ones? According to de Ruiter, three factors are central to determining whether a deepfake is morally problematic:

(i) "whether the deepfaked person(s) would object to the way in which they are represented";
(ii) "whether the deepfake deceives viewers"; and
(iii) "the intent with which the deepfake was created".

(2021, p. 1328)

In the cases involving Hamish Blake and Scarlett Johansson, both expressed their disapproval and objected to the deepfakes of them, as stated in (i). In Hamish Blake's case, deception was involved, and there was an intent to mislead audiences, as mentioned in conditions (ii) and (iii). In Scarlett Johansson's case, while some were misled into believing it was really her (condition (ii)), it is less clear that OpenAI had the intention to deceive users. Using de Ruiter's (2021) three conditions as a guide, which certainly seems to match up with my own ethical intuitions, and possibly yours too, we would conclude that these instances are unethical. The Arnold Schwarzenegger or Shah Rukh Khan deepfakes, on the other hand, might serve to entertain or even be designed for artistic purposes, and we might not expect the actors to object to them. If labelled correctly, they would not mislead anyone.

The three conditions outlined by de Ruiter (2021) are useful in helping us to distinguish ethical from unethical deepfakes; however, one notable omission in the account is an explicit consideration of informed consent. Even if Arnold Schwarzenegger would not object to a deepfake of him being produced, might there be something wrong with the causal sequence of events here—that is, should permission (or consent) be sought before the deepfake is created? Consider an analogy: even if your neighbour would not object to you borrowing their electric drill, it would generally be a good idea to ask first.

This is a difficult question to answer because in some cases, such as in art or entertainment, while it might be considered a polite gesture to ask for consent, it might not be a morally necessary one. For example, it might not be morally necessary for a person to get informed consent before they create an interesting piece of art that involved a deepfake of a famous actor in a well-known film scene, if it was neither deceptive nor sought to mislead. Additionally, in cases where a person has died and consent can never be sought, the issue becomes even more complex. However, of course, in other contexts, such as the one involving Blake and Johansson, consent does seem important. Even if you *think* that the person would not object to the deepfake, the process of getting consent ought to be secured. After all, just like with one's emotions, one's likeness (e.g., their voice, image, characteristics, etc.) might be closely tied to one's personal identity. Individuals might react quite differently. Even though the deepfake might not be real, its resemblance might be so strong that it may make the person feel uncomfortable, even if it's not misleading or deceptive. And even though the deepfake might not be real, you might not want it out there at all.

To be sure, in such cases people would "object to the way in which they are represented", as de Ruiter puts it, so we might not need to account for consent in order to say what would be wrong with such cases. However, it might be hard to know how one would respond without obtaining consent first. Consent would address this ambiguity. The request for consent does however lead to a practical problem. Exactly how people would give consent to others to use their likeness online remains a big challenge. Requiring a famous actor to process multiple consent applications for their likeness to be used seems onerous (compare the impracticality of the frequent cookie pop-up windows that we discussed in the previous chapter). A type of automated consent could potentially be useful here, though it does not seem ideal, as it would seem to require a kind of request process for deepfakes which may not be easy to set up.

On the other hand, regardless of how onerous the process of giving consent may be, it seems morally necessary in other cases, especially since it can be used to blackmail people (see Citron & Chesney, 2019) and also to create deepfake pornography. The recent short film for example, "My Blonde GF: the experience of being deepfaked for pornography", directed by Rosie Morris (2023), tells the story of an individual, Helen, who was the victim of a pornographic deepfake. In the film, Helen describes her traumatic experience—noting the anxiety and fear that followed the deepfake and how it negatively affected her life. She notes, that since she has a public profile as a writer, images of her were available online (similar to the cases above).

An important point of the short film involves her account of how she reported the incident to the police. She notes that they told her there was nothing that they could do, since the deepfaked images were not real, and so not technically "revenge porn"; in other words, there was a loophole in the law (cf. Mubarak et al., 2023). The film ends with the alarming statistic that 96% of deepfakes are non-consensual pornographic material featuring women (Morris, 2023). Even if consent is not something that is morally necessary for all deepfakes, there is a subset of them, such as ones involving pornography, where a failure to get consent is a serious issue.

In the next few years, the law will undoubtedly play an important role in regulating the sharing of deepfakes. In 2023, an Online Safety Bill, which would make the sharing of non-consensual deepfake porn images illegal (Bushby, 2023), was scrutinised by the UK parliament. It was given Royal Assent in October 2023. In Australia, similarly, the Albanese government introduced new laws in 2024 that banned the sharing of *non-consensual* deepfake pornography (see Bovill, 2024). Legal measures may be required to stop pornographic and harmful political deepfakes, but it would seem problematic to ban all non-consensual deepfakes, since there are so many of them now, and not all of them would seem to cause much harm, such as the humorous ones mentioned above. A mechanism that requires subjects to give informed consent could theoretically provide a way for people to manage the sharing of harmful, or undesirable, deepfakes. However, as mentioned above, a challenge would remain with respect to how this would be set up.

Given that it might be easy to produce deepfakes and given that people cannot realistically be expected to manage requests to allow deepfakes themselves, online companies will need to play an important role in managing this space, which might require them to go beyond the law. Social media companies like Facebook or Instagram wield a lot of power in distributing deepfake images or videos. There are, however, already some positive signs that they will be interested in addressing the issue. In May 2024, Meta announced that it would start applying "Made with AI" labels to AI-generated videos, images, and audio posted on its platforms (Paul, 2024). This is a positive step forward, but we might also question whether it goes far enough. As discussed above, some might not want deepfakes out there, even if they are labelled "made with AI".[7]

Here lies an opportunity for companies to welcome external ethics review committees (as discussed in Chapter 4). As deepfake technology gets more sophisticated, and easier to use, we may see its proliferation. If the companies which provide platforms for deepfakes to be shared online are not active in thinking about how to manage their use now, it may be harder to control later.[8] In terms of informed consent, all of this presents a challenge. Harmful deepfakes do not arise because people are not fully aware of what they are consenting to, but rather from a lack of involvement in the process at all.

7.3 Generative AI and Informed Consent

One of the most significant advances in AI over the past few years has been the development of Generative Artificial Intelligence (hereafter, "GenAI"), exemplified by platforms like OpenAI's ChatGPT and Microsoft's Co-pilot. These technologies, based on large language models (LLMs), offer users text-based responses to the prompts they provide. However, their emergence has sparked debate with respect to the implications they have for the future of work and education. Like many of my colleagues who work at a university, for example, it is already common to see students submitting essay questions to ChatGPT and handing in the answers from it as their own work. This raises questions about the purpose of education and the skills students should be learning. Has Gen-AI caused the "death of the essay" (cf. Walsh, 2023b), or will it help students develop their writing abilities? Only time will tell.

How does Gen-AI raise issues about informed consent though? An answer to this question can be found by reflecting on how it functions. In his recent book, *What Is ChatGPT Doing . . . and Why Does It Work?*, Stephen Wolfram gives a basic overview of how ChatGPT works. He says:

> [T]he basic task for ChatGPT is to figure out how to continue a piece of text that it's been given. So to get it "training examples" all one has to do is get a piece of text, and mask out the end of it, and then use this as the "input to train from"—with the "output" being the complete, unmasked piece of text . . . but the main point is that—unlike, say, for learning what's in images—there's no "explicit tagging" needed; ChatGPT can in effect just learn directly from whatever examples of text it's given.
>
> (2023, p. 34)

One of the key features of ChatGPT, as Wolfram points out, is that it can perform "unsupervised learning" (2023, p. 34), from the many examples of text that it is given. Where do these data come from? As Matt Burgess of *Wired* has noted, ChatGPT gets its data from three main sources: the web, data licensed from others, and the text you actually type into it (see Burgess, 2023). An ethical issue about consent arises here due to the obtaining of these data without permission. Some authors, for example, were surprised to discover that their books were amongst the data used to train the model. And according to Wolfram, many books were used. He notes that "5 million digitised books have been made available" (2023, p. 55) on the web. If a percentage of those books were used, should OpenAI have sought consent first?

In July 2023, Ella Creamer (2023) reported in the *Guardian* that the authors Mona Awad and Paul Tremblay had filed a lawsuit against OpenAI, claiming that the company had used their books to train the LLMs without their permission. Books make for good examples to train ChatGPT, of course—compared to say social media posts, or blogs—as the writing is typically of a much higher quality. However, as Creamer (2023) also notes, there is "secrecy" about how many books are used. One estimate noted by Creamer is that the number is close to 300,000. While the litigation might fail, as Dilan Thampapillai notes, he also notes that it "is just the first salvo in a major AI-driven groundshift in copyright" (2023).[9]

Also in 2023, Lucy Knight reported in the *Guardian* that Margaret Atwood, Viet Thanh Nguyen, and Philip Pullman (and 8,000 others) signed an open letter to Open AI asking that *permission* be granted and *compensation* given to the authors whose books were used for training (Knight, 2023). In the letter, the following three demands were asked for:

1. Obtain permission for use of our copyrighted material in your generative AI programs.
2. Compensate writers fairly for the past and ongoing use of our works in your generative AI programs.
3. Compensate writers fairly for the use of our works in AI output, whether or not the outputs are infringing under current law.

> We hope you will appreciate the gravity of our concerns and that you will work with us to ensure, in the years to come, a healthy ecosystem for authors and journalists.
>
> (Authors Guild, 2023)

It is important to note that the open letter does not categorically oppose the use of the authors' books, only that some sort of permission or compensation be offered for the use of their work. The seeking of permission is also important as it provides a kind of symbolic value. If we recall from Chapter 1, there is value in giving people choice, and communicating what is being done with their data. Walker says with respect to the medical consent context that the "opportunity to choose, and even more so being denied that opportunity, *reveals something* about how healthcare professionals see their patients" (2022, p. 62, my emphasis). We might wonder, analogously, what the using of texts without consent reveals about the companies using these data to train their LLMs.

These questions are difficult to address, given the novelty of the technology, but will be important for scholars to focus on, given that LLMs like ChatGPT and Copilot will likely be applied to an increasing number of use cases in the future. One option would be to simply require companies to get permission or consent. For example, Schwitzgebel et al. (2024), have recently published a study on whether LLMs could produce "expert" level philosophy text. In order to answer this question, they of course needed training data from philosophical texts. To do this, they examined the work of Daniel Dennett, who collaborated with the researchers by providing them with the "entire digitally available corpus of his philosophical work" (2024, p. 242)—which was 15 books and over 250 articles. He was thus able to give informed consent for his work to be used. This may work well in small studies such as this one, but how would a large company like OpenAI or Microsoft possibly get consent from all the authors' works they use? This would be difficult to achieve. Not only might some authors be deceased, but it would be hard to know where to start in obtaining consent from thousands of authors.

Might it be possible to compensate users, then, since the texts have already been used? One problem with doing so is that it may be hard to know *how* a certain work contributes to the LLM. In the Dennett example, his work obviously contributed to the project, as the project was focused on his work. But if we are talking about hundreds of thousands of works that collectively train an LLM, it may be hard to know how one single text or group of texts contributed. Commenting on the lawsuit that Awad and Tremblay filed against OpenAI, Andres Guadamuz from the University of Sussex said "ChatGPT may work "exactly the same" if it had not ingested the books themselves" (as cited in Knight, 2023). This is because the LLM could have been trained on discussions about the books from users, blog posts, and so on.

Might OpenAI have benefited from subjecting its training data collection processes to ethics review, of the kind discussed in Chapter 4? Quite possibly. One challenge, however, is that the company may have predicted that there would be objections to their data collection processes and thus not be motivated to be transparent and allow people to scrutinise them, and thus "slow them down". Furthermore, the company may be hesitant to reveal too much about how their practices work in fear that rival companies will learn trade secrets (recall the Transparency Problem from Chapter 3).

On the other hand, given that it is not just authors who are potentially affected by Open AI's data collection processes, but also members of the general public, there may be greater pressure applied to them as more people become aware of how such data are collected. As Uri Gal, Professor in Business Information Systems at the University of Sydney, says "[i]f you've ever written a blog post or product review, or commented on an article online, there's a good chance this information was consumed by ChatGPT" (Gal, 2023). Here, an ethics review committee may have had important suggestions to make about the use of such data, even if their collection at the time was legal.

Of course, ethics review committees may struggle with novel issues, like the rest of us, as there may not be any previous cases to draw upon, and debates about what the company should do may arise. However, they might still be well-placed to offer guidance related to more familiar matters that will also face such companies. For example, in light of some of the issues discussed here, OpenAI added an opt out option on their website in the form of an "OpenAI Personal Data Removal Request".[10] This allows those concerned with OpenAI's use of their personal data to be removed from the data set. An ethics review committee may have suggested that this option should have been given to users from the outset. Furthermore, an ethics review committee may have suggested that OpenAI should have provided more transparency about how the feature works. According to Burgess (2023) of *Wired,* for example, it is not clear that the removal request removes your personal data from the answers that ChapGPT gives, or whether it also removes your data from the training data set. And of course, ethics committees could have worked with OpenAI to make sure that their privacy policy explained such information, possibly even suggesting the use of visuals to help explain certain policies.

7.4 Bluetooth Trackers

If you are like me, and tend to misplace things, you might find the idea of a Bluetooth tracker a lifesaver. In the last few years, various trackers have entered the market. In 2021, Apple for instance released their AirTags, which are compact circular tracking devices that can help Apple users locate their personal items—whether they have lost them or they have been stolen. Other brands, such as Samsung with their Galaxy Smart Tag, and Life360's Tile, have also entered the market. Like all new technologies, ethical challenges can arise in the way we choose to use these devices. One issue is non-consensual tracking. For example, one user put an Apple AirTag in an ex-girlfriend's car without her knowing; and the Sports Illustrated model Brooks Nader found one in her pocket without any idea of how it got there (Ray, 2022).

In their recent piece in *The Verge*, Chin and Song (2022) suggest that there are several specific issues with Apple's AirTags that pertain to the problem of people being tracked without their *consent*. They note that while trackers have been around for years, Apple AirTags raise two unique issues (even though other trackers on the market face similar issues). The first has to do with the size of Apple's network: since the trackers work by connecting with other Bluetooth devices, and since Apple have a large network, this allows for more accurate location data, compared to trackers with smaller networks. This enables people to pinpoint the location of someone with greater accuracy. The second concern they raise has to do with the marketing of the product—that is, it is not marketed as a spying device; and being an Apple product, the abuser might not think they are doing anything wrong by tracking someone.

In the book so far, we have for the most part looked at the problems of informed consent through the lens of the difficulties data subjects face with respect to managing their privacy online. These problems are familiar by now. However, the consent processes involved in the use of AirTags do not neatly fit into this discussion. Certainly, they involve the collection of personal data, namely, the location of a person's whereabouts. But non-consensual tracking, such as non-consensual personal data collection for the purpose of training LLMs, or creating deepfakes, represents a different kind of category altogether.

In contrast, if one has no interest in using Facebook, one can always choose not to use the site, even if the use of so-called "shadow profiles" complicates this (see Quodling, 2018). If you are not comfortable with the idea of Bluetooth tracking, or with your data being used to train LLMs, or to create deepfakes, you cannot simply refrain from using the service (insofar as this is a meaningful choice in other contexts)—you are simply "thrown into the process", so to speak. As such, focusing on improving consent-gathering practices (e.g., through the use of automated consent processes or adding visuals) might be less important than a focus on establishing legal measures in order to ensure individuals' rights are protected.

Nevertheless, there still might be a role for companies to work with ethics committees, in order to ensure that websites, and the technology itself, can protect people's privacy as much as possible. Apple for example has developed some anti-stalking software. If someone is moving with an "unfamiliar" AirTag on their device, for instance, their iPhone can be alerted. Second if the AirTag is parted from its owner for a long period of time, it will make a noise audible enough to alert those who are not aware they are travelling with one. And third, even if you do not have an iPhone, Android users can download a "Tracker Detect app" (cf. Chin & Song, 2022), if they believe they are being tracked.

These approaches show how software design can help with privacy concerns, even though such approaches have flaws. Having to download and install a tracker-detection app may require a user to be tech-savvy. Furthermore, while a notification can be useful, determining when they should be sent remains a vexed question. As Chin and Song note, Apple was initially criticised because the time taken to notify people was too great, namely, 72 hours. This means that a potential victim could be tracked for a long period of time before becoming aware that they were being tracked. Apple has since updated its software, and the current time it takes is around 8–24 hours. Specifying what the right amount of time should be is a difficult question, as there are many factors to consider.[11] If the notifications are too frequent, then users might become annoyed; if they are too infrequent, then security issues could arise. As Chin and Song say, "the longer it takes from the time an AirTag is planted to the point when it alerts the victim, the more information an ex or spouse can potentially collect about their victim's daily activities" (2022).

Questions about what an appropriate window of time looks like, how users should be notified if travelling with unwanted trackers, or whether there are pre-emptive measures one can undertake to disable trackers are difficult questions, but it is important to note that they are closer to normative (ethical), questions rather than technical ones. In this domain, ethics committees could be useful then. The fact that Apple changed the notification time from 72 hours, which was deemed too long, indicates that they are responsive to feedback. Ethics committees could analyse certain practices *before* products are released to the public. As we have seen in this book, it is common for companies to make a change to a policy, or data collection practice, after push back from the public or when they are issued with legal fines. While such mechanisms can prove effective in bringing about change, there remains the issue of the harm done to data subjects during the time between the start and end of the practices. If ethics approval could be sought before products or services were launched, this might be one way in which harm to data subjects could be reduced.

7.5 Blockchains and Informed Consent

Over the past decade, blockchain technologies have captured considerable attention and have been employed in various use cases.[12] If you have been following the rise of cryptocurrencies like Bitcoin (BTC) or Ethereum (ETH) or have been involved in a "smart contract", you may be aware that they use blockchain technologies. Here, I will briefly consider whether they could be used to facilitate informed consent. First, what is blockchain technology? Essentially, it is a ledger system, that is shared by a network of "nodes", which are devices, typically computers (cf. Gonçalves et al., 2024). One of the key features of the technology is that it is decentralised, meaning that no one node on the network has the only copy of it or controls it. One advantage of this is that no one individual can manipulate the ledger to their advantage. Unlike a Word document, or Excel file, on your computer, you cannot simply alter the ledger in whatever way you see fit. The majority of other nodes on the network must verify any changes too. This makes the ledger "tamper-resistant" as Gonçalves et al. (2024, p. 1021) put it. It is only once there is consensus amongst the nodes can information be "stored" in files, which are the "blocks", on the ledger. The linked blocks are called "chains". The ledger is "append-only" meaning that once information is added it cannot be deleted (Gonçalves et al., 2024, p. 1022). There are "permissioned" and "permissionless" types of blockchains, as Gonçalves et al. (2024) point out. They differ in their restrictions of who can join and maintain the network—specifically, who has permission to "publish blocks".

The unique characteristics of blockchain technology have made it appealing to those looking to uphold the integrity of stored information. Since people cannot easily manipulate records until consensus from other nodes is obtained first, a nefarious actor, or even a team of cyber criminals, could not fraudulently change it. This is why smart contracts have been gaining traction. They can self-execute when certain conditions are met, ensuring fairness and enforceability. Once a contract is recorded in the ledger, its details cannot be changed retrospectively, for example. In recent years, there have been discussions about other applications. To pick just two examples. There has been interest in using the technology in the medical context. Shanthapriya and Vaithianathan (2022), for example, note that blockchain technologies could be used to protect medical health records. Additionally, blockchain technology has potential in providing supply chain transparency. Azad et al. (2023), for instance, discuss how blockchain technologies could be used to give consumers awareness of where certain food products originate from. If each step is on the blockchain, then it can be accessed and seen by people, thereby upholding transparency.

Blockchain technologies may lead to many different use cases and could even bring about significant changes to the way that businesses operate and society in general, as some have predicted (see Marr, 2023). But could the technology also help with informed consent? The answer is "quite possibly", as some have already begun to consider how consent forms in the medical context—especially in clinical trials—could take advantage of the technology. In a recent study, Mak et al. (2021) sought to empirically investigate whether informed consent procedures, in clinical trials, could be improved by using blockchain technologies. First, consider their articulation of some of the problems currently facing consent processes in clinical trials:

> The informed consent process, which is predominantly paper-based, is susceptible to errors as consent forms are often long, convoluted, and complex in nature. Additionally, poor communication between parties can lead to a lack of informed consent because of a failure to perform reconsent procedures that may be required prior to the implementation of protocol changes.
>
> (2021, p. 2)

The consent processes that we have examined so far are not paper-based but do suffer from similar problems of length and miscommunication. The results of this study may thus be relevant to our concerns. What did the authors find, then? They ask participants to take part in a "pilot study" where they tested the effects of using blockchain technology. An online portal allowed participants to "grant" or "withdraw" informed consent, and "reconsent" during the trial process; and also allowed them to acquire clinical trial "status data" (2021, p. 3). The experimenters found positive results, noting that 91% of participants "increased their confidence that their safety and well-being were being ensured" (2021, p. 7) and 82% "felt that blockchain technology increased their awareness regarding their trial status and upcoming procedures" (2021) Since the experiment only had a small number of participants, the results should be viewed with caution. However, the experiment does show that the technology could hold promise for consent procedures in general.

Would similar results hold for online consent procedures? It is possible, as the experiment showed that the blockchain technology helped participants gain awareness of what was happening in the clinical trial and provided participants with more engagement about their participation. As we have seen in the book so far, transparency problems are widespread; and there are also general misunderstandings about how our personal data are used online. If data subjects could manage their privacy through blockchain technology, this could prove to be beneficial. However, there is a problem with such a proposal, namely, it has the potential to overwhelm users. A person may only be involved in one clinical trial at a time, whereas a person on the internet gives away a lot of personal information to potentially thousands of companies—managing all of this would be difficult.

A more promising alternative may be to store automated consent settings or agreements on the blockchain. This would allow records to be accessed easily, showing users what companies have used their data. Records could be automatically accessed, and consent preferences honoured. How would this improve informed consent? If it gave users more *confidence* that their settings were being upheld or gave them greater *awareness*, then that would be worth exploring. How could the technology actually help to *inform* users, however? One thing to consider is that the easier data subjects find the process of managing their consent settings, the more confident they will feel about managing their privacy—which is obviously something that can facilitate informed consent.

In a recent article, Porsdam Mann et al. (2021) focused on how blockchain technologies could empower patients, in the context of medical research, by giving them greater control over how their medical data are used. The authors claim that the "use of blockchain technologies could give patients control over who may access their data" (2021, p. 244). In the authors' view, this could increase autonomy, as patients would be able to monitor who has permission to view their medical data. Patients could easily modify permissions by updating blockchain transactions whenever they wanted to do so. Porsdam Mann et al. discuss three different ways in which the system could be used. The first would grant data subjects the "sole power" to determine who accesses their data; the second would "include some default permissions on an opt-out model"; and a third would remove the opt-out option, and thus "mandate data access" (2021, p. 247). If we consider the first option, it is easy to see how it would increase autonomy, as patients would have complete control over who has permission to view their data. On the complete control model, the authors state:

> [A]ccess to sensitive medical data might be kept private or granted only to select entities, whereas less sensitive data might be put up for donation, or, from the point of view of some start-ups, possibly even for sale. The blockchain thus provides a practical means of implementing meta-consent.
>
> (2021, p. 247)

Giving people this type of control appears to address some of the issues we have explored in this book. If a comparable system could be established for data subjects to manage how their personal data are used online, it could be beneficial. However, as mentioned earlier, there may be concerns about burdening users with too great a task. Managing one's medical records is one thing; managing online consent is another. Moreover, implementing such a system could potentially require companies to invest time and resources. Medical practitioners may have a vested interest in using the technology as it could empower patients. It is difficult to see how companies operating in the data economy would be as equally motivated.

Alternatively, blockchain technology could be *combined* with automated consent technology. As discussed in Chapter 6, automated consent functionalities could reduce the burden on users. While blockchain technologies may not directly address informed consent issues, they could help to streamline how individuals manage their privacy, via automated consent, for example, thereby encouraging users to have deeper engagement with their choices. On the other hand, if this can already be achieved through automated consent functionalities, then the use of blockchain technology may become redundant. Much will depend on how both technologies advance.

I will discuss one final challenge with blockchain technology, however, that pertains to the GDPR's requirement that data subjects have a right to be forgotten (see European Union, 2016). We have not spoken much about this problem so far, but it is importantly related to informed consent.

Suppose you have done something embarrassing in the past, or have committed a crime many years ago, or there is just something you just do not want found online. Search engines could still bring up these kinds of information from your past, and in some cases things that are not true. When it comes to blockchain technology, what makes it a secure technology also makes it a potentially dangerous technology. As Wahlstrom et al. suggest: "[t]he right to be forgotten enshrines a legitimate right to request that personal information be erased from the Internet, so that it cannot be found by search engines" (2020, p. 4). Yet at the same time, if you do not give your consent for certain personal data to be there forever, that is an issue. As Gonçalves et al. say, the "GDPR entitles the users to request the deletion of their personal data (barring some exceptions) which is at odds with the immutability of blockchain, a key pillar for enabling trust in those systems" (2024, p. 1022).

Gonçalves et al. suggest a technical solution that could help. They consider whether it is "possible to create a system that overcomes the major challenges of storing personal data in a blockchain", while at the same time upholding the benefits of the blockchain which include, "auditability, verifiability, tamper resistance", and also be GDPR compliant (2024, p. 1021). Their answer is "yes", although their solution is technical, and cannot be explored in depth here. The authors claim that by adding an off-chain storage capacity, data can be protected "keeping the qualities of blockchain, such as tamper-proof and the immutability of records" (2024, p. 1031). Whether such technical solutions will truly work is an open question, but this shows that technical solutions in principle may indeed be sought.

Transparency and awareness are key features that are required for informed consent. If blockchain technology can be implemented to improve these aspects, then their use will be beneficial. On the other hand, the transparency that blockchain technology promises also threatens to undermine privacy. If such issues could be overcome, however, then the technology could be used to help secure informed consent online.

7.6 Conclusion

If we consider what the future might hold for our personal data privacy, one thing seems inevitable: more personal data will be used and collected than is currently the case, as more devices become connected to the Internet of Things. When examining emotional AI, deepfakes, Generative AI, Bluetooth trackers, and blockchain technology, it becomes clear that informed consent needs to be rethought. The process of passing on a "list of facts" to users without ensuring their understanding is unlikely to facilitate comprehension and leave data subjects well placed to provide informed consent.

As the capacity to gather information about us increases—as our discussion revealed—there is the risk that our personal identities could become jeopardised. The effectiveness of ethics committees, visual consent processes, or automated consent mechanisms remains uncertain, but they hold promise. One significant issue is that as companies accumulate more and more data about us, it becomes increasingly challenging for us to self-manage our privacy. I will address this problem in the next chapter, where I discuss the so-called "privacy paradox".

Notes

1 For more information, see their website: https://www.zenus.ai/about.
2 While it is unclear that "engagement" is an emotional state itself, there are several emotional states one could undergo that might suggest that one is "engaged".
3 See National Sleep Foundation (2023).
4 See Brown (2024) for a discussion on the newly proposed *right to mental privacy*. He also discusses some of the language used to advocate for it.
5 See Smith (2024) for a discussion about some of the controversies surrounding the facial recognition company Clearview AI, who "scraped" images from the internet, such as from social media sites (see Chapter 6: "Face Value").
6 The advertisement can be viewed on YouTube here: https://www.youtube.com/watch?v=5WECsbqAQSk.
7 See Dixon (2024, pp. 222–225) for a discussion on how we could develop systems that allow users and applications to verify the authenticity of deepfakes. He discusses the idea of using "attestations" on blockchains which could help "vouch" for the authenticity of deepfakes. This may be useful as deepfakes get so realistic that we may not be able to tell they are deepfakes.
8 For a dystopian example of this, see the *Black Mirror* episode "Joan is Awful" directed by Ally Pankiw (2023). The episode features a woman, Joan, whose likeness and story are used for an AI-generated show without her informed consent. When she tries to object, her lawyer informs her that she actually did provide consent (i.e., express consent), when she signed up for the platform—of course, it is revealed that she did not read the terms and conditions.
9 Creamer (2024) notes that in 2024, two of the copyright infringement lawsuits that were brought against Open AI were "partially" dismissed by a California Court.
10 For more information, see the OpenAI privacy policy, effective January 31, 2024: https://openai.com/policies/privacy-policy.
11 Apple's statement on how they updated their software to address unwanted tracking can be found on their website: https://www.apple.com/au/newsroom/2022/02/an-update-on-airtag-and-unwanted-tracking/.
12 See, for example, Bernard Marr's (2023) book, the *Future Internet*.

8 On the Privacy Paradox

In this final chapter, I will discuss the so-called *privacy paradox*—the phenomenon where people claim to value privacy yet behave in ways that suggest they do not (e.g., fail to read privacy policies and give away large amounts of personal data). While our focus has been on informed consent, questions about privacy are, of course, never far away. Consent allows one to control the personal information one desires to keep *private* and the types one desires to disclose.

I will argue, following Daniel Solove, that the privacy paradox is not much of a paradox at all. The "paradoxical" behaviour people exhibit when they give away large amounts of personal data stems from a problem that lies at the heart of this book, namely, the difficulty of online privacy self-management. Whereas Solove is pessimistic that privacy self-management is something that can be achieved, I remain optimistic that small-scale changes to consent-gathering procedures, of the kind outlined in the book, can make privacy self-management possible. In Section 8.1, I give an overview of the paradox, noting subtle key differences in the various formulations of it. In Section 8.2, I explain why the privacy paradox is not much of a paradox at all. In Section 8.3, I turn to Solove's pessimism about the possibility of privacy self-management and argue that there are grounds for optimism regarding the potential for online privacy self-management.

8.1 What Is the Privacy Paradox?

To get a better sense of what the privacy paradox is, and how it relates to our current concerns about informed consent, I will consider three recent definitions of it. First, Dienlin et al. suggest that the "privacy paradox states that people's concerns about online privacy are *unrelated* to their online sharing of personal information" (2023, p. 1043, my emphasis). Second, Øverby suggests that "[t]he privacy paradox is a concept in which online users state that they are concerned about privacy but disclose personal data

DOI: 10.4324/9781032626048-8

nonetheless" (2021, p. 1). And third, Solove says, "[p]eople express strong concern about privacy yet fail to take easy and inexpensive steps to protect their privacy" (2021, p. 2). In all three definitions, a tension between what people *say* about privacy, and how they actually *behave* when it comes to sharing their personal data, is described. However, while the same basic problem is articulated in each, there are some subtle differences between them that I think are important to point out, in order to see why the privacy paradox might not be so paradoxical at all.

First, Dienlin et al.'s definition suggests that people's concerns about privacy are "unrelated" to their actions when it comes to data sharing. It is worth asking why that is so. After all, if someone shares personal information *because* they are unaware of the risks of doing so—say because they believe data companies do not sell their personal data to data brokers, then they would not be acting paradoxically—they would simply have a false belief about how their data are being used. This is a problem no doubt, but not quite paradoxical. In Øverby's definition, the paradox is stated in terms of the "clash" between people's "concerns" about privacy and the disclosing of their personal data. Again, it is worth asking what the nature of peoples' concerns are, and why they clash with their disclosure of personal data. If they clash due to the fact that people believe they do not have a say in how their data are being used, this may not be so paradoxical either. And in Solove's definition, he stresses the "ease" of the steps users can take to protect their privacy. It is worth questioning whether these steps are really so easy to take.

Regardless of how we understand the fine-grained details of the paradox, there is of course a problem here that deserves our attention. Consider an average internet user who claims to worry about data privacy, and then consider the fact that this same person gives away large amounts of their personal data. One might wonder how such a person can do so, given their concerns about privacy. On the other hand, we might worry that this observation, by itself, might not give rise to a paradox at all. Let us pick a data subject, Graham, who claims to care about data privacy, and also gives his personal data away. Is Graham's behaviour paradoxical? I would say *not necessarily*. It could be that Graham, while privacy conscious, is happy to share his personal data, in exchange for the use of services such as YouTube, Google, or Spotify. Graham, who we may imagine has a lot of time on his hands, may have read all the privacy policies and terms and conditions agreements that apply to him and has a good understanding of exactly what is happening with his data. He may not want the contents of his diary or his family photos (which are printed in photo albums) shared but is happy with his online personal data being collected and used. We can imagine that Graham has seriously considered the implications of sharing his data, and then given his informed consent to companies to use his data.

(For the sake of argument, I assume that companies have been transparent in the privacy policies that Graham has read.) Suppose that Graham spends many hours a week going through privacy policies, making sure that he has a good understanding of them. Whenever he is unsure, he seeks legal advice and consults experts in his country. Again, we can ask, "Is Graham's behaviour paradoxical?" I think the answer is "no", even though Graham states that he is concerned about privacy while also disclosing his personal data.

Now, of course, Graham is not our average internet user, and so possibly, the privacy paradox is not meant to capture this kind of case. However, the example involving Graham highlights that informed consent is quite important to understanding the so-called paradox, even though it might not be explicit in the formulations of it above. In Graham's case, we have an example of a fully informed data subject who actually consents to his data being shared. Nothing seems paradoxical here. Caring about privacy, after all, does not mean that one never wants to share their personal information. Being concerned about privacy, in the personal data context, is better understood as being concerned about having the ability to control who has access to your personal data. In some contexts, for example, a person may want personal data to be shared widely. In other contexts, one may only want a select few people to know something. One may have, for example, a strong desire to share a medical diagnosis *only* with their spouse. One may want to keep the diagnoses hidden from work colleagues because it is a "private matter". To say they wish to keep their medical diagnosis "private" in this context just means that the person wants to *control* who knows the medical diagnosis; or alternatively have *autonomy*, with respect to deciding who gets to know.

What should we say about cases where people assert that they care about privacy but share their data without providing informed consent? There are two types of cases to distinguish here. First, there are cases where people do not provide informed consent and are indifferent to their personal data being shared. The second type involves individuals who assert that privacy matters to them and do have a problem with their personal data being used and collected. The data subjects in the former category are of great interest, but I will not be concerned with them here since such people's behaviours are not paradoxical—even if we say that they *should* be concerned. It is the latter group that I will concern myself with here. It does, at least at first pass, seem paradoxical to assert that "privacy matters" and then give away your own personal data in ways that might be in tension or conflict with your privacy preferences.

Let us take a concrete example: the case of data brokers, of the kind discussed throughout the book. Suppose someone claims to value privacy, and also suppose that this person nevertheless gives express consent for their personal data to be sold to other companies to build a profile about them in order to send them targeted advertisements. Is their behaviour paradoxical? I think the answer depends on what the person understands to be occurring. If they have "shared" their data without understanding whether their data will be used in ways that conflict with their preferences, then it is hard to see how their behaviour is paradoxical. This person may not even possess any beliefs about data brokers because they do not know they exist. Furthermore, we might also imagine that such a person provides consent on a website simply by virtue of using the website (cf. Jones et al., 2018, p. 66). In this last case, one may not even be aware that one has given consent or is sharing their personal data.

We may note that in such cases, people's concerns about online privacy are indeed unrelated to their online sharing of personal information, as Dienlin et al.'s (2023) definition suggests. However, in such cases, it is not clear to me that we should say that anything paradoxical has arisen. In the case above, the lack of any "relation" between the person's privacy concerns and their behaviour can be explained by examining what they believe. In Øverby's (2021) definition of the paradox, he notes that people claim to care about privacy but "disclose personal data nonetheless". Unless, however, we know the nature of the disclosure, we surely cannot say that anything paradoxical has arisen, especially if such disclosures occur without the person's awareness. Data sharing without awareness of course is common and something we have observed throughout the book. So, we cannot simply look at behaviour, then, to establish the paradox. One must also look to psychology. After all, someone who claims to be terrified of sharks and is swimming in shark-infested waters need not be acting paradoxically, if they are not aware the water is shark-infested. According to Solove's (2021) definition, users do not take simple steps to protect their data, even though they supposedly care about privacy. As we have seen in the book, however, it is uncommon that meaningful alternatives are given to data subjects, so that they can take such steps to protect their privacy.

8.2 Is the Privacy Paradox a Myth?

I have provided a somewhat sceptical response to the privacy paradox—that is, I have expressed doubt about the extent to which such data-sharing behaviours are paradoxical, unless some assumptions about a person's psychology and informed consent are also made. In suggesting this, I am aligning myself with others in the literature such as Solove, who call the privacy paradox a "myth" (2021). Solove claims that the privacy paradox is essentially an *illusion*, which is "created by faulty logic, unwarranted generalizations, and conflated issues" (2021, p. 4). But what does it mean to say that the privacy paradox is a myth? According to Solove, it is a myth because people's attitudes and behaviour only "appear to be in conflict" (2021, p. 4). He does not deny that people can behave as if they do not care about privacy but argues that there are some legitimate reasons why people give away personal data while also claiming to care about privacy. First, let us look at a different kind of paradox in order to make a comparison to the privacy paradox.

Consider a widely discussed paradox in philosophy that has attracted a lot of attention, namely, Moore's paradox, named after the English philosopher G.E. Moore. According to Moore's paradox, it would be absurd for someone to assert that *P*, while simultaneously claiming to believe that *P* is not true. For example, if I were to tell you, "Sydney is in NSW, but I don't believe it is" you would most likely be confused about what I have just said. If I don't believe that Sydney is in NSW, then why would I assert that it is? There is a paradox here for the following reason: it is not a contradiction for one to judge (and assert) that Sydney is NSW yet not believe it; yet it would be absurd for someone to say such a thing. Although beliefs and judgements are distinct mental phenomena, after all, it does seem like when one judges something to be the case, they would usually believe it to be the case. To resolve the paradox, as Green and Williams (2007) explain, one needs to address the question "[i]n what does this form of absurdity consist?" (2007, p. 11). One needs to provide an explanation of the seemingly absurd, yet not necessarily contradictory, content of Moore Paradoxical sentences.[1]

While not exactly the same, it is useful to look at the privacy paradox in comparison to Moore's paradox because it encourages us to examine the underlying logic of the privacy paradox. The first thing that we are required to do in analysing Moore's Paradox is to recognise the seeming absurdity of Moore Paradoxical sentences. Yet, as the discussion above suggested, it is not clear there is anything absurd to explain in all instances of the privacy paradox. Suppose that someone asserts that "privacy is important" and then proceeds to use a website that collects and uses their personal data. Is there anything *absurd* or even contradictory about the person's actions? Again, not necessarily, for the reasons given above. What about situations where people do claim to care about privacy and are aware that their data are being collected and used by companies: are there any contradictions there? Certainly, there is tension, and maybe even in some cases contradiction, but it is important to ask *why* this is the case. For example, if a lecturer tells their students that they care about responding to all of their student emails and gets to the end of the week with 100 emails in their inbox, we need additional information before concluding that their behaviour is paradoxical. It might simply be that they are trying their best to respond, but there are simply too many emails coming in. Their behaviour could still be paradoxical, of course, if they asserted that they care and then showed no interest in checking their inbox; but it need not necessarily be paradoxical—and that is the key point.

An explanation of why the "privacy paradox" occurs could thus help us to explain why it might not be so paradoxical at all. One such explanation is given by Solove, who suggests that a failure of self-management is the reason for people's purportedly paradoxical behaviour. He says the following:

> The reason for people's failure to manage privacy effectively I argue, is based on the futility of what I call "*privacy self-management*." Privacy self-management involves the various decisions people must make about their privacy and the tasks people are given the choice to do regarding their privacy, such as reading privacy policies, opting out, changing privacy settings, and so on. Managing one's privacy is a vast, complex, and never-ending project that does not scale; it becomes *virtually impossible* to do comprehensively.
>
> (2021, p. 3 my emphasis)

Here Solove provides a reason why people's behaviours do not necessarily cohere with their assertions about privacy. His answer is that data subjects face the impossible task of self-managing their privacy, so it should not be surprising that they fail to do so. The fact that we "allow" companies to use our data in ways that we might not sign off on if we understood and reviewed each decision, is not a paradox, but a result of our failure to achieve a task that lies beyond the reach of possibility.

The central argument that I have made in this book suggests a similar point. If you cannot review all the privacy policies that apply to you, or keep track of where your data goes, then it is difficult to say that you have offered informed consent to companies to collect and use your personal data. While Solove's (2021) article on the privacy paradox does not contain the word "consent", he does make a reference to it an earlier article which does. In it he says, "[p]rivacy self-management takes refuge in consent" (Solove, 2013a, p. 1880). I take this to mean that consent mechanisms are one of the central ways that we self-manage our privacy. Given that it is "virtually impossible", as Solove suggests, to self-manage our privacy, we would expect informed consent to often fail to be given and obtained for the same reasons.

As was pointed out in earlier chapters: if "ought implies can", and people cannot self-manage their privacy effectively, then it would be unjust to blame them for not doing so. Consider just one of the problems we looked at in Chapter 3, namely, the Re-purposed Data Problem. As data analytics become more sophisticated, there will be greater opportunities to re-use data that have already been collected. This makes it increasingly difficult to self-manage how your data are being used, potentially for many years. Moreover, as more devices connect to the Internet of Things, this task seems virtually impossible. Solove points out that the "best people can do is manage their privacy haphazardly" (2021, p. 5). He goes on to suggest that "[p]eople will never gain sufficient knowledge of the ways in which personal data will be combined, aggregated, and analysed over the years by thousands of organizations" (2021, p. 5). This is certainly a large problem and helps to explain why people claim to care about privacy and yet give their personal data away.

One important reason that I believe it is important to look at this problem through the lens of informed consent is that doing so requires us to focus on what people actually believe about what is occurring with their data (informed consent, recall, requires that people have knowledge of what they are consenting to). Solove is right that privacy self-management is difficult; but it might be so difficult that some might not even recognise the importance of privacy self-management in certain contexts—that is, some might not be aware that their data can be misused. Scrutinising what people believe can help to reveal this. For example, if someone believes that a company would not misuse their data, and there is virtually no risk of their personal data being collected, then it might be hard to motivate them to care about privacy self-management.

Let us consider some examples of this. In her recent book, *I Have Nothing to Hide: And 20 Other Myths About Surveillance and Privacy*, Heidi Boghosian (2021) describes several *myths* that people currently believe about privacy. Here are 10 noteworthy ones that feature in the book, and are titles of various chapters:

1. "I have nothing to hide, so I have nothing to fear" (p. 19);
2. "No one wants to spy on kids" (p. 70);
3. "Police don't monitor social media" (p. 77);
4. "Metadata doesn't reveal much about me" (p. 96);
5. "Congress and the courts protect us from surveillance" (p. 129);
6. "Surveillance doesn't influence how I act" (p. 142);
7. "Teenagers don't care about privacy" (p. 149);
8. "Surveillance affects everyone equally" (p. 156);
9. "Surveillance cannot predict future behaviour" (p. 175);
10. "There's nothing I can do to stop surveillance" (p. 183).

Suppose you believe one of these myths—suppose, for example, that you believe that metadata doesn't reveal much about you. And suppose that you also care about privacy. If you visit a website that states that it collects metadata, you might not be so concerned about understanding how metadata are used, or be motivated to manage your privacy settings, since you might *not* believe that metadata poses any privacy-related risks (cf. Solove, 2013b). If a privacy expert were to observe your behaviour from afar, they might conclude that your behaviour is paradoxical. After all, metadata *can* reveal information about you, and it could undermine your privacy. Similarly, in the case of surveillance or any of the other "myths" that Boghosian describes. If someone believes that there is nothing that they can do to stop surveillance, then why would they bother to spend time reading privacy policies, since their actions cannot make a difference anyway.

Thus, to simply say, as the formulations above suggest, that it is paradoxical that people's behaviours are "unrelated" to their concerns about privacy, fails to take these other considerations into account. This is not to say that the privacy paradox can never arise—of course it could. It is easy to imagine someone asserting that privacy matters to them and then giving away their data with full awareness of what they are doing. Human behaviour can be paradoxical and contradictory at times. When we examine how things operate online, however, we may not wish to ascribe paradoxical attitudes to those behaviours, at least as a general way to explain the phenomenon. Consider what occurred with the Facebook-Cambridge Analytica case: no one was even consulted about what was being done with their data. Or consider the case of Meta's VPN service as looked at in Chapter 5: people likely believed that the VPN would protect their personal data, even though in reality their data were being shared to Meta for advertising purposes. Would we describe these cases as ones where people "gave away" their data? If so, the behaviour is hardly paradoxical, as the issue lies in people's inability to manage how their data are being used.

***

One might respond to this general discussion by pointing out that there are concrete examples of the privacy paradox that have been well-documented.[2] For example, in a recent study conducted by Aleisa et al. (2020), an experiment was performed to test the "existence of the privacy paradox in the Saudi Arabian IoT [Internet of Things] domain" (p. 1). The experimenters aimed to see whether people who care about privacy would continue to use a smart plug, once the experimenters revealed evidence of a specific smart plug's "privacy violations". The experiment involved 46 Saudi Arabian participants, who were given a "smart plug", which allowed them to turn a lamp on or off via their smart phone. The participants were shown the associated smart plug's privacy policy, which, according to the experimenters, none of them read. They "simply agreed to commence with the study" (Bongiovanni et al., 2020). After a couple of hours, the participants were told about how much data the smart plug collected (this was the revealed "privacy violation"). Although "trust" in the product went down, after the reveal, 15 participants continued to use it, while the remaining participants tried to take further precautions—such as hiding personal information or complaining online. The experimenters claimed that "[i]t is clear that a mere increase in awareness is not going to convince everyone to take action to preserve their privacy" (Aleisa et al., 2020, p. 13). And in discussing their results in the *Conversation*, the researchers stated that despite the fact that people were concerned about their privacy, they were still "willing to sacrifice some of it in exchange for the convenience afforded by an internet-connected device" (Bongiovanni et al., 2020).

Do such results undermine the main points I have made above? Do they exemplify the main idea behind the privacy paradox? I contend that they do not. Again, following Solove, I think it is better to interpret these results as illustrating the challenges of privacy self-management, rather than revealing paradoxical behaviour. Consider for example the "privacy violation" that occurred in the experiment. The authors state that they showed the participants "how much of their data the IoT-connected plug was harvesting" (Bongiovanni et al., 2020), but since none of the participants actually read the privacy policy, before using it, it is not clear what they actually believed about what personal data were taken. Should we understand "privacy violations" as ones that pertain to violations of the law, misleading data collection practices, or simply ones that collect personal data? Regardless, you might think it is notable that some participants continued to use the smart plug device, even though *trust* in the device went down. Might that result exemplify the main idea behind the privacy paradox? After all, the experimenters note that the participants' "behaviour did not align with their concerns" (Bongiovanni et al., 2020).

One challenge that makes this question difficult to assess is that it is hard to know what each individual believed—not only regarding their beliefs about the extent to which the convenience of certain IoT devices outweighs their risks, but also about privacy self-management in general. In some circumstances, people might feel like they do not have the ability to negotiate with companies, and thus feel powerless to take any meaningful steps to protect their data. Some might also share their personal information, even if they are uncomfortable with doing so, or do not "trust" a device, because they believe one of the myths examined above—for example, there's nothing one can do to stop surveillance.

One year on from the Facebook-Cambridge Analytica Scandal, one might have thought that large amounts of people would have stepped away from Facebook, thus taking steps that are "easy and inexpensive" as Solove (2021, p. 2) says, to manage their privacy. Yet interestingly, the site's active numbers went up (see Naughton, 2019). What explains this? Did people simply stop being concerned about what Facebook was doing? It is possible that this describes some people, but in other cases, people might simply have been unprepared to lose connection with friends on the site or might have relied on the site for work purposes. The experimenters (Aleisa et al., 2020) might be right that a mere increase in awareness of what personal data are being collected might not convince everyone to *take action*. What is less clear is the extent to which those same people are actually aware of the meaningful alternatives or actions that they could take to self-manage their personal data. There may also be a "fear of missing out" (FoMO) (cf. Tandon et al. 2021), that may prevent users from leaving a website or an app even when they become uncomfortable with the associated data collection practices employed.

Consider, further, some of the results from an Australian Government Report titled "Australian Community Attitudes to Privacy Survey 2017 Report" which found that "[e]ight in ten Australians (79%) are uncomfortable with businesses sharing their personal information with other businesses" (Australian Government, 2017, p. 11). Most people said that they were "concerned about organisations sending their personal information overseas (93%)" (Australian Government, 2017, p. ii). When asked if they care about their personal information being shared online, most people say they do, with 69% of Australians reporting that they were more concerned about their online privacy, compared to five years earlier (in 2012) (Australian Government, 2017, p. 31). However, when asked "[d]o you normally read the privacy policy attached to any internet site?" (Australian Government, 2017, p. 31), 65% of Australians said that they did not (Australian Government, 2017, p. 31).

At first pass, these results may seem to present us with examples of the privacy paradox: people claim to care about privacy yet fail to take simple steps to self-manage their privacy, say by reading a privacy policy and then making an informed choice about how their personal data are shared. It should be clear by this point what is wrong with this response. The task of self-managing our privacy is *not* easy. It is simply not possible for the vast majority of people to read all of the privacy policies that apply to them. And even when one does read a privacy policy, however, one will still struggle at times to successfully self-manage their privacy because companies often fail to be transparent, and do not always offer meaningful alternatives to users (e.g., you can either choose to accept Facebook's terms and conditions or not use the site).

8.3 Is Privacy Self-Management Impossible?

I now turn to Solove's pessimistic conclusion about the impossibility of privacy self-management. Like Solove, I think the privacy paradox is a myth brought about by some of the problems associated with "privacy self-management", particularly the difficulty of providing informed consent to companies regarding the collection and use of our personal data. Solove provides a basic explanation of the problem as follows:

> People will *never gain sufficient knowledge* of the ways in which personal data will be combined, aggregated, and analyzed over the years by thousands of organizations. Resignation is a rational response to the impossibility of privacy self-management.
>
> (2021, p. 5, my emphasis)

In this book, I have reached a similar conclusion. Not only are contemporary privacy policies and terms and conditions lengthy and rarely read or understood, but they often do little to empower individuals to control how their personal data are collected and used. Furthermore, individuals will never be able to read and understand all the privacy policies or terms and conditions that apply to them. And even if they could get through a large percentage of them, they certainly cannot keep pace with the constant changes and the diverse stakeholders who may access their data for extended periods (as discussed in the Re-purposed Data Problem in Chapter 3). Providing informed consent thus becomes difficult, making "resignation" a rational response to this situation, as Solove suggests. Understood in these terms, the so-called privacy paradox starts to look less paradoxical.

Is privacy self-management really impossible, however, and what are the implications of this conclusion if it were true? Certainly, it is currently difficult to self-manage one's privacy, and I agree with Solove that "doing countless tasks to exercise more control is an endless and impractical task—and the control is often illusory" (2021, p. 6). The implications of Solove's conclusion that privacy self-management is impossible seems to point us in the direction of privacy regulation, rather than try to improve privacy self-management. He recommends, as a result that "[p]rivacy regulation can be best strengthened by regulating in ways that don't rely on individuals managing their own privacy" (2021, p. 6). This would seem to follow, since if privacy self-management is indeed impossible, then the solution for improving online privacy should not focus on improving consent provision and collection practises.

Although I agree with Solove that regulation will need to play an important role in restricting the collection and use of personal data, I remain unconvinced that privacy self-management is "impossible". And thus, I reject Solove's idea that privacy regulation should be our central focus for improving privacy concerns. My contention in this book has been that if consent practices could be improved upon, then the task of self-managing one's privacy can become easier, and possibly eventually effective. Recall some of the suggestions offered here. I suggested that ethics committees could help to ensure that companies do not mislead data subjects. I suggested that simpler consent procedures can be developed, some of which could include visual images, or comics, to encourage transparency and understanding. And I also suggested the possibility of consent being automatable in ways that align with data subjects' choices (e.g., through the use of browsers, or applications, that can save user's consent preferences and provide consent for them).

Neither one of these solutions on their own will solve the central problem we have considered here, I have argued, but together they provide an alternative solution to Solove's pessimistic one about privacy self-management being impossible. Of course, I would be the first to admit that these proposed solutions will need to be empirically tested in various contexts before their efficacy really can be demonstrated. Could automated consent really work, for example, on a large scale? Might the novelty of adding visuals to consent procedures fade with time, thus lowering the efficacy of the solutions? Privacy self-management is indeed difficult now, but these potential solutions show that we need not resign ourselves to its impossibility.

8.4 Conclusion

In this chapter, I have argued, following Solove, that the privacy paradox is a "myth". There is a perfectly rational explanation why people's concerns about privacy conflict with their behaviour, namely, the extreme difficulty, at present, of self-managing one's privacy. As I have argued throughout the book, current practices of securing informed consent, the mechanism that allows data subjects some control over what occurs to their personal data, does not currently function well. Yet unlike Solove, I do not take this conclusion to point towards the futility of privacy self-management. I have argued throughout the book that we can improve the practices of providing and obtaining informed consent.

In the last few years, several solutions have started to emerge that together may help us to provide informed consent online. Of course, by themselves, they surely cannot provide the kind of robust privacy self-management that Solove envisions. But by using them together, they may give data subjects a chance to provide informed consent, thus giving them control over what occurs to their data. In our current paradigm, "resignation", with respect to privacy self-management, as Solove suggests, may indeed be the default position for data subjects to take. Yet if the ways of improving online consent that I have presented here turn out to be feasible, then data subjects may actually be able to achieve what Solove claims to be impossible.

Notes

1 In Andreotta (2024), I provide an explanation of why the paradox occurs, namely, that judgements actually give rise to belief. For a book-length analysis on moral paradoxes, see Smilansky (2007). In the introduction of Smilansky's book, he provides an overview of what constitutes a "paradox".

2 My claim is not that the privacy paradox never arises, of course. I only claim that before we can say that the disconnect between an *assertion that privacy is important* and a *data sharing episode* is paradoxical, we first need to understand more about a person's psychology—that is, what the person actually believes.

9 Conclusion

In this book, I have argued that we need to rethink our understanding of informed consent in the big data age. Not only are we often unaware of how our personal data are being used and by whom, but there are also significant harms associated with the misuse of our personal data. These issues threaten to worsen, given that more and more devices are connecting to the Internet of Things, which is giving rise to the growth of the data economy. While some boldly advocate for the end of the "data economy" (see Véliz, 2021, p. 249), this need not be the only way to address the problem.

According to an alternative approach, that I have presented in this book, we should focus on how data subjects can regain control of the way that their data are being collected and used by implementing small-scale-everyday changes to the way that consent is sought and used by data controllers and processors. In looking at the medical context, in Chapter 1, I attempted to locate a starting point for this project. There we saw how the understanding of consent has changed over time. It is no longer something that is there to simply "protect" doctors or physicians. It is now seen as something that can "assist" patients in making decisions and protect them from harm. An analogous change in perspective, I have argued, needs to occur in the online data collection context.

Certainly, there are key differences between the consent provided before a surgical procedure and a Google search, but there are similarities too. Harm can be caused to data subjects from the misuse of personal data, as shown in Chapter 2, just like a medical procedure can cause harm to patients—even if the kinds of harms are different in the two contexts, nonetheless. In both contexts, however, consent provides one with the capacity to self-manage the process and assess the associated risks or harms. Without this knowledge, self-management becomes difficult. In the existing paradigm, online consent is often seen as something there to protect companies. A 10,000-word privacy policy makes sense in this context because it might exist to protect companies from legal fines, of

DOI: 10.4324/9781032626048-9

the kind we have looked at. For data subjects, consent procedures, such as the ones involving privacy policies and terms and conditions are often seen as "obstacles" that prevent them from using the service in question. I have argued that we need to rethink the purpose of online informed consent as something that empowers data subjects, rather than a process that involves the "transfer of information" without considering how that information is understood.

This is where smaller everyday improvements to online consent practices may indeed be effective. While the law may be able to successfully prevent certain deceptive practices, it may be less effective in providing practical advice about how to facilitate more meaningful consent in various contexts. For example, if a company is fined for misleading users, say by telling users it won't share personal data, while actually doing so, the law can help correct this. The law can obviously do much, further, to address the three problems with online consent practices presented in Chapter 3, namely, the Transparency Problem, the Re-purposed Data Problem, and the Meaningful Alternatives Problem. When it comes to context-specific guidance, however, it may be less effective, as was shown in Chapter 4. According to the GDPR, for example, the processing of personal data should be transparent. Achieving this in practice can be a challenge, however. As Lundgren (2020a) has pointed out, a seemingly endless "pop-up spam festival" to self-manage the use of cookies might seem to be transparent, and provide us with meaningful alternatives, but from a practical perspective, it is ineffective, due to the sheer volume of these pop-ups we are required to engage with. So even if laws protect data subjects from the most egregious behaviours from companies, we will need to go beyond them, to ensure that data subjects can successfully self-manage their privacy.

The proposals outlined in this book, which seek to address the question of how online consent practices can be improved upon, of course need to be tested, developed, and refined further based on how data subjects react to them. Although I have provided reasons and argumentation for these proposals, they require empirical validation. Could companies ever be motivated to subject their personal data collection and use practices to ethical review, if they were not legally required to—as we considered in Chapter 4? Would people actually engage with privacy policies or terms and conditions if they were shortened, more comprehensible and engaging, and contained visuals—as examined in Chapter 5? Would automated consent, as outlined in Chapter 6, provide users with the capacity to self-manage their privacy or might it undermine the very notion of informed consent? These important questions must be subjected to empirical analysis. Furthermore, as the technology advances, as explored in Chapter 7, the efficacy of the solutions offered here will need to be re-examined as new challenges emerge. I have, nonetheless, expressed optimism about their viability.

I hope to have convinced the reader of the following: many small-scale changes to consent practices have the potential to make large-scale improvements to privacy self-management. As I argued in Chapter 8, privacy self-management need not be seen as "impossible", as Solove (2021) argues. Certainly, at present, it is very difficult for data subjects to manage the collection and use of their personal data, but we need not resign ourselves to this impossibility.

I also hope that this book generates discussions on the importance of online informed consent and stimulates debate on how we can improve online consent practices moving forward. A collective effort is required from multiple stakeholders: from government agencies, the private sector, and the public. As I have stated many times in the book, large-scale data collection and use presents us with many opportunities in addition to challenges. If we can continue to develop better methods of obtaining and providing online consent, then we may be able to enjoy all the benefits of the data economy, while also being in control of our privacy—achieving the best of both worlds.

References

ACCC (Australian Competition and Consumer Commission). (2020, July 27). *Correction: ACCC alleges Google misled consumers about expanded use of personal data*. https://www.accc.gov.au/media-release/correction-accc-alleges-google-misled-consumers-about-expanded-use-of-personal-data

ACCC (Australian Competition and Consumer Commission). (2022a, August 12). *Google LLC to pay $60 million for misleading representations*. https://www.accc.gov.au/media-release/google-llc-to-pay-60-million-for-misleading-representations

ACCC (Australian Competition and Consumer Commission). (2022b, December 9). *Court dismisses ACCC case against Google*. https://www.accc.gov.au/media-release/court-dismisses-accc-case-against-google

Affectiva. (2024). *Affectiva automotive AI for driver monitoring systems*. https://www.affectiva.com/product/affectiva-automotive-ai-for-driver-monitoring-solutions/

Agarwal, P. (2022, December 31). Emotional AI is no substitute for empathy. *Wired*. https://www.wired.com/story/artificial-intelligence-empathy/

Aleisa, N., Renaud, K., & Bongiovanni, I. (2020). The privacy paradox applies to IoT devices too: A Saudi Arabian study. *Computers & Security*, *96*, 101897.

Allhoff, F. (2003). Business bluffing reconsidered. *Journal of Business Ethics*, *45*, 283–289. https://doi.org/10.1023/A:1024103612716

Andersen, C. B. (2020). Musings on the comic book contract project and legal design thinking. *Journal of Graphic Novels and Comics*, *12*(1), 1–7. https://doi.org/10.1080/21504857.2020.1731563

Andreotta, A. J., & Lundgren, B. (2024). Automated informed consent. *Big Data and Society*, *11*(4). https://doi.org/10.1177/20539517241289439.

Andreotta, A. J. (2021). The hard problem of AI rights. *AI & Society*, *36*, 19–32. https://doi.org/10.1007/s00146-020-00997-x

Andreotta, A. J. (2023). Partial first-person authority: How we know our own emotions. *Review of Philosophy and Psychology*. https://doi.org/10.1007/s13164-023-00698-6

Andreotta, A. J. (2024). Transparency, Moore's Paradox, and the concept of belief. In A. J. Andreotta & B. Winokur (Eds.), *New perspectives on transparency and self-knowledge*. Routledge.

Andreotta, A. J., Kirkham, N., & Rizzi, M. (2022). AI, big data, and the future of consent. *AI & Society*, *37*, 1715–1728. https://doi.org/10.1007/s00146-021-01262-5

Asokan, A. (2024). Amazon appeals privacy fine of 746 million euros. *Bank Info Security*. https://www.bankinfosecurity.com/amazon-appeals-privacy-fine-746-million-euros-a-24094

Associated Press. (2019, September 5). YouTube fined $170m for collecting children's personal data. *The Guardian*. https://www.theguardian.com/technology/2019/sep/04/youtube-kids-fine-personal-data-collection-children-

Australian Government. (2017). *Australian community attitudes to privacy survey 2017 report*. https://www.oaic.gov.au/__data/assets/pdf_file/0024/5739/acaps-2017-report.pdf

Authors Guild. (2023). *Open letter to generative AI leaders*. https://authorsguild.org/app/uploads/2023/10/Authors-Guild-Open-Letter-to-Generative-AI-Leaders.pdf

Autorité de protection des données. (2022). *Case number: DOS-2019–01377. Concerning: Complaint relating to transparency & consent framework*. https://www.edpb.europa.eu/system/files/2022-03/be_2022-02_decisionpublic_0.pdf

Auxier, B., Rainie, L., Anderson, M., Perrin, A., Kumar, M., & Turner, E. (2019). *Americans and privacy: Concerned, confused and feeling lack of control over their personal information*. Pew Research Center. https://www.pewresearch.org/internet/2019/11/15/americans-attitudes-and-experiences-with-privacy-policies-and-laws/

Azad, R. U., Ahammed, K., Salam, M. A., & Efat, M. I. A. (2023). Block-chain aided cluster based logistic network for food supply chain. In M. S. Satu, M. A. Moni, M. S. Kaiser, & M. S. Arefin (Eds.), *Machine intelligence and emerging technologies. MIET 2022. Lecture notes of the institute for computer sciences, social informatics and telecommunications engineering, vol. 491*. Springer. https://doi.org/10.1007/978-3-031-34622-4_34

Baker, R. (2019). *The structure of moral revolutions: Studies of changes in the morality of abortion, death, and the bioethics revolution*. MIT Press.

Bakir, V., Laffer, A., & McStay, A. (2023). Blurring the moral limits of data markets: Biometrics, emotion and data dividends. *AI & Society*. https://doi.org/10.1007/s00146-023-01739-5

Bankwest. (2021). *Pictures make a thousand words in visual style Australia-first*. https://www.bankwest.com.au/about-us/media-centre/news/pictures-make-a-thousand-words-in-visual-style-australia-first

Barnes, T. J. (2013). Big data, little history. *Dialogues in Human Geography*, *3*(3), 297–302. https://doi.org/10.1177/2043820613514323

Barrett, L. F. (2017). *How emotions are made: The secret life of the brain*. Mariner Books.

BBC News. (2019, April 12). Bounty pregnancy club fined £400,000 over data handling. *BBC News*. https://www.bbc.com/news/technology-47908222

BBC News. (2023, March 24). TikTok banned from UK Parliament over security concerns. *BBC News*. https://www.bbc.com/news/uk-politics-65055712

Beauchamp, T. L. (2011). Informed consent: Its history, meaning, and present challenges. *Cambridge Quarterly of Healthcare Ethics*, *20*, 515–523. https://doi.org/10.1017/S0963180111000259

Beauchamp, T. L., & Childress, J. F. (2008). *Principles of biomedical ethics* (6th ed.). Oxford University Press. (Original work published 1979)

Bellan, R. (2020, August 27). Facebook criticizes Apple's iOS14 privacy changes as harmful to small business. *Forbes*. https://www.forbes.com/sites/rebeccabellan/2020/08/27/facebook-criticizes-apples-ios14-privacy-changes-as-harmful-to-small-business/

Bloom, P. (2016). *Against empathy: The case for rational compassion*. Ecco.

Bobek, E., & Tversky, B. (2016). Creating visual explanations improves learning. *Cognitive Research: Principles and Implications*, *1*(1), 27. https://doi.org/10.1186/s41235-016-0031-6

Boghosian, H. (2021). *I have nothing to hide: And 20 other myths about surveillance and privacy*. Beacon Press.

Bongiovanni, I., Renaud, K., & Aleisa, N. (2020, July 29). The privacy paradox: We claim we care about our data, so why don't our actions match? *The Conversation*. https://theconversation.com/the-privacyparadox-we-claim-we-care-about-our-data-so-why-dont-our-actions-match-143354

Borg, J. S., Sinnott-Armstrong, W., & Conitzer, V. (2024). *Moral AI: And how we get there*. Penguin Press.

Bounty. (2023). *Bounty privacy policy*. https://www.bounty.com/info/privacy-policy

Bounty. (2024). *Bounty*. https://www.bounty.com

Bovill, M. (2024, June 2). Federal government to introduce ban on sharing of non-consensual deepfake pornography. *ABC News*. https://www.abc.net.au/news/2024-06-02/deepfake-pornography-sharing-image-based-abuse-criminal-prison/103923814

Bowie, N. E. (1999). A Kantian approach to business ethics. In R. E. Frederick (Ed.), *A companion to business ethics* (pp. 3–16). Wiley-Blackwell.

Brandsen, T., Boogers, M., & Tops, P. (2006). Soft governance, hard consequences: The ambiguous status of unofficial guidelines. *Public Administration Review*, *66*(4), 546–553. http://www.jstor.org/stable/3843940

Brave. (2024). *The browser that puts you first*. https://brave.com/

Bravo-Lillo, C., Cranor, L., Komanduri, S., Schechter, S., & Sleeper, M. (2014). Harder to ignore? Revisiting pop-up fatigue and approaches to prevent it. In *Proceedings of the 10th Symposium on Usable Privacy and Security* (pp. 105–111), Unenix.

Brennan, J. (2016). *Against democracy*. Princeton University Press.

British Medical Journal. (1996). The Nuremberg Code (1947). *British Medical Journal*, *313*. https://doi.org/10.1136/bmj.313.7070.1448

Broadbent, A. (2019). *Philosophy of medicine*. Oxford University Press.

Brown, C. M. L. (2024). Neurorights, mental privacy, and mind reading. *Neuroethics*, *17*, 34. https://doi.org/10.1007/s12152-024-09568-z

Brożek, B., Furman, M., Jakubiec, M., & Kucharzyk, B. (2024). The black box problem revisited. Real and imaginary challenges for automated legal decision making. *Artificial Intelligence and Law*, *32*, 427–440. https://doi.org/10.1007/s10506-023-09356-9

Burgess, M. (2021, August 5). Amazon's massive GDPR fine shows the law's power—and its limits. *Wired*. https://www.wired.com/story/amazon-gdpr-fine-shows-power-limits/

Burgess, M. (2022, May 23). How GDPR is failing. *Wired*. https://www.wired.com/story/gdpr-2022/

Burgess, M. (2023, May 9). How to delete your data from ChatGPT. *Wired*. https://www.wired.com/story/how-to-delete-your-data-from-chatgpt/

Burin, M. (2019, February 27). They resent the fact I'm not a robot. *ABC News*. https://www.abc.net.au/news/2019-02-27/amazon-australia-warehouse-working-conditions/10807308

Burrell, J. (2016). How the machine 'thinks:' Understanding opacity in machine learning algorithms. *Big Data & Society*, *3*(1), 1–12. https://doi.org/10.1177/2053951715622512

Bushby, H. (2023, June 18). Deepfake porn documentary explores its 'life-shattering' impact. *BBC News*. https://www.bbc.com/news/entertainment-arts-65854112

Byrne, E. (2022, August 12). Google fined $60 million for misleading some Australian mobile users about collection of location data. *ABC News*. https://www.abc.net.au/news/2022-08-12/google-fined-60m-misleading-mobile-users-location-data/101329790

Cabinet Office & Dowden, The Rt Hon. O. CBE. (2023). TikTok banned on UK government devices as part of wider app review. *GOV.UK*. https://www.gov.uk/government/news/tiktok-banned-on-uk-government-devices-as-part-of-wider-app-review

Cabitza, F., Campagner, A., & Mattioli, M. (2022). The unbearable (technical) unreliability of automated facial emotion recognition. *Big Data & Society*, *9*(2). https://doi.org/10.1177/20539517221129549

Cain, S. (2017, March 9). How the 20,699-word iTunes T&Cs became this year's hottest graphic novel. *The Guardian*. https://www.theguardian.com/books/2017/mar/08/terms-and-conditions itunes-t-and-c-graphic-novelrobert-sikoryak-interview

Carlson, R. V., Boyd, K. M., & Webb, D. J. (2004). The revision of the Declaration of Helsinki: Past, present and future. *British Journal of Clinical Pharmacology*, *57*(6), 695–713. https://doi.org/10.1111/j.1365-2125.2004.02103.x

Carr, A. Z. (1968). Is business bluffing ethical? *Harvard Business Review*, *46*(1), 143–153. https://hbr.org/1968/01/is-business-bluffing-ethical

Carter, S. E. (2022). A value-centered exploration of data privacy and personalized privacy assistants. *Digital Society*, *1*, 27. https://doi.org/10.1007/s44206-022-00028-w

Cass-Gottlieb, G. (2023). Regulatory intersections between competition, consumer and privacy laws speech. *ACCC*. https://www.accc.gov.au/about-us/media/speeches/regulatory-intersections-between-competition-consumer-and-privacy-laws-speech

Charles Sturt University. (n.d.). *Do I need to apply for ethics approval?* https://research.csu.edu.au/integrity-ethics-compliance/human/do-i-need-ethics-approval#:~:text=Yes%2C%20if%20you%20are%20doing,academic%2C%20divisional%20and%20centre%20staff

Chen, B. X. (2021, April 26). To be tracked or not? Apple is now giving us the choice. *The New York Times*. https://www.nytimes.com/2021/04/26/technology/personaltech/apple-app-tracking-transparency.html

Chin, M., & Song, V. (2022). AirTags are dangerous—Here's how Apple could fix them. *The Verge*. https://www.theverge.com/2022/3/1/22947917/airtags-privacy-security-stalking-solutions

Choi, H., Park, J., & Jung, Y. (2018). The role of privacy fatigue in online privacy behavior. *Computers in Human Behavior*, *81*, 42–51. https://doi.org/10.1016/j.chb.2017.12.001

Chomanski, B., & Lauwaert, L. (2023). Online consent: How much do we need to know? *AI & Society*. https://doi.org/10.1007/s00146-023-01790-2

Citron, D. K. (2022). *The fight for privacy: Protecting dignity, identity, and love in the digital age*. Chatto & Windus.

Citron, D. K., & Chesney, R. (2019). Deep fakes: A looming challenge for privacy, democracy, and national security. *California Law Review*, *107*, 1753–1820. https://scholarship.law.bu.edu/faculty_scholarship/640

Citron, D. K., & Solove, D. J. (2021). Privacy harms. *Boston University Law Review*, *102*, 793–863.

Clark, M. (2023, March 3). BetterHelp shared customer data while promising it was private, says FTC. *The Verge*. https://www.theverge.com/2023/3/2/23622227/betterhelp-customer-data-advertising-privacy-facebook-snapchat

Cockburn, G. (2021, February 28). Bankwest to introduce comic-style version of terms and conditions in bid to get customers to properly read contracts. *The Australian*. https://www.theaustralian.com.au/news/latest-news/bankwest-to-introduce-comicstyle-version-of-terms-and-conditions-in-bid-to-get-customers-to-properly-readcontracts/newsstory/f87f7b4487ac5e00719caad6418bab9f

Coeckelbergh, M. (2020). Artificial intelligence, responsibility attribution, and a relational justification of explainability. *Science and Engineering Ethics*, *26*, 2051–2068. https://doi.org/10.1007/s11948-019-00146-8

Coeckelbergh, M. (2024). *Why AI undermines democracy and what to do about it*. Polity Press.

Cohen, J. E. (2019). *Between truth and power: The legal constructions of informational capitalism*. Oxford University Press.

Cohen, S. (1999). "Good ethics is good business"—Revisited. *Business & Professional Ethics Journal*, *18*(2), 57–68. http://www.jstor.org/stable/27801090

Comic Book Contracts. (n.d.). *The Aurecon visual employment contract*. https://www.comicbookcontracts.com/aurecon-contract

CPRC (Consumer Policy Research Centre). (2020). *CPRC 2020 data and technology consumer survey*. https://cprc.org.au/wp-content/uploads/2020/12/CPRC-2020-Data-and-Technology-Consumer-Survey.pdf

Creamer, E. (2023, July 6). Authors file a lawsuit against OpenAI for unlawfully 'ingesting' their books. *The Guardian*. https://www.theguardian.com/books/2023/jul/05/authors-file-a-lawsuit-against-openai-for-unlawfully-ingesting-their-books

Creamer, E. (2024, February 15). Two OpenAI book lawsuits partially dismissed by California court. *The Guardian*. https://www.theguardian.com/books/2024/feb/14/two-openai-book-lawsuits-partially-dismissed-by-california-court

Crofts, P. (2020). Strategies of denial and the Australian Royal Commission into misconduct in the banking, superannuation and financial services industry. *Griffith Law Review*, *29*(1), 21–42. https://doi.org/10.1080/10383441.2020.1819266

Culnane, C., Rubinstein, B. I. P., & Teague, V. (2019). Two data points enough to spot you in open transport records. *Pursuit: University of Melbourne*. https://pursuit.unimelb.edu.au/articles/two-data-points-enough-to-spot-you-in-open-transport-records

Custers, B. (2016). Click here to consent forever: Expiry dates for informed consent. *Big Data & Society*, *3*(1). https://doi.org/10.1177/2053951715624935

Custers, B., van der Hof, S., & Schermer, B. (2014). Privacy expectations of social media users: The role of informed consent in privacy policies. *Policy & Internet*, *6*(13), 268–295. https://doi.org/10.1002/1944-2866.POI366

Dance, G. J. X., LaForgia, M., & Confessore, N. (2018, December 18). As Facebook raised a privacy wall, it carved an opening for tech giants. *The New York Times*. https://www.nytimes.com/2018/12/18/technology/facebook-privacy.html

Deakin University. (2021). *Human research ethics procedure*. https://policy.deakin.edu.au/document/view-current.php?id=239

De Rooy, R. (2019). *Creative contracts—Who are we and what do we do*. https://www.youtube.com/watch?v=EgshAS6GqOc

De Ruiter, A. (2021). The distinct wrong of deepfakes. *Philosophy & Technology*, *34*, 1311–1332. https://doi.org/10.1007/s13347-021-00459-2

Dienlin, T., Masur, P. K., & Trepte, S. (2023). A longitudinal analysis of the privacy paradox. *New Media & Society*, *25*(5), 1043–1064. https://doi.org/10.1177/14614448211016316

Dixon, C. (2024). *Read write own: Building the next era of the Internet*. Penguin.

Doss, A. F. (2020). *Cyber privacy: Who has your data and why you should care*. BenBella Books.
Driver, J. (2012). *Consequentialism*. Routledge.
Eckstein, L., McWhirter, R., & Stewart, C. (2022). Better mechanisms are needed to oversee HREC reviews. *Public Health Ethics*, *15*(2), 200–203. https://doi.org/10.1093/phe/phac010
EDPB (European Data Protection Board). (n.d.). *Data controller or data processor*. https://www.edpb.europa.eu/sme-data-protection-guide/data-controller-data-processor_en
Englezos, E. (2024, May 23). Scarlett Johansson's row with OpenAI reminds us identity is a slippery yet important subject. AI leaves everyone's at risk. *The Conversation*. https://theconversation.com/scarlett-johanssons-row-with-openai-reminds-us-identity-is-a-slippery-yet-important-subject-ai-leaves-everyones-at-risk-230677
ETI (Edelman Trust Institute). (2023). *Edelman trust barometer: The collapse of the purchase funnel*. https://www.edelman.com/trust/2023/trust-barometer/special-report-brand-trust
European Commission. (2022). *Regulation (EU) 2022/868 of the European Parliament and of the Council of 30 May 2022 on European Data Governance and Amending Regulation (EU) 2018/1724 (Data Governance Act)*. https://eur-lex.europa.eu/eli/reg/2022/868/oj
European Commission, D-GJC (Directorate-General for Justice and Consumers). (2016). The EU data protection reform and big data: Factsheet 2016. *Publications Office*. https://data.europa.eu/doi/10.2838/190200
European Union. (2016). *Regulation (EU) 2016/679 of the European Parliament and of the Council of 27 April 2016 on the protection of natural persons with regard to the processing of personal data and on the free movement of such data, and repealing Directive 95/46/EC (General Data Protection Regulation)*. https://eur-lex.europa.eu/eli/reg/2016/679/oj
Evans, J. (2024, September 11) Facebook admits to scraping every Australian adult user's public photos and posts to train AI, with no opt-out option. *ABC News*. https://www.abc.net.au/news/2024-09-11/facebook-scraping-photos-data-no-opt-out/104336170
Eyal, N. (2019). Informed consent. In E. N. Zalta (Ed.), *The Stanford encyclopedia of philosophy*. https://plato.stanford.edu/archives/spr2019/entries/informed-consent/
Faden, R. R., & Beauchamp, T. L. (1986). *A history and theory of informed consent*. Oxford University Press.
Favaretto, M., De Clercq, E., Schneble, C. O., & Elger, B. S. (2020). What is your definition of Big Data? Researchers' understanding of the phenomenon of the decade. *PLoS One*, *15*(2), e0228987. https://doi.org/10.1371/journal.pone.0228987
Feiler, T., Hordern, J., & Papanikitas, A. (Eds.). (2018). *Marketisation, ethics and healthcare: Policy, practice and moral formation*. Routledge.
Feller, G., & Burroughs, B. (2022). Branding kidfluencers: Regulating content and advertising on YouTube. *Television & New Media*, *23*(6), 575–592. https://doi.org/10.1177/15274764211052882
Filho, L. W., Wolf, F., Lange Salvia, A., Beynaghi, A., Shulla, K., Kovaleva, M., & Vasconcelos, C. R. P. (2020). Heading towards an unsustainable world: Some of the implications of not achieving the SDGs. *Discover Sustainability*, *1*(1), 2. https://doi.org/10.1007/s43621-020-00002-x

Floridi, L. (2012). Big data and their epistemological challenge. *Philosophy and Technology*, *25*, 435–437. https://doi.org/10.1007/s13347-012-0093-4

Floridi, L. (2018). Soft ethics, the governance of the digital and the General Data Protection Regulation. *Philosophical Transactions of the Royal Society A: Mathematical, Physical and Engineering Sciences*, *376*, 20180081. https://doi.org/10.1098/rsta.2018.0081

Floridi, L. (2019). *The logic of information: A theory of philosophy as conceptual design*. Oxford University Press.

Fordham, B. (2023, October 23). 'It's scary'—Hamish Blake warns about latest scam. *2GB Sydney*. https://www.2gb.com/its-scary-hamish-blake-warns-about-latest-scam/

FRA (European Union Agency for Fundamental Rights). (2020). *Your rights matter: Data protection and privacy*. https://fra.europa.eu/sites/default/files/fra_uploads/fra-2020-fundamental-rights-survey-data-protection-privacy_en.pdf

Francis, L. P., & Francis, J. G. (2017). *Privacy: What everyone needs to know*. Oxford University Press.

Francis, T., & Hoefel, F. (2018, November 12). *'True Gen': Generation Z and its implications for companies*. https://www.mckinsey.com/industries/consumer-packaged-goods/our-insights/true-gen-generation-z-and-its-implications-for-companies

Freeman, R. E. (1984). *Strategic management: A stakeholder approach*. Cambridge University Press.

Friedman, M. (1970). The social responsibility of business is to increase its profits. *The New York Times Magazine*, *32–33*, 122–124.

FTC (Federal Trade Commission). (2019, September 4). *Google and YouTube will pay record $170 million for alleged violations of children's privacy law*. https://www.ftc.gov/news-events/news/press-releases/2019/09/google-youtube-will-pay-record-170-million-alleged-violations-childrens-privacy-law

FTC (Federal Trade Commission). (2023, March 2). *FTC to ban BetterHelp from revealing consumers' data, including sensitive mental health information, to Facebook and others for targeted advertising*. https://www.ftc.gov/news-events/news/press-releases/2023/03/ftc-ban-betterhelp-revealing-consumers-data-including-sensitive-mental-health-information-facebook

Gal, U. (2023). ChatGPT is a data privacy nightmare. If you've ever posted online, you ought to be concerned. *The Conversation*. https://theconversation.com/chatgpt-is-a-data-privacy-nightmare-if-youve-ever-posted-online-you-ought-to-be-concerned-199283

Geier, C., Adams, R. B., Mitchell, K. M., & Holtz, B. E. (2021). Informed consent for online research—Is anybody reading? Assessing comprehension and individual differences in readings of digital consent forms. *Journal of Empirical Research on Human Research Ethics*, *16*(3), 154–164. https://doi.org/10.1177/15562646211020160

Gibbons, R. (2010). Transaction-cost economics: Past, present, and future? *Scandinavian Journal of Economics*, *112*, 263–288. https://doi.org/10.1111/j.1467-9442.2010.01609.x

Goldschlag, D., Reed, M., & Syverson, P. (1999). Onion routing for anonymous and private Internet connections. *Communication of the ACM*, *42*(2), 39–41.

Gomer, R., Schraefel, M. C., & Gerding, E. (2014). Consenting agents: Semi-autonomous interactions for ubiquitous consent. *Proceedings of the 2014 ACM International Joint Conference on Pervasive and Ubiquitous Computing: Adjunct Publication* (pp. 653–658). https://doi.org/10.1145/2638728.2641682

Gonçalves, R. M., da Silva, M. M., & da Cunha, P. R. (2024). Olympus: A GDPR compliant blockchain system. *International Journal of Information Security*, *23*, 1021–1036. https://doi.org/10.1007/s10207-02300782-z
Grant, N., Singer, N., & Krolik, A. (2023, August 17). YouTube ads may have led to online tracking of children, research says. *The New York Times*. https://www.nytimes.com/2023/08/17/technology/youtube-google-children-privacy.html
Grant, S. C. (2021). Informed consent—We can and should do better. *JAMA Network Open*, *4*(4), e2110848. https://doi.org/10.1001/jamanetworkopen.2021.10848
Green, M., & Williams, J. N. (2007). Introduction. In M. S. Green & J. N. Williams (Eds.), *Moore's paradox: New essays on belief, rationality, and the first person* (pp. 3–36). Oxford University Press.
Green, S., Hillersdal, L., Holt, J., Hoeyer, K., & Wadmann, S. (2023). The practical ethics of repurposing health data: How to acknowledge invisible data work and the need for prioritization. *Medicine, Health Care and Philosophy*, *26*(1), 119–132. https://doi.org/10.1007/s11019-022-10128-6
Grewal, P. (2018). Suspending Cambridge Analytica and SCL group from Facebook. *Meta*. https://about.fb.com/news/2018/03/suspending-cambridge-analytica/
Hadden, K. B., Prince, L. Y., Moore, T. D., James, L. P., Holland, J. R., & Trudeau, C. R. (2017). Improving readability of informed consents for research at an academic medical institution. *Journal of Clinical and Translational Science*, *1*(6), 361–365. https://doi.org/10.1017/cts.2017.312
Hallinan, B., & Striphas, T. (2016). Recommended for you: The Netflix prize and the production of algorithmic culture. *New Media & Society*, *18*(1), 117–137. https://doi.org/10.1177/1461444814538646
Hawe, P., Rowbotham, S., Marks, L., & Casson, J. (2022). The risk management practices of health research ethics committees may undermine citizen science to address basic human rights. *Public Health Ethics*, *15*(2), 194–199. https://doi.org/10.1093/phe/phab029
Herder, H., & Zhang, B. (2019). Unexpected and unpredictable: Factors that make personalized advertisements creepy. In *ABIS '19 Proceedings of the 23rd International Workshop on Personalization and Recommendation on the Web and Beyond* (pp. 1–6). https://doi.org/10.1145/3345002.3349285
Hern, A. (2017, July 14). Thousands sign up to clean sewage because they didn't read the small print. *The Guardian*. https://www.theguardian.com/technology/2017/jul/14/wifi-terms-and-conditions-thousands-sign-up-clean-sewage-did-not-read-small-print
Hern, A. (2019, April 13). Parenting club bounty fined £400,000 for selling users' data. *The Guardian*. https://www.theguardian.com/technology/2019/apr/12/parenting-club-bounty-fined-selling-users-data
Herschel, R., & Miori, V. M. (2017). Ethics & big data. *Technology in Society*, *49*, 31–36.
Hodge, N. (2022, July 29). One year later, Amazon GDPR fine details remain clouded. *Compliance Week*. https://www.complianceweek.com/regulatory-enforcement/one-year-later-amazon-gdpr-fine-details-remain-clouded/31913.article
Hollingworth, D. (2023, September 1). University of Sydney student data involved in third-party data breach. *Cyber Daily*. https://www.cyberdaily.au/commercial/9502-university-of-sydney-student-data-involved-in-third-party-data-breach
Holzinger, A., Goebel, R., Fong, R., Moon, T., Müller, K. R., & Samek, W. (Eds.). (2022). *xxAI—Beyond explainable AI*. Springer. https://doi.org/10.1007/978-3-031-04083-2_2

Horton, A. (2024, May 14). Inside the rise and fall of Ashley Madison: 'People literally lost their lives'. *The Guardian*. https://www.theguardian.com/tv-and-radio/article/2024/may/14/ashley-madison-netflix-documentary

Huddleston, T., Jr. (2022, February 8). TikTok shares your data more than any other social media app—And it's unclear where it goes, study says. *CNBC*. https://www.cnbc.com/2022/02/08/tiktok-shares-your-data-more-than-any-other-social-media-app-study.html

Hummel, P., Braun, M., & Dabrock, P. (2021). Own data? Ethical reflections on data ownership. *Philosophy & Technology*, *34*, 545–572. https://doi.org/10.1007/s13347-020-00404-9

Hunt, E. (2017, March 15). Amazon Kindle's terms 'unreasonable' and would take nine hours to read, choice says. *The Guardian*. https://www.theguardian.com/australia-news/2017/mar/15/amazon-kindles-terms-unreasonable-and-would-take-nine-hours-to-read-choice-says

Hurd, H. M. (1996). The moral magic of consent. *Legal Theory*, 2(2), 121–146. https://doi.org/10.1017/S1352325200000434

ISO (Information Commissioner's Office). (2019). *Data Protection Act 1988. Supervisory powers of the Information Commissioner. Monetary penalty notice.* https://www.skadden.com/-/media/files/publications/2019/04/privacy-and-cybersecurity-update-april-2019/ico_decision.pdf

Jones, M. L. (2021). Surveillance capitalism online: Cookies, notice and choice, and web privacy. In J. Lauer & K. Lipartito (Eds.), *Surveillance capitalism in America* (pp. 183–202). University of Pennsylvania Press.

Jones, M. L., Kaufman, E., & Edenberg, E. (2018). AI and the ethics of automating consent. *IEEE Security & Privacy*, *16*(3), 64–72.

Kahneman, D., & Tversky, A. (1972). Subjective probability: A judgment of representativeness. *Cognitive Psychology*, *3*(3), 430–454. https://doi.org/10.1016/0010-0285(72)90016-3

Kaiser, B. (2019). *Targeted: The Cambridge Analytica whistleblower's inside story of how big data Trump, and Facebook broke democracy and how it can happen again*. Harper.

Kang, C. (2016, March 7). Verizon settles with F.C.C. over hidden tracking via 'Supercookies'. *The New York Times*. https://www.nytimes.com/2016/03/08/technology/verizon-settles-with-fcc-over-hidden-tracking.html

Kant, I. (1993). *Groundwork of the metaphysic of morals* (3rd ed., J. W. Ellington, Trans.). Hackett. (Original work published 1785)

Karegar, F., Gerber, N., Volkamer, M., & Fischer-Hübner, S. (2018). Helping john to make informed decisions on using social login. *Proceedings of the 33rd Annual ACM Symposium on Applied Computing* (pp. 1165–1174), Association for Computing Machinery.

Kastrenakes, J. (2023, October 30). Facebook and Instagram launch a paid ad-free subscription. *The Verge*. https://www.theverge.com/2023/10/30/23938283/facebook-instagram-ad-free-subscription-eu

Kaye, B. (2023, July 26). Australia fines Facebook owner Meta $14 million for undisclosed data collection. *Reuters*. https://www.reuters.com/technology/australia-court-fines-facebook-owner-meta-14-mln-undisclosed-data-collection-2023-07-26/

Kearns, M., & Roth, A. (2019). *The ethical algorithm: The science of socially aware algorithm design*. Oxford University Press.

Kemp, K. (2023). Your body, our data: Unfair and unsafe privacy practices of popular fertility apps. *UNSW Law Research*. http://dx.doi.org/10.2139/ssrn.4396029

Kemp, K., Gupta, C., & Campbell, M. (2024). *Singled out—Consumer understanding—And misunderstanding—Of data broking, data privacy, and what it means for them.* Consumer Policy Research Centre. https://cprc.org.au/wp-content/uploads/2024/02/CPRC-Singled-Out-Final-Feb-2024.pdf

Kiener, M. (2021). When do nudges undermine voluntary consent? *Philosophical Studies*, *178*, 4201–4226. https://doi.org/10.1007/s11098-021-01644-x

Kiener, M. (2023). *Voluntary consent: Theory and practice*. Routledge.

Kim, N., Oh, H., & Choi, J. K. (2023). A privacy scoring framework: Automation of privacy compliance and risk evaluation with standard indicators. *Journal of King Saud University—Computer and Information Sciences*, *35*(1), 514–525. https://doi.org/10.1016/j.jksuci.2022.12.019

Kindt, E. J. (2013). The risks involved upon the use of biometric data and biometric systems. In *Privacy and data protection issues of biometric applications. Law, governance and technology series* (pp. 275–401). Springer. https://doi.org/10.1007/978-94-007-7522-0_4

Kirkham, N., & Andersen, C. B. (2020). The potential of medical consent contracts using visuals. *American Journal of Biomedical Science & Research*, *8*(3), 165–166.

Klais, B. (2022). New research across 200 iOS apps hints that surveillance marketing is still going strong. *URL Genius*. https://app.urlgeni.us/blog/new-research-across-200-ios-apps-hints-surveillance-marketing-may-still-be-going-strong

Knight, L. (2023, July 20). Authors call for AI companies to stop using their work without consent. *The Guardian*. https://www.theguardian.com/books/2023/jul/20/authors-call-for-ai-companies-to-stop-using-their-work-without-consent

Kosinski, M., Stillwell, D., & Graepel, T. (2013). Private traits and attributes are predictable from digital records of human behavior. *Proceedings of the National Academy of Sciences of the United States of America*, *110*(15), 5802–5805. https://doi.org/10.1073/pnas.1218772110

Kshetri, N., Dwivedi, Y. K., Davenport, T. H., & Panteli, N. (2024). Generative artificial intelligence in marketing: Applications, opportunities, challenges, and research agenda. *International Journal of Information Management*, *75*, 102716. https://doi.org/10.1016/j.ijinfomgt.2023.102716

Kuhn, T. S. (2012). *The structure of scientific revolutions: 50th anniversary edition*. University of Chicago Press. (Original work published 1962)

Kunert, P. (2019, April 12). Pregnancy and parenting club bounty fined £400,000 for shady data sharing practices. *The Register*. https://www.theregister.com/2019/04/12/commercial_pregnancy_club_bounty/

Kurmelovs, R. (2022, September 23). Optus cyber-attack leaves customers feeling 'powerless' over risk of identity theft. *The Guardian*. https://www.theguardian.com/australia-news/2022/sep/23/optus-cyber-attack-leavescustomers-feeling-powerless-over-risk-of-identity-theft

Lamdan, S. (2022a). *Data cartels: The companies that control and monopolize our information*. Stanford University Press.

Lamdan, S. (2022b, November 9). The quiet invasion of 'big information'. *Wired*. https://www.wired.com/story/big-information-relx-privacy-surveillance-data/

Lanier, J. (2013). *Who owns the future?* Simon & Schuster.

Lanier, J. (2018). *Ten arguments for deleting your social media right now*. Picador.

La Quadrature du Net. (2021, July 30). Amazon fined 746 million euros following our collective legal action. *La Quadrature du Net*. https://www.laquadrature.net/en/2021/07/30/amazon-fined-746-million-euros-following-our-collective-legal-action/

Lauer, J., & Lipartito, K. (Eds.). (2021). *Surveillance capitalism in America*. University of Pennsylvania Press.

Lecher, L. (2019, December 7). FTC officially rules that Cambridge Analytica deceived Facebook users. *The Verge*. https://www.theverge.com/2019/12/6/20999078/ftc-cambridge-analytica-facebook-users-official-ruling-privacy-scandal

Le Métayer, D., & Monteleone, S. (2009). Automated consent through privacy agents: Legal requirements and technical architecture. *Computer Law and Security Review*, *25*(2), 136–144.

Levy, S. (2011). *In the plex: How Google thinks, works, and shapes our lives*. Simon & Schuster.

Liu, F. (2022). A Q&A about differential privacy. *Chance*, *35*(4), 52–56. https://doi.org/10.1080/09332480.2022.2145146

Llyod, N., & Jackson, C. (2022). Most Americans say it is increasingly difficult to control who can access their online data. *Ipsos*. https://www.ipsos.com/sites/default/files/ct/news/documents/2022-01/Data%20Privacy%20Topline%2001.07.22.pdf

Lohr, S. (2012, February 11). The age of big data. *The New York Times*. https://www.nytimes.com/2012/02/12/sunday-review/big-datas-impact-in-the-world.html

Lundgren, B. (2020a). How software developers can fix part of GDPR's problem of click-through consents. *AI & Society*, *35*, 759–760. https://doi.org/10.1007/s00146-020-00970-8

Lundgren, B. (2020b). Beyond the concept of anonymity: What is really at stake? In K. Macnish & J. Galliott (Eds.), *Big data and democracy* (pp. 201–216). Edinburgh University Press.

Mackie, J. L. (1977). *Ethics: Inventing right and wrong*. Penguin.

Macklin, R. (2003). *Future challenges for the Declaration of Helsinki: Maintaining credibility in the face of ethical controversies*. Address to scientific session, World Medical Association General Assembly, Helsinki.

Maggetti, M. (2015). Hard and soft governance. In K. Lynggaard, I. Manners, & K. Löfgren (Eds.), *Research methods in European union studies* (pp. 252–265). Palgrave Macmillan. https://doi.org/10.1057/9781137316967_16

Mak, B. C., Addeman, B. T., Chen, J., Papp, K. A., Gooderham, M. J., Guenther, L. C., Liu, Y., Broedl, U. C., & Logger, M. E. (2021). Leveraging blockchain technology for informed consent process and patient engagement in a clinical trial pilot. *Blockchain in Healthcare Today*, *4*, 182. https://doi.org/10.30953/bhty.v4.182

Manson, N. C., & O'Neill, O. (2007). *Rethinking informed consent in bioethics*. Cambridge University Press.

Manwaring, K., Kemp, K., & Nicholls, R. (2021, March 31). (mis)Informed consent in Australia. *UNSW Law Research*. http://dx.doi.org/10.2139/ssrn.3859848

Marr, B. (2023). *The future internet: How the metaverse, web 3.0, and blockchain will transform business and society*. Wiley.

McDonald, A. M., & Cranor, L. F. (2008). The cost of reading privacy policies. *I/S A Journal of Law and Policy for the Information Society*, *4*(3), 543–568.

McGuire, J., & Andersen, C. B. (2019). Improving Aurecon's employment contracts through visualisation. *The University of Western Australia Law Review*, *46*(2), 218–236. https://www8.austlii.edu.au/au/journals/UWALawRw/2019/31.pdf

McNamee, R. (2019). *Zucked: Waking up to the Facebook catastrophe*. Penguin Press.

McNeil, T. (2018, May 17). Did Cambridge Analytica sway the election? *Tufts Now*. https://now.tufts.edu/2018/05/17/did-cambridge-analytica-sway-election

McStay, A. (2020). Emotional AI, soft biometrics and the surveillance of emotional life: An unusual consensus on privacy. *Big Data & Society*, *7*(1). https://doi.org/10.1177/2053951720904386

Mehta, P., Zimba, O., Gasparyan, A. Y., Seiil, B., & Yessirkepov, M. (2023). Ethics committees: Structure, roles, and issues. *Journal of Korean Medical Science*, *38*(25), e198. https://doi.org/10.3346/jkms.2023.38.e198

Mejias, U. A., & Couldry, N. (2024). *Data grab: The new colonialism of big tech and how to fight back*. The University of Chicago Press.

Milmo, D., & Hern, A. (2023, March 18). Why is TikTok banned from government phones—And should the rest of us be worried? *The Guardian*. https://www.theguardian.com/technology/2023/mar/17/why-is-tiktok-banned-from-government-phones-and-should-rest-of-us-be-worried

Milmo, D., & O'Carroll, L. (2023, May 23). Facebook owner Meta fined €1.2bn for mishandling user information. *The Guardian*. https://www.theguardian.com/technology/2023/may/22/facebook-fined-mishandling-user-information-ireland-eu-meta

Mittelstadt, B. D., Allo, P., Taddeo, M., Wachter, S., & Floridi, L. (2016). The ethics of algorithms: Mapping the debate. *Big Data & Society*, *3*(2). https://doi.org/10.1177/2053951716679679

Mittelstadt, B. D., & Floridi, L. (2016). The ethics of big data: Current and foreseeable issues in biomedical contexts. *Science and Engineering Ethics*, *22*(2), 303–341. https://doi.org/10.1007/s11948-015-9652-2

Morris, R. (2023, October 23). My Blonde GF: The experience of being deepfaked for pornography. *The Guardian*. https://www.theguardian.com/technology/ng-interactive/2023/oct/25/my-blonde-gf-a-disturbing-story-of-deepfake-pornography

Morrison, S. (2022, April 29). The winners and losers of Apple's anti-tracking feature. *Vox*. https://www.vox.com/recode/23045136/apple-app-tracking-transparency-privacy-ads

Morse, J. (2022, April 5). How to stop Spotify from sharing your data, and why you should. *Mashable*. https://mashable.com/article/spotify-user-privacy-settings

Mubarak, R., Alsboui, T., Alshaikh, O., Inuwa-Dute, I., Khan, S., & Parkinson, S. (2023). A survey on the detection and impacts of deepfakes in visual, audio, and textual formats. *IEEE Access*, *11*, 144497–144529. https://doi.org/10.1109/ACCESS.2023.3344653

Müller, V. C. (2009). Would you mind being watched by machines? Privacy concerns in data mining. *AI & Society*, *23*, 529–544. https://doi.org/10.1007/s00146-007-0177-3

Murphy, H. (2022, May 23). Optus says it will defend allegations it failed to protect confidential details of 9 million customers in cyber attack. *ABC News*. https://www.abc.net.au/news/2024-05-23/optus-to-fight-in-federal-court/103885104

National Health and Medical Research Council, Australian Research Council and Universities Australia. (2023). *National statement on Ethical conduct in human research*. National Health and Medical Research Council. www.nhmrc.gov.au/about-us/publications/national-statement-ethical-conduct-human-research-2023

National Sleep Foundation. (2023, November). *National Sleep Foundation's 2023 Drowsy Driving Survey*. https://www.thensf.org/wp-content/uploads/2023/11/NSF-2023-Drowsy-Driving-Survey-Report.pdf

Naughton, J. (2019, May 5). The privacy paradox: Why do people keep using tech firms that abuse their data? *The Guardian*. https://www.theguardian.com/commentisfree/2019/may/05/privacy-paradox-why-do-people-keep-using-tech-firms-data-facebook-scandal

NCPHSBBR (National Commission for the Protection of Human Subjects of Biomedical and Behavioral Research). (1979). The Belmont report. *Federal Register, 44*(76), 23192-23197. https://www.hhs.gov/ohrp/regulations-and-policy/belmont-report/index.html

Newson, A. J., & Lipworth, W. (2015). Why should ethics approval be required prior to publication of health promotion research? *Health Promotion Journal of Australia: Official Journal of Australian Association of Health Promotion Professionals, 26*(3), 170–175. https://doi.org/10.1071/HE15034

New York Times. (2024). *The New York Times Company Privacy Policy*. https://help.nytimes.com/hc/en-us/articles/10940941449492-The-New-York-Times-Company-Privacy-Policy

Nguyen, P., & Solomon, L. (2018). *Consumer data and the digital economy: Emerging issues in data collection, use and sharing*. Consumer Policy Research Centre. https://apo.org.au/node/241516

Nimmon, L., & Stenfors-Hayes, T. (2016). The "Handling" of power in the physician-patient encounter: Perceptions from experienced physicians. *BMC Medical Education, 16*, 114. https://doi.org/10.1186/s12909-016-0634-0

Nissenbaum, H. (2011). A contextual approach to privacy online. *Daedalus, 140*(4), 32–48. https://doi.org/10.1162/DAED_a_00113

Nixon, J. (2008). *Towards the virtuous university: The moral bases of academic practice*. Routledge.

Noujaim, J., & Amer, K. (2019). *The great hack*. Netflix.

NSW Health. (2024). *Consent to medical and healthcare treatment manual*. https://www.health.nsw.gov.au/policies/manuals/Pages/consent-manual.aspx

OAIC (Office of the Australian Information Commissioner). (2020). *Australian community attitudes to privacy survey 2020*. Office of the Australian Information Commissioner, Australian Government. https://www.oaic.gov.au/__data/assets/pdf_file/0015/2373/australian-community-attitudes-to-privacy-survey-2020.pdf

OAIC (Office of the Australian Information Commissioner). (2023). *Australian community attitudes to privacy survey 2023*. Office of the Australian Information Commissioner, Australian Government. https://www.oaic.gov.au/__data/assets/pdf_file/0025/74482/OAIC-Australian-Community-Attitudes-to-Privacy-Survey-2023.pdf

Office of the Privacy Commission of Canada. (2020). *News release: Cadillac Fairview collected 5 million shoppers' images*. https://www.priv.gc.ca/en/opc-news/news-and-announcements/2020/nr-c_201029/

O'Flaherty, K. (2021, June 29). Apple's stunning iOS 14 privacy move: A game-changer for all iPhone users. *Forbes*. https://www.forbes.com/sites/kateoflahertyuk/2021/01/31/apples-stunning-ios-14-privacy-move-a-game-changer-for-all-iphone-users/

O'Hara, K. (2020). Big data, consequentialism and privacy. In K. Macnih & J. Galliott (Eds.), *Big data and democracy* (pp. 13–26). Edinburgh University Press.

Olds, D. (2022, May 27). What do those pesky 'cookie preferences' pop-ups really mean? *Wired*. https://www.wired.com/story/what-do-cookie-preferences-pop-ups-mean/

O'Neill, O. (2002). *Autonomy and trust in bioethics*. Cambridge Universes Press.

O'Neill, O. (2003). Some limits of informed consent. *Journal of Medical Ethics, 29*(1), 4–7. https://doi.org/10.1136/jme.29.1.4

Ortega, A. G., Bourgeois, J., Hutiri, W. T., & Kortuem, G. (2023). Beyond data transactions: A framework for meaningfully informed data donation. *AI & Society*. https://doi.org/10.1007/s00146-023-01755-5

Øverby, H. (2021). The privacy paradox. In S. Jajodia, P. Samarati, & M. Yung (Eds.), *Encyclopedia of cryptography, security and privacy* (pp. 1–2). Springer. https://link.springer.com/referenceworkentry/10.1007/978-3-642-27739-9_1619-1

Page, K. (2012). The four principles: Can they be measured and do they predict ethical decision making? *BMC Medical Ethics*, *13*, 10. https://doi.org/10.1186/1472-6939-13-10

Paltiel, M. (2023). Recent amendments to the Australian Privacy Act. *Bioethical Inquiry*, *20*, 161–167. https://doi.org/10.1007/s11673-023-10249-4

Pankiw, A. (2023). Joan is awful (Season 6, Episode 1). In C. Brooker (Ed.), *Black mirror*. Netflix.

Pascalev, M. (2017). Privacy exchanges: Restoring consent in privacy self-management. *Ethics and Information Technology*, *19*(1), 39–48. https://doi.org/10.1007/s10676-016-9410-4

Pasquale, F. (2016). *The Black box society: The secret algorithms that control money and information*. Harvard University Press.

Passera, S. (2017). *Beyond the wall of contract text: Visualizing contracts to foster understanding and collaboration within and across organizations*. Aalto Dissertation Press.

Paul, K. (2024). Meta overhauls rules on deepfakes, other altered media. *Reuters*. https://www.reuters.com/technology/cybersecurity/meta-overhauls-rules-deepfakes-other-altered-media-2024-04-05/

Paulo, N. (2016). Ethics, applied ethics, and law. In *The confluence of philosophy and law in applied ethics* (pp. 11–25). Palgrave Macmillan. https://doi.org/10.1057/978-1-137-55734-6_2

Pearl, J. (2019). The limitations of opaque learning machines. In J. Brockman (Ed.), *Possible minds: 25 ways of looking at AI* (pp. 13–19). Penguins Press.

Personalized Privacy Assistant Project. (2019). *The Personalized Privacy Assistant Project*. https://www.privacyassistant.org

Pollach, I. (2011), Online privacy as a corporate social responsibility: An empirical study. *Business Ethics: A European Review*, *20*, 88–102. https://doi.org/10.1111/j.1467-8608.2010.01611.x

Popkin, H. A. S. (2010). Privacy is dead on Facebook. Get over it. *NBC News*. https://www.nbcnews.com/id/wbna34825225

Porsdam Mann, S., Savulescu, J., Ravaud, P., & Benchoufi, M. (2021). Blockchain, consent and prosent for medical research. *Journal of Medical Ethics*, *47*(4), 244–250. https://doi.org/10.1136/medethics-2019-105963

Powles, J. (2024, January 31). Parking apps are sweeping Australia's cities. Here's what you may not know about them. *The Conversation*. https://theconversation.com/parking-apps-are-sweeping-australias-cities-heres-what-you-may-not-know-about-them-221016

Prinz, J. (2011). Against empathy. *The Southern Journal of Philosophy*, *49*, 214–233. https://doi.org/10.1111/j.2041-6962.2011.00069.x

Queensland Health. (2023). *Guide to informed decision-making in health care: Interim update version 2.3*. https://www.health.qld.gov.au/__data/assets/pdf_file/0019/143074/ic-guide.pdf

Quodling, A. (2018, April 13). Shadow profiles—Facebook knows about you, even if you're not on Facebook. *The Conversation*. https://theconversation.com/shadow-profiles-facebook-knows-about-you-even-if-youre-not-on-facebook-94804

Raab, E. L. (2004). The parameters of informed consent. *Transactions of the American Ophthalmological Society*, *102*, 225–232.

Radesky, J., Chassiakos, Y. L. R., Ameenuddin, N., Navsaria, D., & Council on Communication and Media. (2020). Digital advertising to children. *Pediatrics*, *146*(1), e20201681. https://doi.org/10.1542/peds.2020–1681

Ray, H. (2022, January 10). Model shares warning after she says a stranger used an Apple AirTag to track her. *CBC News*. https://www.cbsnews.com/news/brooks-nader-model-apple-airtag-stranger-track/

RCOG (Royal College of Obstetricians and Gynaecologists). (2015). *Obtaining valid consent: Clinical Governance Advice No. 6*. https://www.rcog.org.uk/media/pndfv5qf/cga6.pdf

Realeyes. (2022). Realeyes—Education use case. *YouTube*. https://www.youtube.com/watch?v=BbEHjlxzUsk

Reuters. (2023, December 30). Google agrees to settle $5bn lawsuit claiming it secretly tracked users. *The Guardian*. https://www.theguardian.com/technology/2023/dec/29/google-lawsuit-settlement-incognito-mode.

Richards, N. (2021). *Why privacy matters*. Oxford University Press.

Richards, N., & Hartzog, W. (2021). A duty of loyalty for privacy law. *Washington University Law Review*, *99*, 961–1021.

Robins-Early, N. (2024, May 21). ChatGPT suspends Scarlett Johansson-like voice as actor speaks out against OpenAI. *The Guardian*. https://www.theguardian.com/technology/article/2024/may/20/chatgpt-scarlett-johansson-voice

Romm, T. (2018, April 26). Facebook didn't read the terms and conditions for the app behind Cambridge Analytica. *The Washington Post*. https://www.washingtonpost.com/news/the-switch/wp/2018/04/26/facebook-didnt-read-the-terms-and-conditions-for-the-app-behind-cambridge-analytica/

Rose, F. (2021). *The sea we swim in: How stories work in a data-driven world*. W.W. Norton & Company.

Roth, E. (2023, August 31). X wants permission to start collecting your biometric data and employment history. *The Verge*. https://www.theverge.com/2023/8/31/23853618/x-privacy-policy-update-biometrics-job-history

Rowan, J. R. (1998). Informed consent as an ethical principle for business. *Business & Professional Ethics Journal*, *17*(1/2), 95–111. http://www.jstor.org/stable/27801055

Ruohonen, J. (2021). The treachery of images in the digital sovereignty debate. *Minds and Machines*, *31*, 439–456.

Ruohonen, J., & Mickelsson, S. (2023). Reflections on the Data Governance Act. *Digital Society*, *2*, 10. https://doi.org/10.1007/s44206-023-00041-7

Rusbridger, A., MacAskill, E., & Gibson, J. (2015, May 23). Edward Snowden: A right to privacy is the same as freedom of speech—Video interview. *The Guardian*. https://www.theguardian.com/us-news/video/2015/may/22/edward-snowden-rights-to-privacy-video

Russell, N. C., Reidenberg, J. R., Martin, E., & Norton, T. B. (2018). Transparency and the marketplace for student data. *Center on Law and Information Policy*, *4*. https://ir.lawnet.fordham.edu/clip/4

Sabbagh, D. (2023, May 17). UK bans TikTok from government mobile phones. *The Guardian*. https://www.theguardian.com/technology/2023/mar/16/uk-bans-tiktok-from-government-mobile-phones

Saqr, M. (2022). Is GDPR failing? A tale of the many challenges in interpretations, applications, and enforcement. *International Journal of Health Sciences*, *16*(5), 1–2.

Scanlon, T. M. (1998). *What we owe to each other*. The Belknap Press.

Schermer, B. W., Custers, B., & van der Hof, S. (2014). The crisis of consent: How stronger legal protection may lead to weaker consent in data protection. *Ethics and Information Technology*, *16*, 171–182. https://doi.org/10.1007/s10676-014-9343-8

Schneble, C. O., Elger, B. S., & Shaw, D. (2018). The Cambridge Analytica affair and Internet-mediated research. *EMBO Reports*, *19*(8), e46579. https://doi.org/10.15252/embr.201846579

Schwitzgebel, E., Schwitzgebel, D., & Strasser, A. (2024). Creating a large language model of a philosopher. *Mind & Language*, *39*(2), 237–259. https://doi.org/10.1111/mila.12466

Selbst, A. D., & Powles, J. (2017). Meaningful information and the right to explanation. *International Data Privacy Law*, 7(4), 233–242. https://doi.org/10.1093/idpl/ipx022

Shanthapriya, R., & Vaithianathan, V. (2022). Block-healthnet: Security based healthcare system using block chain technology. *Security Journal*, *35*, 19–37. https://doi.org/10.1057/s41284-020-00265-z

Shead, S. (2021, July 30). Amazon hit with $887 million fine by European privacy watchdog. *CNBC*. https://www.cnbc.com/2021/07/30/amazon-hit-with-fine-by-eu-privacy-watchdog-.html

Sikoryak, R. (2017). *Terms and conditions*. Drawn and Quarterly.

Singel, R. (2009, December 17). Netflix spilled your Brokeback Mountain Secret, Lawsuit claims. *Wired*. https://www.wired.com/2009/12/netflix-privacy-lawsuit/

Smilansky, S. (2007). *10 moral paradoxes*. Wiley-Blackwell.

Smith, M. (2024). *Techno: Humans and technology*. University of Queensland Press.

Solomon, R. C. (1999). Business ethics and virtue. In R. E. Frederick (Ed.), *A companion to businessethics* (pp. 30–37). Wiley-Blackwell.

Solon, O. (2018, April 5). Facebook says Cambridge Analytica may have gained 37m more users' data. *The Guardian*. https://www.theguardian.com/technology/2018/apr/04/facebook-cambridge-analytica-user-data-latest-more-than-thought

Solove, D. J. (2013a). Privacy self-management and the consent dilemma. *Harvard Law Review*, *126*(7), 1880–1903.

Solove, D. J. (2013b, 13 June). 5 myths about privacy. *The Washington Post*. https://www.washingtonpost.com/opinions/five-myths-about-privacy/2013/06/13/098a5b5c-d370–11e2-b05f-3ea3f0e7bb5a_story.html

Solove, D. J. (2021, January 21). The myth of the privacy paradox. *George Washington Law Review*, *89*(1), 1–51.

Solove, D. J., & Hartzog, W. (2022). *Breached! Why data security law fails and how to improve it*. Oxford University Press.

Spotify. (2023). *Spotify privacy policy*. https://www.spotify.com/us/legal/privacy-policy/#2-your-personal-data-rights-and-controls

Stewart, E. (2019, December 10). Why every website wants you to accept its cookies. *Vox*. https://www.vox.com/recode/2019/12/10/18656519/what-are-cookies-website-tracking-gdpr-privacy

Suleyman, M., & Bhaskar, M. (2023). *The coming wave: Technology, power, and the twenty-first century's greatest dilemma*. Crown.

Swisher, K. (2018). Mark Zuckerberg wanted Facebook to change the world. And it has—But not for the better. *NBC News Think*. https://www.nbcnews.com/think/opinion/mark-zuckerberg-wanted-facebook-change-world-it-has-not-better-ncna897701

Taddeo, M., & Floridi, L. (2018). How AI can be a force for good. *Science*, *361*(6404), 751–752.

Tandon, A., Dhir, A., Almugren, I., AlNemer, G. N., & Mäntymäki, M. (2021), Fear of missing out (FoMO) among social media users: A systematic literature review, synthesis and framework for future research. *Internet Research*, *31*(3), 782–821. https://doi.org/10.1108/INTR-11-2019-0455

Telford, T. (2021, 30 July). E.U. regulator hits Amazon with record $887 million fine for data protection violations. *The Washington Post*. https://www.washingtonpost.com/business/2021/07/30/amazon-record-fine-europe/

Tendler, C., Hong, P. S., Kane, C., Kopaczynski, C., Terry, W., & Emanuel, E. J. (2023). Academic and private partnership to improve informed consent forms using a data driven approach. *The American Journal of Bioethics*, *24*(4), 8–10. https://doi.org/10.1080/15265161.2023.2250330

Tepper, J., & Hearn, D. (2018). *The myth of capitalism: Monopolies and the death of competition*. Wiley.

Terzon, E., & Xiao, A. (2023, April 18). Inside the 'opaque' property tech sector that helps real estate agents decide who gets a lease in a rental shortage. *ABC News*. https://www.abc.net.au/news/2023-04-18/choice-rent-tech-data-renters-apply-snug-regulation-data/102231206

Thaler, R. H., & Sunstein, C. R. (2008). *Nudge: Improving decisions about health, wealth, and happiness*. Yale University Press.

Thampapillai, D. (2023). Two authors are suing OpenAI for training ChatGPT with their books. Could they win? *The Conversation*. https://theconversation.com/two-authors-are-suing-openai-for-training-chatgpt-with-their-books-could-they-win-209227

Thompson, S. A., & Warzel, C. (2019, December 20). How to track President Trump. *The New York Times*. https://www.nytimes.com/interactive/2019/12/20/opinion/location-data-national-security.html

TikTok. (2024). *Privacy policy*. https://www.tiktok.com/legal/page/row/privacy-policy/en

Till, C. (2023). Spotify as a technology for integrating health, exercise and wellness practices into financialised capitalism. *Big Data & Society*, *10*(2). https://doi.org/10.1177/20539517231210278

Topol, E. (2019). *Deep medicine: How artificial intelligence can make healthcare human again*. Basic Books.

Touma, R. (2022, July 19). TikTok has been accused of 'aggressive' data harvesting. Is your information at risk? *The Guardian*. https://www.theguardian.com/technology/2022/jul/19/tiktok-has-been-accused-of-aggressive-data-harvesting-is-your-information-at-risk

Tsamados, A., Aggarwal, N., Cowls, J., Morley, J., Roberts, H., Taddeo, M., & Floridi, L. (2022). The ethics of algorithms: Key problems and solutions. *AI & Society*, *37*, 215–230. https://doi.org/10.1007/s00146-021-01154-8

Tunney, C. (2020, October 29). Mall real estate company collected 5 million images of shoppers, say privacy watchdogs. *CBC News*. https://www.cbc.ca/news/politics/cadillac-fairview-5-million-images-1.5781735

UWA Research Impact. (2020). *Comic book contracts*. https://researchimpact.uwa.edu.au/research-impact-stories/comic-book-contracts/

Véliz, C. (2021). *Privacy is power: Why and how you should take back control of your data*. Penguin.

Véliz, C. (2023). The surveillance delusion. In C. Véliz (Ed.), *The Oxford handbook of digital ethics* (pp. 555–574). Oxford University Press.

Wachter, S., Mittelstadt, B., & Floridi, L. (2017). Why a right to explanation of automated decision-making does not exist in the general data protection regulation.

International Data Privacy Law, 7(2), 76–99. https://doi.org/10.1093/idpl/ipx005
Wahlstrom, K., Ulhaq, A., & Burmeister, O. (2020). Privacy by design: A Holochain exploration. *Australasian Journal of Information Systems*, *24*. https://doi.org/10.3127/ajis.v24i0.2801
Walker, T. (2012). Informed consent and the requirement to ensure understanding. *Journal of Applied Philosophy*, *29*(1), 50–62. https://doi.org/10.1111/j.1468-5930.2011.00550.x
Walker, T. (2022). Value of choice. *Journal of Medical Ethics*, *48*, 61–64. https://doi.org/10.1136/medethics-2020–106067
Walsh, T. (2023a). Will AI end privacy? How do we avoid an Orwellian future. *AI & Society*, *38*, 1239–1240. https://doi.org/10.1007/s00146-022-01433-y
Walsh, T. (2023b, November 30). A year of ChatGPT: 5 ways the AI marvel has changed the world. *The Conversation*. https://theconversation.com/a-year-of-chatgpt-5-ways-the-ai-marvel-has-changed-the-world-218805
Warren, S. D., & Brandeis, L. D. (1890). The right to privacy. *Harvard Law Review*, *4*(5), 193–220. https://doi.org/10.2307/1321160
Warzel, C., & Ngu, A. (2019). Google's 4,000-word privacy policy is a secret history of the Internet. *The New York Times*. https://www.nytimes.com/interactive/2019/07/10/opinion/google-privacy-policy.html
White, L. (2019, April 18). Parenting support club bounty fined in 'unprecedented' data breach. *Data Protection Report*. https://www.dataprotectionreport.com/2019/04/parenting-support-club-bounty-fined-in-unprecedented-data-breach/
Williams, J. J., Foster, J., & Watson, T. (2022, September 26). What does the Optus data breach mean for you and how can you protect yourself? A step-by-step guide. *The Conversation*. https://theconversation.com/what-does-the-optus-data-breach-mean-for-you-and-how-can-you-protect-yourself-a-step-by-step-guide-191332
WMA (World Medical Association). (2013). World Medical Association Declaration of Helsinki: Ethical principles for medical research involving human subjects. *JAMA*, *310*(20), 2191–2194. https://doi.org/10.1001/jama.2013.281053. (Original work published 1964)
Wolford, B. (n.d.-a). What is GDPR, the EU's new data protection law? *GDPR.EU*. https://gdpr.eu/what-is-gdpr/
Wolford, B. (n.d.-b). Data sharing and GDPR compliance: Bounty UK shows what not to do. *GDPR.EU*. https://gdpr.eu/data-sharing-bounty-fine/
Wolfram, S. (2023). *What is ChatGPT doing . . . and why does it work?* Wolfram Media.
Wolmar, C. (2023, December 6). Driverless cars were the future but now the truth is out: They're on the road to nowhere. *The Guardian*. https://www.theguardian.com/commentisfree/2023/dec/06/driverless-cars-future-vehicles-public-transport
Wylie, C. (2019). *Mindfuck: Inside Cambridge Analytica's plot to break the world*. Profile Trade.
Xu, H., & Shuttleworth, K. M. J. (2024). Medical artificial intelligence and the black box problem: A view based on the ethical principle of "do no harm." *Intelligent Medicine*, *4*(1), 52–57.
Zan, B., Andersen, C. B., & Toohey, L. (2023). Assessing the efficacy of visual contracts: An empirical study of transaction costs. *Applied Economics*, *55*(40), 4712–4726. https://doi.org/10.1080/00036846.2023.2174942
Zenus. (n.d.-a). *Ethical facial analysis*. https://www.zenus.ai
Zenus. (n.d.-b). *We stand behind our values*. https://www.zenus.ai/about

Zenus AI. (2021). Zenus AI: Promo video. *YouTube*. Retrieved June 22, 2024, from https://www.youtube.com/watch?v=BR5bCckd1dE

Ziffer, D. (2024, February 5). Unintended consequences and more work to do: Five years after the banking royal commission. *ABC News*. https://www.abc.net.au/news/2024-02-05/banking-royal-commission-five-years-on-asic/103423072

Zuboff, S. (2019). *The age of surveillance capitalism: The fight for a human future at the new frontier of power*. Profile Books.

Index

Note: Page numbers in *italic* indicate a figure on the corresponding page.

FSC
www.fsc.org
MIX
Papier | Fördert gute Waldnutzung
FSC® C083411

Kolibri 360 GmbH
Ferdinand-Jühlke-Straße 7
99095 Erfurt, Deutschland
produktsicherheit@kolibri360.de